BELIZE

'In nature-watching terms, a coral reef is the very opposite
of a rainforest. Where a trek through the jungle will, unless
you're very lucky, usually involve a lot of fruitless searching,
down among the coral there's always something to look at –
shoals of multicoloured fluorescent fish, scuttling lobsters,
spiny scary sea urchins and, of course, the coral itself.'

Joseph Fullman and Nicola Mainwood

About the Guide

The **full-colour introduction** gives the author's overview of the country, together with a suggested **itinerary** and a regional '**where to go**' **map** and **feature** to help you plan your trip.

Illuminating and entertaining **cultural chapters** on local history, wildlife, conservation and food and drink give you a rich flavour of the country.

Travel covers the basics of **getting there** and **getting around**, plus entry formalitie The **Practical A–Z** deals with all the **essential information** and **contact details** tha you may need, including a section for disabled travellers.

The **regional chapters** are arranged in a loose touring order, with plenty of public transport and driving information. The author's top '**Don't Miss**' ⭐ sights are highlighted at the start of each chapter.

A **language guide**, ideas for **further reading** and a comprehensive **index** can be found at the end of the book.

Although everything we list in this guide is **personally visited and recommended** our authors inevitably have their own favourite places to eat and stay. Whenever you see this **Authors' Choice** ⭐ icon beside a listing, you will know that it is a lit bit out of the ordinary.

Hotel Price Guide

Luxury	$$$$$	US$120 and above
Expensive	$$$$	US$80–119
Moderate	$$$	US$40–79
Inexpensive	$$	US$26–39
Budget	$	US$25 and under

About the Authors

Joseph Fullman and Nicola Mainwood are fast becoming Central American old hands, having already worked together on Cadogan's Guide to Costa Rica as well this new guide to Belize. Together and separately, the authors have written and contributed to guides to Andalucia, Berlin, England, Las Vegas, London, Turkey and Venice.

1st Edition Published 2006

01 INTRODUCING BELIZE

Above: Ambergris Caye, p.119; Lamanai, p.210

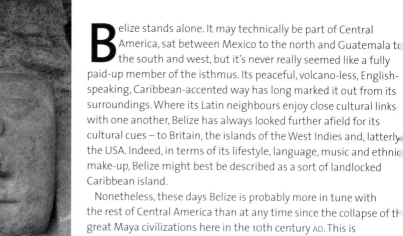

Belize stands alone. It may technically be part of Central America, sat between Mexico to the north and Guatemala to the south and west, but it's never really seemed like a fully paid-up member of the isthmus. Its peaceful, volcano-less, English-speaking, Caribbean-accented way has long marked it out from its surroundings. Where its Latin neighbours enjoy close cultural links with one another, Belize has always looked further afield for its cultural cues – to Britain, the islands of the West Indies and, latterly the USA. Indeed, in terms of its lifestyle, language, music and ethnic make-up, Belize might best be described as a sort of landlocked Caribbean island.

Nonetheless, these days Belize is probably more in tune with the rest of Central America than at any time since the collapse of the great Maya civilizations here in the 10th century AD. This is principally due to the large numbers of Guatemalan and Mexican migrants who have settled in the west and north of the country over the past couple of decades, and who have brought with them their own more Latin-orientated culture. Thankfully, a few grumbles about the dominance of Spanish over English in these areas aside, the absorption of these newcomers into the general population has been relatively smooth. But then, Belize is generally a very tolerant, welcoming sort of a place in which its many and varied ethnic groups – Creoles, mestizos, Garifuna, Chinese, Guatemalans, Mexicans, Mennonites, Maya, ex-pat Americans – seem to rub along together pretty well.

Unlike much of the rest of the region, Belize has rarely let its political or social tensions ignite into conflict, either internal or external. Its last major battle, which saw the Belizeans fend off Spain's attempt to annex it into its American Empire, was fought over 200 years ago. There has never been a Belizean civil war. Even

Above: San Pedro, p.122

*Opposite page:
Flowering tree*

the country's release from British Imperial rule in the early 1980s, which was much delayed (the process began in the early 1960s) and which saw much protesting on the streets, was still conducted largely peacefully.

To be honest, if Belize did decide to pick a fight with another country, it would have to choose its target very carefully to have any hope of success. It's a tiny place – encompassing just 8,866 square miles (22,963 sq km) – with a correspondingly tiny population. The latest estimates put the total number of people living in Belize some-where between 250,000 and 300,000. To put it into context, that's roughly the size of a small city in Europe or the USA. And with so few potential taxpayers, the country's public expendi-ture is necessarily extremely limited. That's not to say Belize is exactly destitute, just not particularly rich. But despite its relative impoverishment, the country does still manage to operate commendably enlightened polices toward the provision of education – which is compulsory and provided free of charge up until the age of 14 – healthcare and conservation. Nonetheless, there's a limit to what can be realistically achieved with the available funds, which is one of the principal reasons why the government is currently so keen to promote tourism and get people visiting the country, as it's hoped that the revenue generated can be used to plug any fiscal gaps. This is the bit where you come in.

For around a decade now, Belize has been a global pioneer in the field of ecotourism, the so-called 'golden bullet' solution to conservation, whereby – so the theory goes – the natural environ-ment is preserved by charging visitors who want to see it for its upkeep. It's a simple idea, but one that needs careful monitoring if it's to be made to work. Pristine natural environments and hordes of eager tourists don't always make for the most accommodating of bedfellows. Still, as more of Belize's area – some 40 per cent – is protected against development than any other country, you could argue that if it's going to work anywhere, it's going to work here.

So, the million (Belizean) dollar question is – why should you take part? What does Belize have to offer that might tempt you to pay it a visit and contribute to its great ecological pension plan? It's not an easy question to answer. Not because Belize is a particularly mysterious or complex place, but because, for such a modestly sized country, it's got an almost immodest amount of attractions, including the world's second longest barrier reef, the world's only jaguar reserve, and the remains of over 30 major Maya cities, to name just a handful.

In broad brush terms, Belize main tourist draws can be classified under three main headings: **coastal life** – sunbathing on golden sands, swimming in crystal clear seas, snorkelling amid the multicoloured fish and coral of the barrier reef; **jungle exploration** – scouring the forest depths on the lookout for jaguars, pumas and (more realistically) monkeys; and **historic wonders** – exploring the country's great Mayan ceremonial centres. But, of course, these basic categorizations don't even begin to tell the whole story. As with any trip, the great joy of Belize comes in the individual details, in the unplanned moments – the charming little towns, the happy welcomes, the spray-spattered boat rides, the bumping banging car journeys, the glorious sunsets over the Maya Mountains. Perhaps the best reason anyone can give you for why you should visit Belize is that you'll probably like it. And if you like sunshine, friendly people, lots of wildlife, beautiful views and a relaxed, easygoing way of life, then you'll definitely like it. And if you don't, there's always Milton Keynes.

Above: Belize City, p.93

Below: Xunantunich, p.163; reef, p.123

Opposite page: Cockscomb Basin Wildlife Sanctuary, p.187

Where to Go

Home to a little over 70,000 people, Belize's 'big city' – **Belize City** – is as urban, bustling and congested as Belize gets, which is to say not very. With a (rather exaggerated) reputation for dodginess, the city tends not to feature too highly on most people's Belizean itineraries. However, as it's the site of the country's only international airport, the main water taxi terminal for trips out to the cayes and the docking point for international cruise liners, you will probably end up spending a portion of your holiday here, even if it's only to pass on through to somewhere else. Stick around a while, however, and you may be pleasantly surprised. It's a vibrant place with a handful of decent museums and art galleries, and its collection of superior hotels and restaurants make it a good base for exploring the attractions of the surrounding area, which include Belize Zoo, the Monkey Bay Wildlife Sanctuary, the Mayan site of Altun Ha and the Crooked Tree Wildlife Sanctuary.

The **Northern Cayes** (pronounced 'keys'), a group of islands near the border with Mexico's Yucatán peninsula, represent Belize at its most touristy, but also its most idyllic. The two main islands of Ambergris Caye and Caye Caulker offer sweeps of palm tree-lined golden sand beach, an easygoing lifestyle, and access to the country's great barrier reef with its superabundance of colourful marine life. They also offer the country's most highly developed tourist infrastructure, with numerous resorts (including some of the very grandest in all Belize), hotels, bars, restaurants, shops, as well as a plethora of tour operators and dive shops, many of which are situated in San Pedro, the jaunty little capital of Ambergris Caye.

Cayo District and the West is the most topographically intense region in Belize, which is otherwise rather flat. Here, the country's only mountain range, the Mayan Mountains, looms over the southwest – as much as a collection of peaks that barely exceed 3,280ft (1,000m) can loom (the country's highest summit, Victoria Peak, is just 3,674ft high). The district is framed to the east by the country's rather bland, purpose-built capital, Belmopan, and to the west by the much livelier Spanish-accented market town of San Ignacio, just a few miles from the Guatemalan border. The latter makes a good base for exploring some of the region's main attractions, which include a couple of Belize's most impressive Maya ruins, Xunantunich and Caracol, and the Mountain Pine Ridge Forest Reserve, the country's largest protected area, comprising over 300 square miles (777 sq km) of forests, rivers, waterfalls, cave systems and wildlife.

With much of its area still blanketed in thick broadleaf forest, the humid **South** is Belize's wildest region, boasting a number of extensive nature parks, chief among them the Cockscomb Basin

Chapter Divisions

Wildlife Sanctuary, the world's only jaguar reserve. And yet, it's also the country's most tamed area, particularly along the beach-lined Placencia peninsula where development – the erecting of condos, hotels and resort complexes – is happening at a feverish pace. Many ex-pats (mainly, but not exclusively, American) have invested in holiday homes here, thereby adding to a diverse racial mix that already includes Creoles, Garifuna and several Maya communities.

The **North** is primarily agricultural, its great flat expanses dominated by sugar cane and banana plantations. In among all the farmland, however, you'll also find some of the country's best nature reserves (including the Rio Bravo Conservation and Management Area, the largest private reserve in the country, and the 22,000-acre Shipstern Nature Reserve), the ruins of a number of Mayan ceremonial centres, including Lamanai (one of the few cities to survive the great collapse of the 10th century), and some charming little towns, such as Orange Walk and the Spanish-flavoured Corozal.

Clockwise from top left:
Reef life; jellyfish;
marine turtle

Sea Life

Just off the shore of Belize lies the world's second longest barrier reef (after Australia's), comprising over 180 miles of delicate, multicoloured corals, which grow in all manner of shapes – fans, horns, tubes, feathers – and which provide a home to an equally varied assortment of wildlife, including brightly patterned iridescent fish, gently pulsing jellyfish and primeval-looking marine turtles. Snorkelling the reef down amongst the coral is Belize's number one tourist attraction.

Getting Around the Belizean Way

With Belize boasting some 180-plus miles of coast and over 450 offshore islands, known as 'cayes', not to mention numerous inland rivers and waterways, boats are unsurprisingly one of the principal means of getting around the country. Belize City Harbour welcomes visitors from international cruise ships all year round, and you can also catch a water taxi from here to the main tourist resorts of Ambergris Caye and Caye Caulker. Out on the cayes, the main modes of transport are bikes and golf carts, which are used to trundle up and down the largely unmade roads. They've become so popular that in San Pedro, the capital of Ambergris Caye, it's quite common to get stuck in a golf cart jam.

Houses in the Air

Belize's clapboard architecture is very distinctive, with the houses' charming pastel colours neatly contrasting with the surrounding tropical greenery. Many houses are set off the ground on stilts, for a number of different reasons. In those settlements built on reclaimed swamp land (such as Belize City) this can help to prevent against flooding. Stilt-set houses also absorb less ground heat and are better able to catch the breeze, making them considerably cooler. Finally, these elevated homes lie out of reach of all but the most determined termites, for whom wood is their favourite food.

Above: Belize City Harbour, p.93; Belize City architecture, p.93

Opposite page: Mayan site, Lamanai, p.210

Mayan Ruins

The mighty pyramids, mask carvings and intricate friezes of Belize's great Mayan sites – including Lamanai, Xunantunich and Caracol – never fail to impress. Their construction, between 1500 BC and AD 1000, seems all the more remarkable when you consider that it was done without the aid of wheeled transport, domesticated animals, metal tools or arches, none of which were invented by the Maya. Nonetheless, they still managed to leave their mark. The main palace at Caracol remains Belize's tallest man-made structure, over a thousand years after it was built. The reason why this great civilization, capable of erecting such architectural wonders, collapsed suddenly in the 10th century continues to baffle historians.

Tumbling Water

Belize is home to the tallest waterfall in Central America, the slightly misleadingly named Thousand Foot Falls (it's actually over 1,600ft high), which lies deep in the centre of the Mountain Pine Ridge Forest Reserve.

Jungle Life

Forty per cent of Belize is protected in a network of parks, reserves and sanctuaries. Indeed, it's estimated that over 70 per cent of the country is still blanketed in thick jungle, which supports a glorious abundance of plant and animal life. Some of the creatures most commonly encountered include howler monkeys, spider monkeys, giant blue morpho butterflies (which are most commonly spotted near the banks of rivers and streams) and the national bird, the keel-billed toucan, which, with its giant multicoloured bill, is pretty difficult to miss.

Above: Thousand Foot Falls, p.168; blue morpho butterfly; spider monkey

Opposite page: Toucan

Street Food

Belize does not have any international fast food franchises. Its version of McDonald's and KFC are the street-side huts and street vendors who serve up cheap, simple fare – *empanadas*, tacos and tortillas – for a couple of dollars.

Fresh Market Produce

Belize's street markets stock a glorious array of fresh produce – mangos, pineapples, breadfruit, yams, peppers and more. Every major town has a market, which, if you're self-catering, is usually your best bet for picking up cheap fresh fruit and vegetables.

*Clockwise from above:
Tortilla press, p.56;
Market produce;*

Street Scenes

Belize's towns are great places to wander around, taking in the street scenes and views of people going about their everyday lives – shopping at the market, browsing the local stores, cycling to work, or making lunch.

Itinerary
The Best of Belize in Two Weeks

Day 1 Tour Belize City, taking in the Swing Bridge, the museums, the city centre bustle and one of the better restaurants.

Day 2 Take the water taxi to Caye Caulker for some gentle snorkelling at the Split, followed by a relaxing evening, watching the sunset and revellers at the Lazy Lizard or I&I Reggae Bar.

Day 3 Take the water taxi to Ambergris Caye. Spend the day sunbathing, exploring San Pedro by golf cart (or bike), before catching the island water taxi to the northern half of the island for dinner at the Rojo Lounge or one of the other fancy restaurants.

Day 4 Take a trip to the Hol Chan Marine Reserve for close-up encounters with nurse sharks, rays and groupers.

Day 5 Take a day trip via water taxi (or, if feel like splashing out, by plane) to Corozal on the mainland, near the border with Mexico, to walk the beaches, explore the Mayan site of Chetumal and, if you've got a spare day, visit the Shipstern Nature Reserve.

Day 6 Take the water taxi back to Belize City, to pick up a 4WD hire car (most rental companies will bring the vehicle to meet you at the taxi terminal), and then set off up the Northern Highway to the Mayan site of Altun Ha (as featured on the Belikin beer bottle labels). If you've got the funds, pamper yourself with a night at the exclusive Marubu Restaurant and Spa.

Day 7 Drive to Orange Walk Town, park up the car and take a boat ride along the jungle-fringed New River to the Mayan site of Lamanai, followed by dinner and a night-time bat walk at the Lamanai Outpost Lodge.

Day 8 Back to Orange Walk, pick up the car and drive south down to Gales Point on the Southern Lagoon. Spend the evening watching the wildlife on the lake from Manatee Lodge.

Day 9 Take a trip out onto the lagoon to spot manatees. In the evening, if in season (May–Oct), take a tour to see marine turtles nesting on nearby beaches.

Day 10 Drive west to Belmopan and spend the morning looking for wildlife and giant trees at Guanacaste National Park. In the afternoon take a river-tubing trip with Ian Anderson's Caves Branch Adventure Company.

Day 11 Drive west to San Ignacio, where you can spend the day exploring the Belize Botanical Gardens and the Mayan ruins of Xunantunich, and the night at the Lodge at Chaa Creek.

Day 12 Take an early morning bird-watching tour around the grounds of Chaa Creek, followed by a trip through the Mayan ruin-filled Barton Creek Cave.

Day 13 Brave the unmade roads into the Mountain Pine Ridge Forest Reserve. Visit the Hidden Valley Falls, the Thousand Foot Falls, before ending the day with a picnic at the Río On Caves. Overnight at one of the reserve's fancy lodges, such as Blancaneaux.

Day 14 Horse-ride through the pine forest with one of the reserve's various stables, followed by a trip to the Río Frío Cave.

Day 15 Endure the bumpy drive south to Caracol and be rewarded with a tour of one of the country's finest Mayan sites.

Day 16 Leave the west and head southeast down the beautiful Hummingbird Highway to Dangriga, from where you can take a trip out to one of the nearby cayes, such as Coco Plum Caye or Tobacco Caye.

Day 17 Take an early morning trip to the Cockscomb Basin Wildlife Sanctuary on the lookout for jaguars and howler monkeys, followed by a drive south down to Placencia. Spend the afternoon strolling around the town, before enjoying dinner at a beach-front restaurant.

Day 18 Snorkel out to the barrier reef or a join a tour to Gladden Spit to watch whale sharks.

Day 19 Take a tour along the Monkey River on the lookout for turtles, iguanas, crocodiles, howler monkeys and birds.

Day 20 Drive south to Punta Gorda where you can enjoy a historical bike tour of the town, and a trip to the Mayan site of Lubaantun.

Day 21 Back to Belize City and home.

Previous page, from top: Ambergris Caye, p.119; Guanacaste National Park, p.148

Above, from top: Caracol, p.171; coral reef; Cockscomb Basin Wildlife Sanctuary, p.187; spider monkey

CONTENTS

Contents

Contents

Reference

Maps and Plans

History and Culture

Belize hasn't been Belize for very long. From 1862 to 1981 it was British Honduras, a colony of the British Empire. Before that it was the Honduran Bay Settlement, a small amorphous piece of territory founded by bandits and loggers, the precise extent, international status and political attachments of which were somewhat ill-defined. Spain regarded it as part of the Spanish Empire, essentially a province of neighbouring Guatemala. Britain regarded it as a sort of unofficial addendum to the British Empire. The people who lived there regarded it as neither.

02

Indeed, Belize never wore its subsequent imperial status particularly comfortably. The irony was that it remained yoked to an imperial master longer than most. The country's independence was one of the last spluttering gusts of the 'winds of change', the process (as described by British Prime Minister, Harold Macmillan) which saw Britain relinquish nearly all of its colonial holdings in the decades following the Second World War.

As eager as Belize was to finally cut the colonial cord, the relationship with its imperial mother had lasted long enough to have had a profound influence upon the country. Today, Belize has a markedly different culture from the rest of the isthmus. Firstly, it's English-speaking, at least officially, although the arrival of refugees from various Central American conflicts in the past couple of decades means that Spanish speakers now outnumber English ones in the country's western and northern regions. Its parliament and system of government are based upon the British model, with an elected lower house and an appointed upper house, and, again as with Britain, the country's legislature is presided over by a prime minister who is the leader of the largest parliamentary party. Furthermore, the British Queen is still the head of state and her portrait still adorns the country's banknotes. Actually, in this regard, the Belizeans have departed slightly from the British template. Whereas Britain regularly updates its monetary portraits of the monarch to mark the passing of the years, Belize's banknote queen remains trapped in time, forever young. For her, it is always 1953 and the winds of change have barely begun to blow.

History

Prehistory and the Emergence of the Maya

The first peoples to inhabit the area that makes up modern Belize probably arrived around 10,000 years ago. This would have marked the culmination of a migration that began 50,000 years previously, at the height of the last Ice Age, when frozen seas formed an ice bridge across the Bering Strait linking Asia with North America. From here, Asian nomads headed down the new continent, each generation reaching further and further south, until arriving in the tropics just about the time when the final snows of the Ice Age were melting away. These

So Why is it Called Belize?

Good question. Nobody is quite sure. Back in the 17th century, one of the first settlements founded by the British loggers, who made up the majority of the population at that time, was named 'Belize Town', which would go on to become Belize City, the country's largest urban centre and, until 1970, its capital. That much is clear. What's rather less clear is where the name came from. Various theories have been put forward, some more convincing than others. A number of authorities claim that it is a simple corruption of the Maya word 'Belix', which means muddy (the town was founded on swampy ground, after all). Others contend that it is a contraction of 'Belikin' (like the beer), another Maya word meaning 'road to the east'. Another suggestion has it as a mispronunciation of the name 'Wallace' (that's quite some mispronunciation), a Scottish pirate who settled here in 1620, while yet another theory argues that the pirate's name was in fact 'Willis' (which does at least sound a bit more like Belize), that he was English and settled here in 1638. There's no definitive answer. Take your pick.

wandering hunter-gatherers would, over the next few thousand years, begin to utilize simple forms of agriculture, cultivating maize and beans, which in turn obliged them to settle down into (semi-)permanent communities.

From this simple protocivilization would emerge something much more complex, the **Maya**, who from around 1500 BC to AD 1000 would develop a culture and a form of social organization as advanced as anything in contemporary Europe (not that the two continents had the slightest idea of the other's existence, of course). For two and a half millennia, great advances would be made in the fields of astronomy, science, architecture and sculptural art. The Maya would create great forest-clearing cities filled with temples, devise complex writing, counting and religious systems, and fashion tiny intricate pieces of jewellery from jade, which they regarded as the most precious of all materials. And then, almost in the blink of an eye, the whole thing would vanish. The great cities would, in just a couple of generations, be abandoned and reclaimed by the jungle; the centuries worth of accumulated learning would be lost. And nobody is exactly sure why. Indeed, trying to discover the definitive reasons for the collapse of Mayan civilization in the 10th century AD has become one of the great historical detective puzzles.

The Age of Maya Dominance

It is generally accepted that there were three main groups of Maya: the Northern Lowland Maya of Mexico's Yucatán peninsula; the Highland Maya of the Guatemalan highlands; and the Lowland Maya of eastern Guatemala and Belize. The history of the Maya can be further divided into three periods: Preclassic, Classic and Postclassic. **Preclassic** (1500 BC–AD 300) describes the period when the Maya civilization was still in its infancy, when the first permanent large communities were being founded, when systems of belief and ritual were still being codified, and when great astronomical and scientific breakthroughs were being made. This was followed by the **Classic Period** (AD 300–900), which represents the great flowering of this civilization, when all the major advances and breakthroughs were put into practice. It was during this period that all the colossal structures you see today – the mighty pyramids of Caracol, Tikal, Xunantunich etc. – were built, and when the Bacalar Chico trading canal separating the Yucatán peninsula from Ambergris Caye was dug. Such was the Mayan success at this time, in terms of agricultural production and social organization, that the Belize River valley was able to support dozens of separate communities. Indeed, there were far more people living in the area during this period than there are now, with Caracol and Tikal alone supporting populations of over 100,000 each.

Though Mayan urban centres are often described as 'cities', it's an imperfect label. Mayan communities didn't function in the way of modern metropolises. They were first and foremost ceremonial centres, not places of residence or business. Their great structures were not homes, but tombs and temples, platforms on which the religious social elite performed complex rituals (including blood-letting), which they believed honoured their ancestors, appeased the gods and brought fertility to the soils. The religious élite, who inherited their positions (making them, in effect, a

The Mayan World View

There are over thirty significant ancient Maya centres in Belize. And these are just the ones that are known about. The country's jungles have by no means revealed all of their secrets yet, with ruins of this ancient civilization still being discovered every year. While each centre is different – Maya cities were separate entities with a common culture, not part of single empire under a single administrative control – they nonetheless share many characteristics. They tend to have largely similar layouts with great open plazas around which are arranged a collection of significant structures, the most notable being the giant step pyramids, the stelae (inscribed tablets that recorded events) and the ball courts (for more on these, *see* box on p.23). With religion lying at the very heart of Maya society and forming the basis of their world-view, these structures served a primarily ceremonial purpose.

The Maya saw the world and the heavens as one interconnected whole, at the centre of which stood the cross-shaped 'World Tree' whose branches held in place the sky, the earth and the underworld (or Xibalbá, which was considered the realm of the gods). This world, and the gods who controlled it, worked, so the Maya believed, according to readable, predictable astrological rules which could only be revealed via the intense study of the movement and arrangement of heavenly bodies. As a result, the Maya developed an incredibly precise calendar system that could accurately predict the solar year, the lunar months and even exact events, such as eclipses. Indeed it was only slightly less accurate than the calendars we use today.

Of course, religion was not just a matter of determining divine intentions; the gods also had to be placated via worship and sacrifice. This often took the form of blood-letting, whereby the city's leaders would symbolically nourish the gods of the underworld with their blood, just as the gods nourished the earth with rain. Incidentally, it is believed that the similarity between much Maya and Christian iconography – the cruciform imagery, the importance of blood – made the job of the Spanish missionaries sent to convert the heathen population that much easier, as there would have been much about the new religion that would have seemed familiar to the Maya.

The precise look and layout of Maya architecture was extremely significant. Their great ceremonial structures were, as might be expected, carefully aligned with the stars so as to enhance their sacred nature, and their shapes were (so many experts now believe) designed to mirror elements of the natural world. According to this theory, every component of a Maya urban centre was in fact a stylized representation of some other part of the earth – pyramids were mountains, doorways were caves (caves were particularly sacred to the Maya being regarded, quite literally, as gateways to the underworld), stelae were trees while the plazas were fields. Thus, the Maya cityscape could be seen as their attempt to harness and control the great primeval forces of nature and reduce the gods down to human proportions.

The construction of the Maya cities required the invention and development of some very advanced building techniques, the sophistication of which seems all the more remarkable when you consider what the Maya didn't invent – namely the wheel, or metal tools (their most precious material was jade, not gold). Indeed, in European terms, they were essentially a Stone Age culture. Not only did the Maya not have any wheeled transport, they also didn't employ beasts of burden, which means that every single stone in a Maya city had to be brought there and placed in position by hand. They took their religion extremely seriously.

closed aristocracy), occupied the very heart of Mayan society, making decisions based on astronomical calculations that pervaded all aspects of the culture. Only they were allowed to inhabit the ceremonial centre of city, around which the rest of the population was arranged in concentric rings of importance and influence. Next closest to the centre would be artisans and traders, those responsible for building and bringing wealth to the city, while on the outskirts would be the farm workers and peasants, who of course made up the bulk of the population.

Just as it's erroneous to think of Mayan urban centres as cities in the modern sense, so it's equally anachronistic to regard these urban centres as forming a single unified state or empire. Each community was a self-governing entity, maintaining social, cultural and trading links with other states – and occasionally going to war with each other – but remaining essentially separate. Though there was clearly a great cross-fertilization of ideas between the Mayan communities, who shared much the same religious beliefs, the fundamental relationship between the cities was that of rivals, not compatriots. At times, certain cities did manage to achieve a degree of regional supremacy – particularly Tikal and Caracol in the late Classic period – but this could never be described as an imperial-like dominance. There was no such thing as a Maya kingdom, ruled by a monarch or government. The Maya were a shared culture, but with numerous separate points of focus. It was an unstable, undefined, unspecific form of social organization, based on shifting allegiances and ongoing power struggles, which nonetheless seemed to work perfectly well for several hundred years – until it suddenly stopped working altogether, for reasons that are still not fully understood. It appears that, from around the mid-8th century onwards, social relations between the great Mayan cities grew increasingly strained. Trade became more infrequent, wars much more frequent. A period of mass social upheaval followed, which in just a couple of generations saw most of the Mayan cities abandoned and left to decay.

Various theories have been put forward to explain why the Maya self-destructed on such an epic scale (the most outlandish involving some form extraterrestial intervention), the latest of which take as their starting point the notion that, at the end of the Classic Period, the Maya passed its Malthusian limit. In other words, its population grew too big for the land to support, a situation that precipitated a deadly sequence of events.

Mayan Ball Games – It's a Serious Business

It always catches your attention when scanning a map of a Maya site. In among the mass of temples, tombs, pyramids, plazas and stelae, there's always a ball court (sometimes more than one). Ah, you think, so the Maya weren't always so desperately serious. It wasn't all wars and blood-letting and appeasing the gods. At least they sometimes let their hair down and enjoyed themselves. Except they didn't, because even their games seem to have fulfilled a deep religious purpose. The Maya, along with all of the region's other major civilizations, placed great importance on the playing of a game in which two teams of men competed to get a stone ball (or perhaps rubber; the experts are divided) from one end of a court to the other. Silly as this sounds, it's no more daft than the idea of a few men kicking a ball around a pitch commanding the attention of billions of people around the world and generating billions of pounds worth of revenue.

Very little is known about the Maya ball game, but what seems clear is that it was no mere sport, but a solemn ritual, the results of which probably served some sort of predictive, oracular purpose. The ball courts of Lowland Maya sites usually adhere to the same pattern. Laid out at the ceremonial centre of the city, they consist of two sloping banks facing a central channel where the players (nobody knows how many there were on each side) would have competed to move a heavy stone ball from one end to the other, without using their hands, their feet, their head or anything else that might make it easy. Instead, players had to rely on a sort of kneeing or hipping their way to victory. And just to give it an extra competitive edge, it's believed that the members of the losing team may have been put to death.

Thin tropical soils are, despite the abundance of life they sustain, notoriously poor supporters of agriculture. In order to feed a population as large as the Maya, a very large amount of land would have had to be cleared. However, as the years passed, this would have become less and less productive, returning poorer and poorer crop yields, which in turn would have lead to the clearance of more and more forest. Forest clearances on a really large scale would, so it's been argued, have lead to localized (but severe) climate changes, resulting in long periods of drought. As food became scarce, and the mass of the population began to starve, so the people would have turned for help to their rulers in the great cities, whose job it was to appease the gods and ensure the fertility of the soil. But when the traditional rituals failed, the rulers began to blame the problems on each other, starting an ever escalating series of conflicts between the cities. As a consequence, peasants started to spend more time fighting than toiling in the fields, thus further reducing agricultural output. And as the problems got worse, so the unkempt, illiterate masses on the outskirts of society began to turn on the pampered literate élite at the centre. Soon the whole region was in crisis and a mass collapse of a great civilization under way.

It's a theory, but one that, of course, remains essentially unprovable. Whatever the truth, the end came about extremely quickly. While it seems bizarre that an entire population could, in just a few decades, abandon dozens of previously prosperous urban centres, and give up on a centuries-old way of life, that seems to be exactly what happened. Except, that is, in those few places where it didn't. In fact, a few cities in northern Belize and the Yucatán survived the great Mayan collapse into the Postclassic Period (AD 900–1530). Indeed, some were still thriving at the time of the Spanish conquest for reasons that are no more fully understood than why their compatriots imploded.

A Spanish Interlude

When the Spanish began to make their initial incursions into Central America from around 1530 onwards, the great Mayan civilization had long since extinguished. Northern Belize, however, was still home to a number of Mayan communities, most of whom were vociferously opposed to the Spanish presence. Over the course of the next century, Spain would make sporadic attempts to gain control of the land and subjugate the population, but it never seemed like its heart was really in it. Belize certainly didn't see anything like the ferocious offensives being waged against the Aztecs in Mexico at the time, but then Belize had none of the abundant deposits of silver (as had been found in Mexico) or gold (as had been found in Peru) that would have made a more sustained campaign worthwhile.

The Spanish did enjoy some initial success beating back the Mayan resistance, and by the late 16th century had founded a town on Lake Bacalar and a missionary base (from which to convert the local population) at Lamanai. This was about as good as it got, however. The Spanish failed to consolidate their position, and by the early 17th century the Mayan opposition was growing. This culminated in outright rebellion in 1640, with the Maya rising up to force the Spanish from the region.

With so much of the rest of the continent to concentrate upon conquering and subduing, the Spanish never again made a concerted attempt to pacify the Belizean Maya. Nonetheless, they clearly regarded the area as belonging to them, even if they exerted no direct control over it. Which is why the arrival of the country's next set of inhabitants in the 18th century, British pirates-turned-loggers, caused such friction between the governments of Britain and Spain.

The British are Coming

For much of the 16th and 17th centuries, British pirates, with the tacit approval of the British Crown, attacked Spanish ships all the way along the Central American coast. Just as fast as the Spanish looted the wealth of the Americas' indigenous inhabitants, so the British would in turn try and loot it back off them as they attempted to sail it across the Atlantic back to Spain. Many of these buccaneers launched their raids from bases on the islands off Belize's Great Barrier Reef. However, as time went on and the supply of plunderable treasure began to dwindle, so these pirates began to look around for another source of income. They found it in inland Belize in the shape of the forest's abundant logwood trees, from which a valuable blue-purple dye could be extracted for use in Britain's rapidly expanding woollen textiles industry.

Although these buccaneers, who had taken to calling themselves by the more socially acceptable name of '**Baymen**' (because they operated out of the Bay of Honduras), were no longer directly stealing Spanish wealth, Spain still wasn't too happy with their activities. Believing all of Central America to be their sovereign territory (the future Belize they considered simply to be a province of neighbouring Guatemala), Spain made numerous official complaints to the British Crown about the 'illegal' activities of the loggers. The lack of any formal Spanish presence in the area, however, meant that the Baymen were able to continue logging largely free from interference, save for the occasional Spanish raid.

By the 18th century, the loggers had established permanent settlements at Belize Town (later Belize City) and on St George's Caye, which became known collectively as the Honduran Bay Settlement, and, having shipped over several thousand African slaves, had expanded their operation to include the harvesting of mahogany, then becoming a popular building material in Europe.

The British Crown's attitude to the Baymen was somewhat ambivalent. Though it was loath to acknowledge the Central American settlement as being 'officially' British, and thus risk a major diplomatic row (or worse) with Spain, they none-theless welcomed the revenues that logwood brought (which then retailed for around £100 a ton, an absolute fortune). The two countries did sign a number of treaties regarding the land, whereby the Spainish agreed to let the Baymen continue logging in return for Britain recognizing that the area belonged to Spain. The Baymen were explicitly forbidden from forming a government, raising an army or pursuing any other form of agriculture (which begs the question, what did the Spanish expect the British to eat exactly?). But the fact that a new treaty had to be drawn up every few years shows what little effect they had in reality.

In the event, Spain decided that its patience had been tested long enough, and so launched a full scale attack in 1798 with the intention of driving the Baymen out once and for all. Unfortunately for Spain, the all-out nature of the offensive obliged the British government to make up its mind whether it considered the Baymen to be British citizens (and thus worthy of British protection) or not. In the end, the Baymen were given official recognition and a naval sloop and several hundred soldiers were sent to bolster their forces (which also included a number of slaves who may have erroneously believed that they were fighting to gain their freedom).

Although the Spanish had the superior numbers (they mustered no fewer than 12,000 troops), they had the inferior (or, at least, less suitable) boats. At the **Battle of St George's Caye** Spain's large cumbersome ships were relatively easily routed by the Baymen's small manoeuvrable craft, so bringing to an end Spain's spectacularly unsuccessful involvement in Belize's history. She would never again try to conquer the country.

Welcome to the Empire

And so the British phase of Belize's history began, at least semi-officially. In fact, its international status would remain vague for decades to come, as it continued to operate as a sort of semi-independent, informal adjunct of the British Empire, only finally being incorporated into the Empire, as the colony of British Honduras, in 1862. Nonetheless what the battle had shown, very clearly, was the way the geo-political wind was blowing, demonstrating in microcosm a global shift of power. Britain was on the up, set to dominate world affairs for the next century, while Spain was very much caught in a downward spiral. She would lose most of her American territories within a few decades, as a popular independence movement swept across the region. Central America, an area she had never had much fondness for anyway, was relinquished more or less without a fight once her beloved Mexico had torn itself free from the imperial grasp in 1820. For most Central American countries, news of their independence arrived with a despatch at the head of mule train, rather than at the point of a rebel gun. It must have come as a shock, which perhaps explains why most of the countries of the isthmus seemed reluctant to go it alone at first, with Guatemala, El Salvador, Honduras, Nicaragua and Costa Rica banding together to form the relatively short-lived Central American Federation.

Belize, however, stood aside. Its destiny remained, at least for now, outside the realm of the Spanish-speaking world. Life in Belize continued much as it had done for the past century, albeit more peacefully now that its inhabitants no longer had to fight off regular Spanish attacks. The country's population began to grow, augmented by a new wave of British settlers, and its urban centres, particularly Belize City, began to expand. In 1838 slavery was abolished, after which the Creole descendants of those former slaves went on to become the country's largest ethnic group. The country grew more confident. Its borders, previously sketched faintly in pencil, were inked in more firmly. Unfortunately, this growing boldness provoked a hostile reaction from one of Belize's neighbours. In the 1850s, **Guatemala** began to assert a claim to Belizean territory, based on the belief that, as the inheritors of

Spanish authority in the region, Spain's former claim to the country had now passed to it. Guatemala argued that the treaties agreed between Britain and Spain prior to the Battle of St George's Caye (which gave the British logging rights to the forest, but not ownership of the land) still applied. Britain successfully negotiated its way out of the problem, however, signing a new treaty with Guatemala in 1859, according to the terms of which Guatemala agreed to recognize Britain as the official owner of Belize, provided that Britain built Guatemala an access road through Belize to the Caribbean Sea. It was the perfect solution, except for the fact that Britain never bothered to build the road, conveniently forgetting all about it once the treaty was signed. Guatemala, however, remembered, and remembers still, the dispute having rumbled on in a low-key way till today.

Britain's decision to make Belize (or British Honduras, as it became known) a full member of the **British Empire** a few years later can be seen largely as an attempt to head off any further Guatemalan protests. Prior to 1862, Belize had been governed in a rather ad hoc way by a superintendent (essentially a representative of the army), but from that year onwards would be in the charge of an official Colonial Governor, despatched from London, who would administer affairs from the then capital, Belize City.

The latter part of the 19th century saw Belize absorbing a significant influx of Mayan and mestizo refugees, fleeing the Caste Wars of the Yucatán, who would go on to found many of the country's northern towns, including Corozal and Orange Walk. The **Caste Wars** were a particularly savage conflict that erupted in 1847 when Yucatán Maya, who had since the time of the Spanish conquest been regarded as a subservient, second-class people, revolted against the *iadinos*, the Spanish-speaking ruling class. Three centuries worth of racial tension exploded in an orgy of Mayan violence. The Spanish retaliated and the situation soon escalated with violent reprisal following violent reprisal and both sides committing atrocities. By the war's end, over half the entire population of the Yucatán was either dead or had fled.

Though the worst of the conflict was over by the 1870s, the wars rumbled on intermittently until 1901, with a group of hard-core Mayan rebels, known as the Cruz Maya (because they had developed a system of religion based on the worship of a 'Talking Cross' which had promised them ultimate victory), camped out on the Belize border. Indeed the Cruz Maya made several applications to join the British Empire, each time without success.

Mexico did eventually reassert her sovereignty over the Cruz Maya's territory, although it was prompted into action as much by economic concerns as political ones, the area bordering Belize having been found to be thick with sapodilla trees, from which could be extracted chicle, the principle ingredient of chewing gum at that time.

Goodbye to All That – Towards Independence

The late 19th century to the 1960s saw the gradual weakening of Britain's hold over Belize. Though Belizeans fought bravely in both World Wars, disillusionment with the 'mother country' had begun to set in, particularly among the black population, who suffered from widespread discrimination. By the 1920s, a black consciousness movement was under way, which in turn fuelled demands for Belizean independence. A tour of Belize by the Jamaican Marcus Garvey, leader of the UNIA (United Negro Improvement Association), a body dedicated to raising funds to repatriate New World descendants of slaves back to Africa, caused riots among Belize's Creoles and no little uneasiness for the British. Calls for Belizean independence increased in volume during the Great Depression of the 1930s, which brought much economic hardship to the region (as it did, of course, to most of the world).

Though dissenting voices were necessarily muted during the Second World War, many in the country believed the aftermath of the conflict to be the perfect time to start piling on the pressure. Britain had been seriously weakened by the conflict – she was largely bankrupt, her place on the world stage had been ceded to the USA and the USSR and she was becoming increasingly powerless to resist the anti-colonial movement spreading throughout the world. In 1948, she was forced to give up the country she regarded as the 'jewel' in her imperial crown, India. Inspired by the subcontinent's example, **George Price**, a young Belizean councillor founded a new political party, the PUP (People's United Party) dedicated to achieving Belizean independence. It caught the popular mood, and in the 1954 elections the party was overwhelmingly returned to power, forcing Britain to act. Though still unwilling to grant Belize full sovereignty, the imperial mother was obliged to loosen the guide reins a little, so as to prevent a full-scale revolt. In 1964, Britain allowed Belize to become a self-governing, if not yet fully independent, country.

Still, most Belizeans believed it wouldn't be too long before they'd be able to go it alone. And, when in 1973 the country's name was officially changed from British Honduras to Belize, independence seemed tantalizingly close, only for a ghost from the past to reappear threatening to derail the entire process. Guatemala, which had never officially relinquished its claim to Belizean territory, first expressed in the mid-19th century (its constitution proclaimed the country as Guatemala's 23rd state), began to flex its military muscles. Twice in the 1970s Guatemalan troops massed on the Belizean border, forcing Britain to send reinforcements to the area in order to prevent an invasion. As inconvenient as this was, Britain was able to use the ongoing dispute as an excuse to delay granting independence – and indeed there were many in Belize fearful of a future unsecured by the British military – prompting the UN to try and force its hand. In 1980, it passed a resolution demanding that Britain cede to Belize full independent control of its own affairs.

Months of negotiations followed between the British, the Belizeans and the Guatemalans. In the event, it was agreed that Belize would become a fully independent self-governing country within the British Commonwealth, retaining the British monarch as head of state, but entirely responsible for her own self-governance. Britain, for her part, agreed to guarantee the country's safety should Guatemala ever threaten to invade, and still maintains a significant army presence in the country, although this has been scaled down in recent years. Guatemala, far from happy with the deal, has in the years since engaged in much sabre-rattling – with successive governments loudly proclaiming their territorial ambitions – but little action. The Belizeans, meanwhile, got on with the task of (finally) governing their own country, electing George Price, the leader of the PUP, as the country's first prime minister in 1981.

Culture

Government and Politics

Today, Belize enjoys a **parliamentary democracy** very similar to Britain's, on which it is, after all, based. The Parliament (or National Assembly) is split into two houses – an elected lower house (the House of Representatives) whose job it is to make the laws, and an appointed upper house (the Senate) which fulfils a function largely similar to Britain's House of Lords – scrutinizing, reviewing and suggesting amendments to these laws, but, crucially, having no power to insist upon any changes. Indeed, as five of the Senate's nine members are appointed by the ruling party of the day, it often acts as little more than a rubber stamp for the House of Representatives' decisions. The country is led by a prime minister, who is the leader of the largest elected party, and governs with the assistance of an appointed cabinet.

The political landscape is dominated by two main political parties: the left of centre PUP (People's United Party), who played a prominent role in the campaign for independence during the years of colonial rule; and the more right-wing, market-orientated UDP (United Democratic Party). They've more or less shared power since independence. Indeed, whichever party happens to be returned at election time seems to quickly disillusion the electorate who almost invariably vote in their rivals the next time round, although the last election did prove an exception with the PUP (under PM Said Musa) enjoying an unprecedented second consecutive term in office.

National elections must be held every five years, although (again, as with Britain) it is in the Prime Minister's power to call an early election if he feels it to be to his advantage, or if his position has become untenable. Suffrage has been universal since 1954. The voting age is 18.

The Economy

Belize is not, nor has it ever been a rich country. Fortunes have been made here throughout its history, first through piracy and later through the more legitimate pursuits of logging and chicle harvesting, but in general the country's economic history can be characterized as a succession of short-lived monocultures, the rewards of which have quickly been exhausted. These days, the mainstay of the economy is agriculture, with **banana-growing** the single largest employer. This is followed close behind by **tourism**, which is expanding all the time as the country begins to market its ecological and archaeological charms – the Great Barrier Reef, its swathes of tropical forest, its abundant Mayan ruins – more effectively, and the government increases investment in the country's infrastructure.

Indeed, on the northern cayes (particularly Ambergris and Caye Caulker), tourism has already overtaken the more traditional businesses of lobster-fishing and boat-building as the prime employer, largely because over-fishing led to a crash in the lobster population (and the imposition of a strict season to allow stocks to recover), forcing the native population to seek other sources of revenue.

Since the turn of the century, Belize City has also become a major cruise ship destination, with nearly a million people visiting the city in this way in 2005. To put this in perspective, that's around four times the total population of the country.

It seems certain that tourism will become the country's dominant economic force in the near future. For many Belizeans worried about the creation of a Free Trade Area of the Americas, this can't come soon enough. First proposed in the early part of the century, the implementation of the area has been delayed several times as arguments about its terms and conditions drag on. In particular, many in Belize believe that the end to tariff protection that this will signal could drive agricultural prices down and cause a significant recession, which is why there is such eagerness to expand the provision of tourism to fill any fiscal gaps.

Some have even expressed fears that the ultimate consequence of signing the free trade treaty may be the termination of the fixed exchange rate with the US (which currently guarantees one US dollar for every two Belizean), resulting in a devaluation of the entire currency.

The People

Belize is a small, sparsely populated country. Until the 1980s, the majority of its inhabitants were **Creoles**, the descendants of the original British settlers and the slaves they brought over from the 17th century onwards to work in the logging industry. They speak a form of English known as Creole (or Kriol). These were augmented by small numbers of **Mopan** and **Kekchi Maya**, the descendants of Lowland Maya, most of whom live in the south of the country, and from the mid-19th century onwards, by much large numbers of **Northern Maya**, who arrived here as refugees from the savage Yucatán Caste Wars (see p.27), and went on to found many of the country's northern towns, including Corozal and Orange Walk, as well as establishing the first settlements on Ambergris Caye and Caye Caulker.

The 19th century also saw the arrival of the **Garifuna** (also known as the Garinuga), the progeny of African slaves shipwrecked off the island of St Vincent in the early 17th century and Carib Indians (the island's original inhabitants). They were ousted from the island in the late 18th century by the British, who wanted to turn the land into sugar plantations, and sent to an island off the coast of Honduras. From here they eventually made their way to Belize in the 1820s, since when they have founded a number of towns on the country's coast, the largest of which are Punta Gorda, Hopkins and Dangriga. Today they make up around eight per cent of the total population (see box, p.175).

Since then, the most significant waves of immigration have taken place in the 20th century, beginning in the 1930s with **Chinese** refugees fleeing the Japanese invasion of mainland China. Today, several of the region's towns, notably San

Ignacio and Orange Walk, have significant populations of people claiming Chinese ancestry. In the 1950s the country become the latest home for a group of **Mennonites**, a German-speaking religious sect whose extremely rigid beliefs and strict, spartan way of life deliberately removed from mainstream society had led to them being ejected from a number of countries. Belize proved a more tolerant host, however, and the country now has six Mennonite communities – Shipyard, Little Belize, Blue Creek and Progresso in the north of the country, and Barton Creek and Spanish Lookout in the west. The most traditional of the Mennonites pursue a steadfastly simple agrarian existence, making do without electricity, modern appliances, modern fashions or motorized vehicles. Despite their physical separation from the wider community – they do not vote, send their children to non- Mennonite schools, use non-Mennonite financial institutions, serve in the armed forces or marry outside the community (something which is beginning to cause problems, as the Mennonite gene pool is shrinking and birth defects are becoming ever more common) – the Mennonites have nonetheless achieved a good level of success in the one sector of society they don't consider to be off limits, the marketplace, running successful dairy, furniture- and house-making businesses that have bolstered the Belize economy as a whole (*see also* p.213).

In the past few decades, the country's population has also been bolstered by large numbers of refugees fleeing the various conflicts sweeping the rest of Central America. It's estimated that as many as 40,000 **mestizos** may have arrived since 1980, a huge influx for a country whose total population at that time barely topped 200,000. The upshot of this is that Spanish-speakers now outnumber English ones away from the central Creole heartland of Belize City and Belmopan, although English continues to be the official first language taught in schools. While there have been inevitable tensions, the newcomers' absorption into the country has been largely trouble-free, a welcome consequence of the Belizeans' peaceful, non-confrontational nature.

Since the 1990s, the most significant new arrivals have been western tourists, usually referred to here, as elsewhere in Central America, as gringos. Many North Americans now live or have holiday homes in the major tourist hot spots of Ambergris Caye, Placencia and San Ignacio, and are joined in the peak season months of December to May by thousands of short-stay tourists. However, this migration is not entirely one way. Every year, many educated Belizeans leave the country to take up jobs elsewhere, mainly in the US, where their language skills make them eminently employable. The money sent home by these expatriates contributes significantly to the country's overall GDP.

Art and Music

Though accounting for only around eight per cent of the country's total population, most of whom live in just a handful of towns, the Garifuna people have had a disproportionately large influence on the development of the nation's culture. The country's most famous and influential artist, **Benjamin Nicholas**, is Garifuna, turning out colourful naive-style representations of his people's history from his studio in Dangriga (*see* p.178), while the country's most acclaimed musical style is **Punta Rock**, a combination of Punta, a traditional Garifuna music, with modern sounds and influences. It was invented by **Pen Cayetano**, another of the country's celebrated Garifuna artists, in the 1970s as a way of getting Garifuna youth interested in their heritage. Cayetano augmented the traditional drum-based arrangements of Punta with more up-to-date instruments (principally electric guitar) and rhythms and wrote songs highlighting the political and social concerns of the Garifuna people. It proved a huge success with both Garifuna and non-Garifuna alike, and is now popular throughout the country, and indeed in much of Central America. Popular exponents to look out for include the Turtle Shell Band (Cayetano's original band), the Cultural Legend Band, the Punta Boyz, Sopps Sanchez, Aurelio Martinez and the Banda Blanca (a Honduran band, whose success highlights the music's region-wide popularity). To sample the sound, go to *www.stonetreerecords.com*, the website of Stone Tree Records, the country's leading record label, which has a large catalogue of Punta Rock releases.

Another traditional music, this time of Creole origin, still performed on occasion is '**brukdown**', a needs-must sort of entertainment invented by loggers in the early 1800s utilizing whatever instruments lay to hand (or, for want of any instruments, anything that could be hit to make a sound). Thus a melody would be played on a guitar, an accordion, a banjo or a harmonica to a percussive backing of coconut shells, rum bottles, blocks of wood and even animal jawbones (the teeth of which could be rattled with a stick to produce a grim facsimile of maracas).

The music of the country's northern and western regions is strongly influenced by the bordering countries of Mexico and Guatemala (from where the majority of the populations in these areas are derived), so expect to hear lots of **Latin rhythms** when touring these locales.

Jamaican music, particularly **reggae** and **dancehall**, is extremely popular in the Creole heartland of Belize City, while out on the northern cayes you'll hear plenty of international hits aimed at tourists, plus of course regular bursts of Bob Marley. But then you can say that about anywhere; these days there's barely a bar in the world where you can spend an entire evening without hearing 'No Woman No Cry' at least once.

The government of Belize has tried to take a more active role in the promotion of its culture in recent years. In 2003, it set up the **National Institute of Culture and History** (NICH) in order to bring the activities of a number of previously separate cultural bodies under a single administrative control. There are four principal branches of the NICH: the Institute of Creative Arts (ICA), based at the Bliss Centre for the Performing Arts in Belize City, which stages performances of music, dance, drama, etc. and runs workshops and classes; the Museums of Belize and the Houses of Culture, which, as the name implies, oversee the Museum of Belize in Belize City (*see* p.97) and the country's three houses of culture in Belize City, Orange Walk and Benque Viejo del Carmen, where concerts and exhibitions are staged and arts classes offered to the local community; the Institute of Archaeology, which administers the country's multitude of Mayan sites; and the Institute of Social and Cultural Research, which provides scholars and students with access to a library and an archive of significant material on Belize history.

Wildlife and
the Environment

Belize is a little country with a lot of wildlife. The lack of pressure on the country's land, a consequence of its extremely small population – at least in the thousand or so years since the collapse of the Maya civilization – combined with a concerted campaign by environmentalists in recent decades and a far-sighted conservation programme by the country's government, has resulted in around 40 per cent of Belizean territory being preserved against future development, by far the largest percentage in the whole of Central America.

MEXICO

GUATEMALA

BELIZE

03

Indeed, it's estimated that some 70 per cent of the country's land is still blanketed in forest, much of it millennia-old primary forest (and not reclaimed farmland, as is the case with a good deal of the preserved territory in the region's other main conservational hot spot, Costa Rica), which supports thriving populations of native wildlife, including such 'superstar' animals as jaguars, tapirs and black howler monkeys. If forests were all Belize had to offer, it would still be one of the region's prime ecotourism destinations, but it's probably even better known for its offshore habitats, chief among them the mighty 184-mile-long barrier reef which provides a home to an absolute superabundance of sea life.

From the big cats of the forest depths to the colourful birds of the canopy and the scaly shiny creatures of the deep, Belize offers some of the best wildlife-spotting opportunities to be found anywhere in the Americas.

Habitats

Marine Habitats

The Barrier Reef

Belize's barrier reef, the second largest in the world, runs along the entire coastal length of the country, from Mexico to the Bay of Honduras. The reef is essentially a build-up of hard, rock-like calcium carbonate that's been deposited by millions of generations of coral. Although corals often resemble large, single organisms – many look like plants or flowers – each 'individual' coral is actually made up of a community of much smaller creatures, known as polyps, that band together to form the coral shapes. At the start of a reef's life, these polyps attach themselves to a hard, sturdy base, usually a piece of rock, from where they feed by filtering small creatures (plankton) from sea water. As they grow, the polyps produce calcium carbonate, which they use to build supportive skeletons for themselves. When the coral dies, so the calcium skeletons mesh together causing the reef to expand, in the process providing a home to a whole array of other animals – including fish, octopuses, crabs, lobster, sponges, anemones and sea urchins.

Coral reefs are one of the most sensitive of all marine habitats and their health, or otherwise, is a good indicator of the general state of the environment. Coral won't grow just anywhere; conditions needs to be just so. The water must be tropical with an average temperature of over 70°F/20°C, clear enough to allow the algae that grows on the surface of the coral (and from which the coral derives most of its oxygen) to photosynthesize, have stable salinity and (somewhat surprisingly) be low in nutrients. And, even if the conditions are right, coral still grows extremely slowly, by no more than a couple of inches annually. A reef the size of Belize's is thousands of years in the making. So, be sure to exercise special caution if snorkel-ling or diving near a reef, as coral formations are extremely delicate, and can be easily damaged by just the slightest touch (see Reef Safety, opposite). Unfortun-ately, all around the world, coral is coming under increasing threat from human interference, both local (increased development polluting the waters, greater numbers of tourists coming into contact with coral) and international global

Reef Safety

There's much more than just your safety to worry about. In fact, most snorkelling and diving is done in the sheltered waters west of the reef, away from the worst of the waves and currents, and is pretty innocuous stuff. However, you will need to be a competent, confident swimmer, and undergo thorough training, in order to tackle some of the more outlying dive spots.

You're unlikely to encounter anything particularly hazardous in Belize's coastal waters. Large sharks and crocodiles are rare. Small sharks (nurse sharks, lemon tip sharks, etc.) and rays are more common, but largely harmless ('labradors with fins' is how some locals describe nurse sharks). Those few things you do need to keep an eye out for tend to come under the heading 'small and irritating' rather than 'big and deadly'. These include black sea urchins (you'll see them pointing spikily out of holes in the coral), whose sharp spines can get lodged under the skin, and jellyfish, who can deliver a nasty sting.

Of more concern than your protection, of course, is making sure you help to protect the well-being of the coral. Being careful does not just mean refraining from actively grabbing hold of the coral (although, you should take this as read, obviously), but making sure you're co-ordinated enough to avoid accidentally hitting it. Flippers can be rather cumbersome objects, especially once you've stopped swimming forward. Remember, you're a lot longer with them on, so keep a safe distance from the coral: a careless swipe can cause a lot of damage. Also, be careful not to let your flippers stir up any sand as this can clog up the coral polyps' filter feeding mechanism.

If you're not an experienced snorkeller, put in some practice first away from the reef. Several of the hotels on the northern cayes feed the fish by their piers, which provides a good opportunity both to practise using the gear (getting used to the mouthpiece, clearing the mask and stopping the flippers from flipping over when treading water) and see some wildlife.

If you're not a strong swimmer, don't let pride be your guide. Be prepared to wear a life jacket, or to hold on to a life preserver (life jacket) in order to prevent yourself from getting into difficulties and perhaps grabbing hold of or (even worse) standing on the coral.

If planning on snorkelling away from the shallow areas of reef near Ambergris Caye and Caye Caulker, where – so long as you're careful – solo snorkelling is possible, you should engage the services of a professional guide (or go on an official snorkelling/dive trip). Not only will they know the best places to go in order to encounter the maximum amount of wildlife (and help identify what you find), but they'll be able to forewarn you about any hidden dangers, such as the strong currents that often occur in gaps (or 'cuts', as they're known) in the reef.

Don't feed the fish (or any other aquatic life forms) as this can lead to them changing their natural behaviour patterns.

It is illegal to remove any coral (even dead coral) from its location to take back as a souvenir.

warming has led to the 'bleaching' and, in certain circumstances, death of much tropical coral.

The Cayes

On the western shore side of the barrier reef lie over 200 islands, known as cayes (from the Spanish *cayo* meaning 'islet'), which mark the uppermost parts of a great limestone ridge stretching down from the Yucatán peninsula. Many of the islands are tiny, just a few yards across and extending just a couple of feet out of the water. Without the protection of the reef, which acts as a barrier against the erosive effects of the waves, most would have been worn away to nothing by now.

There are three types of caye: very low-lying ones that are only revealed at low tide and support little in the way of life; slightly higher-lying, bare, rocky outcrops that might provide a home to a sheen of algae and the odd resting sea bird, but not much else; and sandy islands. These last are where a bare rocky outcrop has over time acquired a covering of sand dense enough for plants to take root, which in due course has come to provide a home for communities of animals. The very largest, Ambergris Caye (which, at 25 miles long and 1–4 miles wide, is by far the biggest caye) and Caye Caulker, now also support small human populations.

Atolls

East of the barrier reef, Belize's seas are also home to three atolls – ring-shaped formations of coral surrounding a lagoon. These are Glover's Reef, the Turneffe Islands and Lighthouse Reef, the last of which boasts the country's most famous offshore feature, the Blue Hole, a giant submerged limestone cavern (the giant blue circle marks the point where the cavern roof collapsed beneath the weight of the sea water above it).

Coastal Habitats

Mangroves

Mangroves, with their ability to thrive in coastal areas where the freshwater of rivers meets the saltwater of seas, provide a unique environment; their stilt-like roots systems act as ecosystems for a great variety of wildlife including Morelet's crocodiles, crabs and a large numbers of birds. They also perform an important role in the creation of new land, with the mud that collects around their roots eventually being laid down as soil.

There are four species of mangrove in Belize, the most common of which are the red mangrove and the black mangrove.

Sea Grass Beds

The cayes' calm protected waters provide the perfect environment for sea grasses, which are only able to lay down roots in the stillest, most gentle of conditions. For any visitor to the cayes, the great greeny-black beds of sea grass lying just off the shore will soon become a familiar sight, as will the piles of dead fronds littering the sand (except at the better class of resort, that is, who pay people to clean them up). The thickness of the grass can make swimming difficult from the shore, although many hotels provide piers extending beyond the beds' limit. The grass provides a home and a food source to a great range of wildlife, including, in certain areas, manatees, who graze on a particular type of grass known as turtle grass (the largest populations can be found in the Southern Lagoon, near San Pedro, and Swallow Caye, see p.136).

Beaches

Belize's best beaches are found on the northern cayes and along the Placencia peninsula, where the gradual erosion of the coral offshore has lead to the laying down of fine, white and golden sands onshore. As a consequence, these areas are among the most developed in the country. While certain stretches are carefully maintained by adjoining hotels and resorts, other parts are becoming increasingly litter-infested. Do your bit by helping to remove as much as you can – particularly any plastics you may find.

The beaches near Gales Point on the mainland provide important nesting sites for marine turtles (*see* pp.109–110).

Inland Habitats

The narrow landmass of Central America has long acted as an ecological gateway between the temperate zones of the north and the tropics of the south. It's an environmental bottleneck into which the creatures of two continents have been funnelled to adapt, evolve and thrive among a vast array of habitats, topographies and microclimates. With so much of Belize's natural vegetation *in situ*, undisturbed by human interference, the country is one of the best places to observe the extra-ordinary biological diversity that once blanketed the entire isthmus. The statistics are stunning: over 4,000 species of flowering plants (including over 250 species of orchid), over 700 species of tree, over 600 species of bird, over 130 species of mammal and over 700 species of insect live in Belize. No matter how short your stay in the country, you're bound to see something remarkable.

Forests

To the untrained eye, a forest is just forest, a load of trees all in one place, but to a naturalist, there are many subtly different types. And there are plenty of variables to be taken into account before any stretch of forest can be given an official name. Belize's forests may look (and especially at certain times of the year feel) like rain-forest, but according to most scientific classifications, this is exactly what they're not, as they do not receive sufficient or steady enough rainfall, even in the humid south of the country. Instead, forests here go by variety of other titles: 'moist tropical forest', 'coastal forest', 'riverine forest', etc. There are essentially three main types in Belize:

Broadleaf Forest

This is the most abundant form of forest in Belize, blanketing much of the interior, particularly in the southern and western regions, and on the lower flanks of the Maya Mountains. It's a dense, damp, abundantly fertile environment thick with all manner of life. Broadleaf forests are made up of four main layers. The lowest is, of course, the forest floor, which is carpeted with a dense litter of fallen vegetation that provides a rotting feast for fungi, mushrooms and insects. There's little in the way of flowers or greenery down here, however, as the flat-topped trees of the canopy compete so effectively for sunlight that very little gets through to the ground below (less than 10 per cent where there's full coverage). Above this is the second layer, the understorey, essentially the area between the forest floor and the canopy. Here you'll notice how many trees use buttresses – great undulating supports extending from their trunks – to secure their positions. Tropical soils are typically very thin and often waterlogged, providing very insecure bases for trees that can grow in excess of 70ft/21m.

At the top of the understorey sits the canopy, a dense interlocking network of branches and flat, leathery (so as to cut down on water loss) leaves that provides support, shelter and food for a glorious cross-section of bird, mammal and insect life. The upper branches of the forest are also home to numerous epiphytes, including bromeliads and orchids. These are perhaps best described as plant squatters who attach their roots to the canopy (once a seed has been dropped there by a passing bird) in order to gain access to greater supplies of water and sunlight. The tree receives no benefit in return, but then neither does it suffer, the relationship being non-parasitical. And overlooking all of this are the emergents, the kings of the forest, who make up the sparsely populated fourth and final layer. These are giant trees that have managed to outgrow the rest of the canopy and now command all the sunshine and moisture they desire.

Coastal Forest

Also known as coconut forest, cohune palm forest and tropical palm savannah, this somewhat indistinct label describes much of the coastal landscape, which tends to be rather open and sparse (it's certainly much less densely packed with vegetation than broadleaf forest), dotted with palm trees (both cohune and coconut) and often fringed at its margins by mangroves.

Pine Forest

This is probably not what you'd expect to see in a tropical country, but the dry, sandy soils of Belize's elevated western climes, just south of San Ignacio, do support a large, albeit somewhat incongruous-looking, swathe of pine forest. Its appearance is all the odder at the moment because much of it has been destroyed in the past two decades by a particularly voracious pine beetle, leaving behind a landscape of bare dead trunks interspersed by bright saplings that represent the new unaffected growth. When healthy, much of this pine is harvested (sustainably) and used in the local building trade (for more information, see p.166–7).

Belizean Trees

A few of the more notable of the country's 700-plus species of tree include:

Breadfruit – Not a native of Belize, the breadfruit tree was brought to the Caribbean from Tahiti in the late 18th century by Captain James Bligh during perhaps the most famous botanical voyage of all time (it was the trip that inspired the 'Mutiny on the Bounty'), to be used as a cheap source of food for slaves. The trees can grow over 60ft/18m tall and produce large (12in/30cm diameter) oval-shaped fruit, which feature heavily in Caribbean cooking. It's known locally as 'mazopan'.

Cashew – From where the famous snack nut is harvested. This is a much more long-winded and complicated process than you might imagine. Each nut grows on the bottom of a pear-like fruit (which can be eaten and is used in local cooking), from which it must be detached (carefully as the seed contains toxic oils) and then roasted in an oven. It takes quite a long time and several cashew trees to produce a single bag of nuts (which is why they're so expensive).

Ceiba – Or silk-cotton tree, the ceiba was regarded as sacred by the Maya for whom it represented the 'World Tree', which held together the heavens, the earth and the underworld. In more modern times, it has found a more commercial use. Its seed pods contain kapok, a superlight, waterproof fibre often used for stuffing mattresses and pillows and as soundproofing insulation in recording studios.

Coconut Palm – One of the more dominant forms of vegetation in coastal areas – particularly on Ambergris Caye which used to be largely given over to coconut plantations. It can be easily identified by the great clusters of greeny-yellow fruit dangling from the top of its trunks.

Cohune Palm – Also found mainly in coastal areas, the cohune palm played an important role in Mayan society, who regarded as a symbol of agricultural fertility, and is still one of the country's most widely utilized trees: its large, distinctive, feather-shaped leaves are used to thatch roofs, its palm hearts are considered a delicacy and regularly turn up on local menus, while its palm kernels yield an oil which can be used for cooking.

Guanacaste – A great wide-trunked giant, the guanacaste tree can grow over 130ft/39m tall. There's a particularly large and impressive specimen in Guanacaste National Park (after which the park was named, see p.148). The tree's wood has traditionally been used to make canoes.

Gumbolimbo – One of nature's neat little balancing acts, the gumbolimbo tree contains the only known cure for blisters and rashes caused by the poisonwood tree (see below), and, rather handily, can often be found growing in close proximity. Rub the bark on the affected area.

Logwood – The tree that first attracted modern settlers to Belize. The British 'Baymen' began harvesting logwood from the 17th century onwards, boiling up its wood to produce a strong (and extremely valuable) blue-purple dye used in the clothing industry. It's usually found growing near rivers and can be identified by its distinctive yellow flowers, and the thorns adorning its trunk and branches.

Mahogany – Belize's national tree, from which many of the country's early fortunes were made, when the dark hardwood began to become popular with European furniture makers in the late 18th century. It has sweet-scented bark and produces small white flowers.

Poisonwood – It's well named; the poisonwood's dark black sap can, if touched, cause very painful blisters and rashes. You needn't suffer long, however, as the only known cure, the gumbolimbo tree, can often be found growing nearby (see above).

Sapodilla – Another stalwart of the country's early economy, sapodilla trees used to be tapped for chicle, a type of rubber that formed the constituent ingredient of chewing gum until the 1960s when synthetic rubbers were developed. You can still see the v-shaped cuts, via which the latex was harvested, on the trunks of trees. In recent years, sapodilla 'tapping' has begun again on a small scale to service the growing demand for 'natural' chewing gum in Japan.

Seabean – Found almost exclusively in coastal areas, the seabean's name derives from its hard, waterproof seeds, which are designed to be washed out to sea and carried on the tide to different areas.

Strangler Fig – The strangler fig in action, its choking roots wrapped tight around another tree, is one of the iconic images of the jungle. Once deposited on a host tree by a passing bird, a strangler fig seed will start extending its root system around the tree's trunk, starving it of sunlight and oxygen until it eventually dies and rots, leaving behind the hollow tree-shaped lattice of the fig.

Yemeri – Easily identified by its yellow leaves. If passing by a swathe of forest with what looks like a bright burst of sunshine at the centre, that's a yemeri tree.

Wildlife-watching Guide

Whatever you want to spot, be it jaguars prowling the forest depths (an unlikely one, but you might as well aim high), spider monkeys swinging through the canopy, rays gliding their way through the ocean, manatees feasting on turtle grass, or 'gardens' of coral gently swaying in the current, you're best off doing it in the company of an experienced guide. Guides aid wildlife-watching in a number of ways. First, and most obviously, they know the best places to go where the chances of encountering animals will be highest. From a safety perspective, they can help prevent you getting lost, eaten, drowned or succumbing to any other potential disaster. Conversely, they can also steer you away from any activities that might cause damage to the environment. Finally, a good guide will prove invaluable in spotting things you might miss. This particularly applies to wildlife-watching in the forest, where much of the activity takes place 100ft/30m above your head and requires an expert eye to pick out. A guide will help you to spot animals camouflaged in the undergrowth, will identify tracks and calls, and will recognize that log-shaped silhouette for what it truly is. And, if the animals aren't putting in the appearances, guides can also draw your attention to the many and varied plants of the forest, which to the uninitiated can look like mass of indistinguishable greenery.

If staying near a protected area, your hotel should be able to put you in touch with a recommended local guide or tour operator/dive shop. Otherwise, *see* p.64.

Marine Wildlife

The majority of visitors to Belize come with the intention of getting wet, of spending a good portion of their holiday submerged in coastal waters gazing at the rich abundance of life there. And it really is quite some abundance. Beginning on the reef, the main draw, there are 110 species of **coral** (74 hard corals, 36 soft corals, although only around 40 are commonly seen). These come in all manner of shapes (tubes, spheres, fans, feathers) and colours (greens, browns, pinks, oranges, fluorescent blues), and all have been given highly evocative (not to say highly descriptive) names (brain coral, leaf coral, stag horn coral, fan coral, feather plume coral) making their identification all the easier.

Living among the coral is an equally wondrous, effervescent, chocolate-box assortment of **fish**. There are over 600 species – butterfly fish, angelfish, trumpet fish, blue tang, parrotfish and more – plus an almost equally large number of invertebrates – lobsters, octopuses, anemones, sea urchins, sponges... the list goes on. Indeed, you could easily spend your entire holiday underwater and still not see a fraction of all the life there is. The fish can be somewhat harder to identify than the coral, although help is usually at hand if you go on an official snorkelling/dive trip. Most dive boats carry laminated cards with pictures of fish to help you recognize what you see, which is why most snorkelling trips follow the same routine: dive, look, surface, check; dive, look, surface, check, etc.

Larger inhabitants of the reef include barracuda, grouper and sea bass, as well as nurse, reef, lemontip and hammerhead sharks (none of which is considered a great

Tips for Spotting Wildlife in the Jungle

Don't believe the hype. Your guidebook may have a close-up image of a jaguar on its front cover, but your chances of seeing one in the wild are virtually zero (in fact, the cover picture may well have been taken in a zoo – why do you think it's a close-up?). You may see plenty of wildlife during your time in the forest (although this is more likely to be birds and monkeys than big cats) or you may not see anything much at all. Adjust your expectations accordingly and be patient. This is a natural environment, not a theme park.

There are, however, a few tips you can follow in order to give yourself the best chance of seeing as much as possible.

• Go as early as you can. Most animals are at their most active shortly after dawn. This particularly applies to birds (and howler monkeys).

• Keep looking. In the forest, most of the activity takes place in the canopy. Keep scouring the tops of the trees for telltale signs of movement.

• Bring a good pair of binoculars.

• Move slowly so as not to alarm the animals.

• Listen. You'll often hear things (monkeys crashing their way along branches, etc.) way before you see them.

• Be quiet. You're not going to hear anything if you make too much noise. And nothing is more likely to drive the animals away than constant chatter.

• And, once again, be patient.

Safety Tips

• It may seem obvious, but if you're planning to do several hours' worth of hiking through a swathe of thick, humid jungle, you'll need to make sure that you're physically up to the task. There have been too many examples of couch potatoes using Belize's jungle trails to undertake their first serious piece of exercise in years, only to succumb to exhaustion after just a few kilometres. If you know you're coming, get in training early.

• Try to travel as light as possible.

• But be sure to bring plenty of water with you.

• Bring light, easily portable waterproof clothing.

• Wear proper fitted hiking shoes.

• Bring a strong DEET-based insect repellent and reapply regularly. Bugs love humid conditions.

• If exploring without a guide, never leave the marked trail.

Responsibilities

Exploring the jungle is not just about getting your fill of wildlife-spotting. Remember you also have responsibilities to bear in mind.

• Never try and attract animals by offering them food. This can upset their natural feeding patterns.

• Never leave any litter in the forest.

• Never remove any vegetation.

• Obey all the signs at all times.

threat to humans) plus the occasional school of bottlenose dolphins. The very largest visitor of all to Belizean waters, however, is the whale shark, the world's biggest fish, which can grow up to 70ft/21m long and is regularly spotted near Gladden Spit off the coast of Placencia between March and June. Numerous companies offer tours, see pp.191–2. Sort of orangey-grey with white stripes, the great ocean behemoth is, despite its bulk, completely harmless, feeding only on plankton which it filters from the water in the manner of the baleen whales after which it's named.

Terrestrial Wildlife

Mammals

Jaguars

It's not just visitors to the region who find jaguars endlessly fascinating. These elusive jungle killers have long held a near-mystical status in Central America. The Maya, in particular, considered them to be sacred animals. In part, it's the very nature of the beast – the silent, invisible assassin that reveals itself only at the moment of attack – that lends itself so well to mythologizing.

They're the largest carnivores in the Americas; a fully-grown male weighs up to 350lbs/158kg and measures over 6ft 4in/2m, nose to tail. Despite their relative bulk, they're extremely graceful creatures, their distinctive patterning – yellowy-orange fur marked with clusters of black rosettes – allowing them to blend in seamlessly with their jungle surroundings and creep up unawares on their prey, which consists mainly of smaller mammals such as peccaries and coatis, as well as fish and birds.

In theory, jaguars have a range that stretches from the tip of Argentina to the bottom of Mexico, but in reality the population is restricted to a few isolated pockets. Definitive numbers are hard to come by, but it's believed that Belize has the healthiest population of jaguars on the isthmus. Your best chances of seeing one (although be aware that 'best' still means practically no chance) are at the Rio Bravo Conservation Area and the Cockscomb Basin Wildlife Sanctuary, which displays pictures of recent sightings in its visitor centre. Of course, the closest you're likely to get is to some of the animal's droppings or to a tree that's been used as a scratching post (one such tree features on one of Cockscomb's official trails). The camouflage, wariness and predatory skill of these animals mean that, even if you were close by, the chances are, you'd never know. If you're particularly determined to track one down, you could try listening out for their call – which, apparently, sounds a bit like a large dog gently clearing its throat.

Other Cats

Next on the 'must see' list for most wildlife watchers is the **puma**, also known slightly misleadingly as the mountain lion. Its territory extends to lowland as well as highland areas. Indeed, it tends to turn up wherever it can find its main prey of deer, porcupines and peccaries. Not quite as glamorous as the jaguar, and sporting a slightly duller coat – it's a uniform sandy brown with a paler throat and belly – it is nonetheless slightly more regularly seen.

Belize's other three cats are all considerably smaller than the jaguar and puma. The most distinctive are **ocelots** and **margays**, both of which look a bit like miniature, more delicate versions of jaguars (ocelots are slightly bigger) with yellow fur and black markings. The **jaguarundi**, which, despite its name (which unlike 'ocelot' or 'margay' does suggest a miniature jaguar), is actually a small reddish brown cat. It's extremely shy, living deep in the forest depths, and, as a consequence, little studied or understood. And should you need reminding of the distinguishing characteristics of any of the above, remember that all can be very easily spotted in Belize Zoo (*see* pp.106–8).

Monkeys

There are two species of monkey native to Belize. **Black howler monkeys**, which are known colloquially as 'baboons' in Belize, are one of six species of howler found in Central America. While populations of the other five are relatively healthy across the region, black howlers have had their numbers severely reduced in recent years through a combination of hunting (for food) and the destruction of their native forests. Today, they are found in only a few isolated pockets of northern Guatemala, southern Mexico and, most significantly, Belize, where the greatest efforts are being made towards their conservation. The monkeys are well named, with the males of the species greeting and bidding farewell to each day with a prolonged chorus of rasping, reverberating howls, which they produce by forcing air past a hollow bone in their throats. The sound can travel for several miles in the forest and, it is believed, is used to literally 'sound out' a group's territory.

Living in small groups of around four to eight individuals, howler monkeys tend to spend their days lazing at the tops of their favourite trees (all that howling must take it out of them) and, even when active, tend not to stray too far. They operate across a small range of territory, slowly moving from tree to tree on the hunt for leaves. Your best chance of spotting them is probably at the Community Baboon Sanctuary (*see* p.111).

In contrast to howler monkeys, which (when not howling) tend to be sleeping, **spider monkeys** always seem to be on the move. Smaller than howlers with black body hair offset by a white face and breast, they are, at times, quite spectacularly gymnastic, flinging themselves from branch to branch as they make their acrobatic way through the jungle, using all four of their long spidery limbs (hence the name) and strong prehensile tail, which seems to act as a sort of safety harness. (And they do need one; spider monkeys often seem to miss the branch they're aiming for, but miraculously also always seem to manage to grab the one below just in time and recover.) Feeding primarily on fruit, spider monkeys require a lot of territory. Forest clearances have in recent decades severely reduced their numbers. Their cute appearance has also led to them often being captured as pets or put on display in private zoos where they rarely thrive.

Baird's Tapir

Unless told, most people assume it must be the jaguar. In fact, the national animal of Belize is this gentle, reclusive herbivore. But then, when you consider the country's largely conflict-free history, it does seem a more appropriate choice. Tapirs are not often spotted in the wild. Despite their bulk – an adult male can weigh up to 650lbs/290kg, making it Central America's largest land animal – they're very shy, rarely straying from the forest depths. Strange, primeval-looking beasts with short, dark grey (verging on black) fur and small ears and eyes behind a long prehensile snout, they look a bit like a missing link diagram showing the evolution of the elephant (though they are, in fact, a distant relative of the rhino). Slow and lumbering (when out of water, where they spend much of their time feeding) with poor eyesight, tapirs are peaceful vegetarians and unlikely to be aggressive, unless with young. Their distinctive appearance has clearly been very successful. According to fossil records, tapirs have existed in this area for at least 20 million years.

Bat Facts

• Bats guide themselves using a form of natural sonar far more sophisticated and much more powerful than anything developed by humans.

• Some of Belize's caves provide a home to over a million bats.

• Mother bats find their young in among the vast crowds by listening out for their unique cries.

• Bats mate for life, which in some species may be as long as 30 years.

• If food sources become scarce, bats can go into hibernation. Never deliberately disturb a bat, as it has to use around 20 days' worth of hibernation-state food reserves gearing up its metabolism to escape.

• Bats are closely related to primates, as can be seen by their wings, which are essentially a thin membrane of skin stretched across a hand-like structure of four fingers and a thumb.

Bats

Statistically speaking, the mammal you're most likely to see is a bat. Of Belize's 130-plus species of mammal, over 70 are bats. The country's cave-riddled landscape provides the perfect habitat for these nocturnal winged hunters to roost during the day, before emerging to feed at twilight, which is when you're most likely to see them. Most species of Belizean bat eat insects. In fact, if staying in a rural area, a good way to spot them is simply to leave an outside light on, which will soon attract an audience of insects and in due course probably attendant numbers of feasting bats. The country also has a number of nectar-feeding bats and fishing bats, as well as a couple of species of vampire bat, from whom there is a small risk of rabies, although they prey primarily on cattle (and are, in any case, very rare).

Peccaries

Tales of fearful confrontations in the jungle usually involve, not as you might suspect, jaguars or pumas or even tapirs with young, but these small, dark-haired wild pigs. There are two types – the collared peccary and the white-lipped peccary – neither of which is particularly large (2–2½ft/70–80cm and up to 20kg when full grown), but they do move around in large packs of up to 50 individuals and can be highly territorial. They've been known to surround unwary travellers and clack their teeth aggressively, although they're unlikely to attack. The standard advice, if you come across a group acting menacingly, is to climb a tree, after which they should quickly lose interest and move on.

Coatis

Coatis are members of the racoon family. They're about twice the size of North American racoons, with brown fur, white markings around their snout and a ringed tail, which they hold in a distinctive upright stance when they walk. Despite their somewhat lumbering gait, they're agile climbers, scampering up trees in the search for insects and fruit. They're omnivorous and fairly commonly spotted in forests.

Kinkajous

Another relative of the racoon, the nocturnal kinkajou is around the size of a domestic cat with light sandy-brown wool-textured fur and a long prehensile tail. They're rarely seen, at least in the wild, although they have featured in a few life-style programmes of late since Paris Hilton got herself one as a pet a couple of years ago. Their large night-vision eyes are undeniably cute, but kinkajous are ill-suited to domesticity and only reluctantly active in daylight.

Other Land Mammals

Other mammals that might put in an appearance in the jungle include **armadillos** (North American, naked, tailed and nine-banded), **anteaters** (tamanduas and silky anteaters), **porcupines**, **skunks**, **agoutis** (a small rodent that looks a bit like a sort of wiry rabbit) and **pacas**, another small nocturnal rodent, whose meat is highly prized and regularly turns up on the menus of local restaurants, where it's known by the colloquial name of 'gibnut'.

Manatees

West Indian manatees, the world's only aquatic mammalian herbivore, are found in larger numbers in Belize than anywhere else in the Caribbean. As impressive as this sounds, it still only amounts to a few hundred individuals, most of whom can be found in the Southern Lagoon, near San Pedro, and Swallow Caye (*see* p.136). They're certainly rather difficult to miss if you come across one, being around 13ft/4m long and weighing over 1,000lbs/450kg (they look a bit like enormous, inflated seals). Unfortunately their population is currently in serious decline because of pollution, the destruction of their feeding grounds and injuries caused by boat collisions (a consequence of their habit of drifting near the surface).

Reptiles and Amphibians

Crocodiles

Belize's coastal waters provide a home to two types of crocodiles: the smaller freshwater **Morelet's crocodile** (which grows to around 8ft/2.4m in length) and the much larger (and scarier) saltwater **American crocodile** (up to 20ft/6m), which is usually found out at sea. Sometimes the two species come into contact in the brackish water of an estuary, but otherwise inhabit different worlds.

Both are unfortunately endangered and thus only rarely spotted. You're most likely to see them bobbing near the surface like partially submerged logs, or basking on mud and sandbanks. Though unlikely to attack, these are still potentially very dangerous animals and, if encountered, should be given a wide berth.

Turtles

Four types of marine turtle lay their eggs on Belize's beaches and can occasionally be seen in its coastal waters – **hawksbill**, **loggerhead**, **leatherback** (which, incidentally, is the world's largest reptile – a fully grown male leatherback can measure up to 8ft/2.5m long and weigh over 1,000lbs/450kg) and **green** turtles. Unfortunately numbers of all are in decline as development continues apace along the country's beaches, destroying nesting sites, and turtle eggs continue to be harvested by the local population – they're regarded as an aphrodisiac and fetch a good price. Only the hawksbills enjoy any kind of serious official protection and then only on a single stretch of beach near Gales Point, where you can undertake night tours to watch these great aquatic giants clambering clumsily up the shore to dig their nests and lay their eggs from May to October (*see* pp.109–110).

Snakes

Judging the potential danger of snakes is always a matter of subdivisions, of finding the Russian doll within the Russian doll. So, of Belize's 50-plus species of snake, only around half are venomous. Of these, only a handful have venom strong enough to kill a human. These include the eyelash pit viper, the hognose viper and the jumping viper, although you're very unlikely to encounter any of them (and their bites, in any case, rarely prove fatal). There are just two species you really need to watch out for. One is the **coral snake**, the most venomous of all Central American snakes, which is around 2–3ft/60–90cm long and has a black body adorned with thick red bands and thin yellow ones. However, it's not aggressive and will only attack if directly threatened (or trodden on). The other, the **fer-de-lance**, known colloquially as the yellow jay tommygoff, is another matter. This is the smallest Russian doll of all (despite its 5–8ft/1.5–2.4m length), responsible for most of the region's fatal bites. Though not as deadly as the coral snake, it has a reputation for being liable to attack at the slightest provocation. Thankfully, it's nocturnal and rarely seen, although its brown, black and white camouflage can make it difficult to pick out. Nonetheless, there's no need to be overly alarmed. Most visitors to Belize do not encounter a single snake during their time in the country. Just be sure to take special care when walking through dense undergrowth or grassland, particularly at dawn or dusk, when snakes are most likely to be active.

Lizards and Frogs

There are plenty of lizards in Belize. One of the most common is the **black iguana**, (also known as the 'common iguana' and 'spiny tailed iguana'), which is predominantly grey with black bands along its body. They're strange, primeval-looking beasts with nobbly heads, spiky protrusions along the length of their spines, and side-set legs, which make them look a bit like mini dinosaurs (which, essentially, is what they are). They can often be spotted basking in the sun at the side of the road. The very largest can grow up to 3ft/90cm long. Most are considerably smaller.

Their larger, more brightly coloured cousins, **green iguanas**, are much less common, although in recent years a couple of captive breeding programmes have been set up, by the Monkey Bay Wildlife Sanctuary (see p.108) and the San Ignacio Hotel (see pp.155–6), to try and increase their numbers. A fully grown green iguana can be up to 6ft/1.8m long, nose to tail.

You'll probably have an easier time spotting the country's profusion of small **Anolis lizards**. Around 4in/10cm long, they can often be seen scampering around the foliage of restaurants and hotels. They tend to be a uniform colour, ranging from dark brown to bright green, although the males also possess a throat pouch which, when inflated, shines bright red and is used as a warning display against rivals (which often seems to include people).

Belize is also home to over 30 species of frog and toad, including that perennial postcard favourite, the **red-eyed tree frog**.

Birds

For its relatively small size, Belize is home to an astonishing variety of birdlife. In total, including migratory birds, over 500 species have been recorded here. These range from the tiny (the **bumblebee hummingbird**, the world's smallest bird) to the huge (the **jabiru stork**, the largest bird in the Americas); from the colourful (the **keel-billed toucan**, the national bird) to the dowdy (**pigeons** and **blackbirds**); and from the rare (**scarlet macaws**, of which there are less than 200) to the abundant (various species of **parrot**). Every day, whether actively spotting or not, you're bound to see several different species. Bird-watching tours are offered throughout the county and many rural lodges can provide spotting packages. The best places for watching are on the edge of an area of forest, out on the open plains, on the sea-front and, for wildfowl, in wetland areas (the Crooked Tree Wildlife Sanctuary's 16,000 acres of wetlands and lagoons provide probably the best opportunities for spotting wildfowl, *see* p.115). Though the heart of the forest may contain a good deal of birdlife, the denseness of the vegetation can make spotting rather tricky.

Just to demonstrate the country's ornithological abundance, here's a list of all the birds we saw during a single two-hour early morning bird-watching tour near San Ignacio: white-crowned parrot, white-fronted parrot, red-lored parrot, rufous-tailed hummingbird, black-headed trogon, violaceous trogon, golden-fronted wood-pecker, brown-crested flycatcher, great kiskadee, rose-throated becard, masked tityra, clay-coloured robin, hooded warbler, crimson-collared tanager, blue-grey tanager, black-headed saltator, white-collared seedeater and melodious blackbird.

Hummingbirds

These tiny, hyperactive, brightly coloured whirligigs are among the most wondrous of all birds. Belize's 26 species come in a mad variety of shimmering shades (oranges, blues, violets, blacks and iridescent greens – their feathers acting as tiny prisms refracting the light) and an even stranger array of names: the green-breasted mango, the violet-crowned woodnymph, the black-crested croquette, the white-necked jacobin, the violet sabre-wing. But, what they all have in common is their size – they're absolutely minute. Most are under 4in/10cm long. The very smallest, the bumblebee hummingbird, is just 2in/5cm long, making it the smallest bird in the world. Not traditionally a native of Belize, this tiny creature has recently been spotted on Ambergris Caye, where it's believed to have migrated from Cuba. It's well named, being so small that it's often mistaken for an insect.

Hummingbirds possess the ability, unique among birds, to hover. Specially jointed bones and super-fast twitch muscles allow them to beat their wings at up to 100 times per second (impossible for the naked eye and even most high-speed cameras to pick out), enabling them to remain motionless in front of the flowers on which they feast. This frenzied beating produces the faint whirring sound from which they get their name. They use their long tongues to feed on nectar, which they must consume in vast quantities in order to keep their feverish metabolism ticking over – their pulse beats at an astonishing 1,200 times per minute. Some species can eat up to eight times their own body weight in a single day. To compensate for their hectic lifestyle, many hummingbirds go into a sort of mini-hibernation each night, lowering their heartbeat and body temperature and slowing their metabolism until morning. Their speed and tiny size can make it quite difficult to tell species apart, although any hummingbird is a wonder to behold, whether correctly identified or not.

Sea Birds

Belize's coastal areas support several regularly spotted, easily recognizable species, including **pelicans**, with their large beaks and great saggy throat pouches, and **frigate birds**, which have very distinctive V-shaped wings. In the mating season, male frigate birds also sport bright red inflatable neck pouches. There's no need to go out into the wilds to see either of these as both are commonly spotted on the seafront in Belize City.

Birds of Prey

Belize's birds of prey include peregrine falcons, kestrels, ospreys, kites, 12 species of owl and 17 species of hawk. One of the most commonly spotted is the **roadside hawk**, which, true to its name, can often be found in rural areas perched on low posts by the roadside. There are also three species of **vulture** in Belize: turkey, black and king. Indeed, if you spend any length of time driving around the countryside, you're almost guaranteed to come across the rather ominous sight of a group of these naked-headed carrion eaters sat on a fence at the side of the road, waiting for something to go wrong (at which point, you can't help but check the petrol gauge).

Insects

Unlike the rest of the country's wildlife, when it comes to insects, there are probably as many species you want to avoid – including mosquitoes and sandflies – as seek out. For these, make sure you have plenty of DEET-based repellent and good luck. On the opposite side of the scale are **butterflies**, which are extremely plentiful. There are hundreds of species in Belize, many of which are large, brightly coloured and active during the day – in other words, a spotter's delight. The top spot is probably the blue morpho, with its vibrantly coloured six-inch wings, which is common along river banks. To guarantee a sighting, pop along to the Blue Morpho Butterfly Breeding Centre at Chaa Creek Lodge (*see* p.161) or the Green Hills Butterfly Ranch (*see* p.153), which captive-breeds over 30 species.

Moving your gaze from the skies to your feet, you'll find the forest floor alive with all manner of **ants** (it's estimated that for every hectare of forest, there are nine million ants), including leafcutters. They move in regimented lines, each individual carrying a tiny piece of vegetation back to the nest where it is collected for food (the ants don't actually eat the plant matter itself, but rather a fungus which they cultivate on its surface). Slightly less charming are army ants, which launch voracious campaigns through the forest, devouring any small creatures in their path. If encountered, simply move to the side and let the column continue on its way. If walking through any stretch of Belizean forest, you'll no doubt see what look like giant soil footballs hanging from the branches of various trees. These are termite mounds, made from partly digested wood.

Arachnophobia is one of the more common phobias and many visitors to the tropics express a fear of encountering a **tarantula**. This is by no means an impossibility – there are nine species native to Belize, after all – but it is highly unlikely. If fact you'd probably have to put in several hours of dedicated searching to find one, as they're primarily nocturnal and live in camouflaged underground burrows. Your best chance of seeing one is as part of an organized night tour.

Conservation

04

Belize probably operates the most successful and wide-ranging conservation programme in the whole of Central America. It's often held up as a sort of shining beacon of environmental integrity, whose example puts the rest of the isthmus to shame. This does seem rather unfair. While there's much to admire about Belize's conservation policy, it has to be said that its implementation has been a good deal simpler than could have been the case in any of the region's other countries. And for one very simple reason – there are considerably fewer people. Not only does Belize have the lowest population density in all Central America – the total population is less than 300,000 – and thus less pressure on its land (although this is growing), but throughout its modern history settlers here have tended to engage in economic pursuits that have caused little environmental damage.

Indeed, there was a good deal more pressure on the land 1,100–1,400 years ago at the height of the Maya Classic Period (in fact, it may have been this pressure that led to the Maya's eventual undoing, *see* pp.23–4), than there has been in the past 200 years. Where the Maya created over thirty major forest-clearing settlements, the largest of which supported populations in excess of 100,000, modern Belize supports less than half that number of urban centres, only one of whose populations tops 70,000 (Belize City). Belize has never been subjected to the great mass clearances of forests that characterized the development of agriculture in the region's other countries (particularly over the last 100 years), nor has it enjoyed much of a population explosion. Almost everything about the country's history seems to have been almost wilfully designed to have had as little environmental impact as possible. The first Spanish to arrive in Belize, in the early 16th century, were never able to establish a permanent base, while British immigrants who arrived here from the 17th century onwards were after specific resources, not great chunks of land, practising selective logging of logwood and hardwood trees, and later tapping sapodilla trees for chicle (a form of rubber that for a long time formed the main constituent ingredient of chewing gum).

Though Belize's population has grown in the past few decades, it certainly hasn't boomed. Most of its urban centres are small coastal towns, and there are still great swathes of the country, particularly in the southwest on the lower slopes of the Maya Mountains, that support almost no human habitation and have no paved roads, but are instead blanketed with thick jungle. Indeed, the country's road network comprises just four major arteries. Thus the 40 per cent of Belizean land that's been preserved against future development, while an important laudable effort, does not represent land wrestled from the developer's greedy grasp, the result of prolonged battles between environmentalists and capitalists, but rather land that almost nobody was using anyway. The same cannot be said for Belize's neighbours.

Conservation Problems

Of course, just because Belize has managed to preserve a significant proportion of its territory, this does not mean that all is well on the ecological front. The country still faces a good number of environmental challenges. Some of these – such as the plague of pine beetles that devastated over 90 per cent of the country's western pine forest in the past couple of decades, *see* p.167 – lie largely beyond human control. Others can be more readily addressed, providing the political will is there.

Much of the northern half of the country is given over to **large-scale agriculture**, its flat plains now supporting vast plantations of sugar cane and (Belize's principal agricultural export) bananas. While this has necessitated the clearing of a good deal of land, the environmental problems that arise here stem less from the decision to grow crops, as the manner in which they are grown. Banana production, in particular, is one of the most chemically intense farming practices on earth, requiring the use of a whole host of powerful pesticides to keep the plants free from the various blights and ailments to which they are susceptible, traces of which regularly end up in local water courses, causing a good deal of damage to the surrounding protected 'wild' environment.

Furthermore, as Belize's population increases (it has swelled by around 40–50,000 in the past couple of decades, most of these refugees from the region's various conflicts), so it prompts a concomitant increase of the country's infrastructure. The construction of the controversial **Chalillo hydroelectric dam** in the west of the country on the Macal River can be seen in this context. The project was delayed for years while environmentalists launched a series of legal challenges, their chief complaint being that the dam would cause the flooding of a valley that represented one of the country's few remaining habitats for rare scarlet macaws. Eventually, Britain's Privy Council (the highest Court of Appeal for a Commonwealth country) gave the scheme the go-ahead, and construction is now under way. The government, despite having a generally good record on environmental matters (several of the first laws passed here following independence related to environmental protection), have consistently voiced their support for the dam project, which they saw as a means of improving the country's electricity supply for very little public expense, the project being largely funded by the Canadian firm, Fortis (who will, of course, also derive most of the profits). Indeed, the dam controversy neatly highlights the dilemma currently facing the government – namely, how both to improve the country's infrastructure while at the same time preserving the environment, especially when there's very little money available to do either.

Most of the official funding for environmental projects is derived from the US$3.75 conservation tax levied on everyone exiting the country and the 20 per cent commission on cruise ship passenger fees. As useful as this is, it's by no means a huge sum and mainly goes on administration costs. This is where private investment comes in, without which it could be claimed that Belize simply wouldn't have much of a conservation programme at all. In fact, the prime impetus behind the modern conservation movement in Belize was not the government, but the **Belize Audubon Society**, a private body founded in 1969 to promote environmental issues, who were instrumental in the drawing up of the country's national parks system. Today, the society manages several major parks and wildlife sanctuaries, including Crooked Tree Wildlife Sanctuary, Cockscomb Basin Wildlife Sanctuary, Half Moon Caye Natural Monument, Guanacaste National Park, St Herman's Blue Hole National Park and the Shipstern Nature Reserve. Of the money they make, most is ploughed straight back into the parks system, 10 per cent goes to the government while 20 per cent is put aside in a fund for developing other environmental projects. The society's work – alongside that of several other prominent private companies and NGOs involved in the administration and funding of Belize's conserved areas (including the Programme for Belize, *www.pfbelize.org*, which looks after the Rio Bravo Conservation Area, and the Friends of Belize Nature, *www. friendsofbelizenature.org*, which manages Laughing Bird Caye) – serves to take the pressure off the cash-strapped government.

Ecotourism – the Perfect Solution?

In its search to find a way to fund the upkeep of the environment, Belize's government is – as with several of the region's other countries, most notably Costa Rica – currently keen to explore the possibilities of **ecotourism**. Over the past few years, it's begun investing heavily (as much as it can invest heavily) in the country's tourist infrastructure and started marketing its natural wonders more aggressively in the hope of making it a more attractive destination for foreign (principally rich US) visitors. The logic of such a scheme is easy to understand – get people to come and pay to experience the country's natural environment, and use the money derived to fund the environment's upkeep. Unfortunately, while there's much merit in this approach, things aren't always that easy. Pristine natural environments and hordes of visitors don't always make the easiest or most accommodating of bed-fellows. Delicate ecosystems tend not to react well to being trampled over day after day. In the interior of the country, this isn't yet a major problem, as visitor numbers to the national parks and forests have yet to reach overwhelming levels. On the coast and on the northern cayes (particularly Ambergris Caye), however, it's a different story. Here growing numbers of vacationers have fuelled a significant expansion of the region's resorts with scores of new hotels, condominium complexes and holiday homes being built. As welcome as this investment is, some of the country's tourism hot spots, most notably Placencia, are beginning to show worrying signs of **overdevelopment**. Many people have expressed concern over whether the country's basic infrastructure – especially water provision, and sewage and litter disposal – will be able to cope with the pace of construction. Certainly litter levels on those stretches of beach not maintained by a resort or hotel are becoming worryingly high. It's also been claimed that several development projects have been given the go-ahead without the benefit of proper prior environmental impact studies. These are particular concerns because, of course, anything that happens onshore will in due course begin to affect what's happening offshore on the coral reef, one of the most delicate and easily damaged of all habitats.

Coral can be adversely affected in a number of different ways: from increased levels of toxins in the water (which may result from the overuse of pesticides on the mainland); from topsoil being washed into the sea in areas where the natural vegetation has been cleared, which can disrupt the polyps' filter feeding mecha-nisms; and from increased exposure to human interference. Such is the extremely fragile nature of coral that simply touching it can often cause it to die. Worst of all, the coral's achingly slow growth rate – it can grow little more than a couple of inches a year – mean that these losses cannot easily be replaced. Furthermore, because coral provides a habitat for a whole host of other creatures – including fish, octopuses, crabs, sponges, lobster, urchins and anemones – its destruction can lead to a whole series of knock-on environmental effects. In certain instances it can even lead to the collapse of entire mini-ecosystems. For this reason, you should always exercise extreme caution whenever snorkelling or diving near coral. For tips on reef safety, see p.35.

The demands of tourists, who naturally want to see as much wildlife as possible, as quickly as possible, have also led to some tour guides and hotels using food to attract large shoals of fish to a specific and easily accessible viewing area. While this may guarantee visitors good views, it can have a deleterious effect on the wildlife, changing their natural feeding habits.

Involving the Local Community

Of course, while there may be problems inherent in the task of raising visitor numbers while at the same time maintaining the integrity of the natural environment, ecotourism still represents the best way of funding the country's preservation. However, in order for it to be truly effective, it needs to benefit society as a whole, which means a lot more Belizeans need to have access to the profits being made from environmental protection than is currently the case.

To date, Belize's conservation movement has largely been led and funded by foreign interests (principally Americans), who have also reaped the rewards. The Belize Audubon Society, the country's pre-eminent conservation group, was, when founded, largely made up of foreigners (although more Belizeans are involved these days), and most of the country's major resorts, particularly in the tourist hot spots of Ambergris Caye, Placencia and the Pine Ridge Mountain Reserve, are American-owned. This could have far-reaching consequences. As the population continues to grow, there are going to be increasing demands placed on the country's land and resources. If the government wants this pressure to translate into people getting jobs in the ecotourism industry and starting projects to showcase the country's natural wonders, rather than ransacking the environment for their immediate agricultural or housing needs, then these people need to be able to benefit eco-nomically from doing so. Many Belizeans have found employment in tourism, but this mostly takes the form of low-level service jobs, acting as guides, hotel staff etc. The few examples there are of local communities being involved at a more intrinsic, operational level – notably at the Community Baboon Sanctuary and the Cocks-comb Basin Wildlife Sanctuary – tend to be small-scale concerns. That said, they do perhaps give some idea of the way forward, giving people an economic impetus to get involved in preservation. However, as things stand, it appears very difficult for locals to raise the capital needed to fund larger, more ambitious tourism projects. And, until this problem is addressed, there will always be a flaw at the heart of the ecotourism argument. For, if the environment is to be maintained for the benefit of everybody, then everybody needs to benefit from it. If the profits from conservation are largely being enjoyed by rich foreigners, it's perhaps no surprise if poorer locals occasionally decide it's not worth the effort. The ideal conservational solution would see Belize's natural wonders preserved, tourism managed in a way that doesn't impact on the environment (or, at least, only minimally), and the profits of tourism used both to help maintain the environment and to get local communities involved with, and benefiting from, its preservation. It's a difficult circle to square.

Belize's Protected Areas

There are over 60 officially protected areas in Belize – some government-owned, many private – which are split into eight categories: marine reserves, private reserves, national parks, national monuments, archaeological monuments, wildlife sanctuaries, forest reserves and nature reserves. These classifications can be slightly confusing. For instance, Laughing Bird Caye is not classed as a marine reserve, but a national park, while the Blue Hole is deemed a national monument. Similarly, the

Monkey Bay Wildlife Sanctuary is not officially designated as a wildlife sanctuary, but a private reserve. To clarify matters, we have used just three categories to describe the areas: Marine Nature Reserves, Terrestrial Nature Reserves and Archaeological Reserves. Not all of the country's protected areas can be visited; some are simply spawning grounds for fish. Those featured in the book are listed below.

The government body that oversees the administration of the country's protected areas, and distributes the funds raised from the US$3.75 conservation tax paid by every visitor leaving the country, and the 20 per cent commission on cruise ship passenger fees, is **PACT** (Protected Areas Conservation Trust), which can be contacted at 2 Mango Street, Belmopan, **t** 822 3637, *www.pactbelize.org*.

Marine Nature Reserves

Name	Type	Chapter	Page
Bacalar Chico	Marine Park	The Northern Cayes	p.119
Blue Hole	Natural Monument	The Northern Cayes	p.142
Caye Caulker	Marine Park	The Northern Cayes	p.134
Gladden Spit	Marine Park	The South	p.175
Glover's Reef	Marine Park	The South	p.182
Half Moon Caye	Natural Monument	The Northern Cayes	p.145
Hol Chan	Marine Park	The Northern Cayes	p.125
Laughing Bird Caye	National Park	The South	p.196
South Water Caye	Marine Park	The South	p.182
Swallow Caye	Wildlife Sanctuary	The Northern Cayes	p.136

Terrestrial Nature Reserves

Cockscomb Basin	Wildlife Sanctuary	The South	p.187
Community Baboon	Wildlife Sanctuary	Belize City & District	p.111
Crooked Tree	Wildlife Sanctuary	Belize City & District	p.115
Five Blues Lake	National Park	The West	p.150
Gales Point	Wildlife Sanctuary	Belize City & District	p.109
Guanacaste	National Park	The West	p.148
Mayflower Bocawina	National Park	The South	p.181
Monkey Bay Sanctuary	Private Reserve	Belize City & District	p.108
Rio Bravo	Private Reserve	The North	p.212
St Herman's Blue Hole	National Park	The West	p.149
Shipstern Nature Reserve	Private Reserve	The North	p.218

Archaeological Reserves

Altun Ha	Archaeological Monument	Belize City & District	p.112
Cahal Pech	Archaeological Monument	The West	p.155
Caracol	Archaeological Monument	The West	p.171
Cerro Maya	Archaeological Monument	The North	p.216
El Pilar	Archaeological Monument	The West	p.160
Lamanai	Archaeological Monument	The North	p.210
Nim Li Punit	Archaeological Monument	The South	p.201
Santa Rita	Archaeological Monument	The North	p.216
Xunantunich	Archaeological Monument	The West	p.163

Food and
Drink

This chapter contains information
on the specialities of Belize cuisine
and what you can expect to find
on restaurant menus when you
go out to eat. Recommended
restaurants, cafés and bars are listed
in the 'Eating Out' sections of the
regional chapters.

05

The Cuisine

There is no true native Belizean cuisine, at least not in a country wide sense, although the country's numerous cultural groups do all have their own culinary specialities to offer. Instead, the country's restaurants serve up a sort of mishmash of Caribbean, North American, Latin American and British flavours. As varied and exciting as this sounds, for many Belizeans these influences have been reduced down to just two main dishes – **rice and beans**, and its inverted sibling, **beans and rice**. The standard recipe for Belizean rice and beans utilizes white rice and red beans which are cooked together in coconut milk giving the dish a slightly moister, creamier consistency to that served in most other Central and South American countries, which tends to feature black beans and be flavoured with cilantro (coriander). It can be eaten on its own, although it's frequently served with a piece of fried chicken, fish or stewed meat and perhaps a small portion of coleslaw, potato salad or fried plantain. Beans and rice, also known as **stew beans with rice**, is a slightly different concoction, albeit not a million miles away from rice and beans. Here, the beans are cooked separately from the rice – often with a pig's tail or another cheap cut of meat added for flavour – until it forms a thick juice which is poured over the rice. Again, this is often served with fried or stewed meats or fish. As cheap and filling as rice and beans is, it's also a bit bland, and its appeal can quickly begin to pall if you're obliged to eat it every day – though many Belizeans happily manage it. Thankfully, there are plenty of other dishes on offer than will give your taste buds a bit more of a work-out.

Unsurprisingly for a country with a 200-mile-long Caribbean coastline, there's plenty of fish and seafood to be had in Belize. The prime (and priciest) catch is **lobster**, available in all the main coastal tourist hot spots, such as Ambergris Caye, Caye Caulker and Placencia, where you can expect to see it crowbarred into all manner of dishes, from pastas to curries, during the open season of mid-June to mid-February. Lobster fishing is banned for the rest of the year in order to preserve stocks, over-fishing having led to a crash in the lobster population in the 1980s. Do not order or accept an offer of lobster outside the official season. When there's no lobster to be had, **conch** (pronounced 'konk') tends to take its place on the menu. This chewy (sometimes too chewy) delicacy is often used in *ceviche* (a mixture of fish, seafood, onions, peppers and spices 'cooked' in lime juice) or dipped in batter, fried and served in the form of **conch fritters**. The open season for conch is October to June. Red snapper, barracuda, sea bass and shrimp are also available and served in a variety of ways – barbecued, fried, stewed, as part of a soup or perhaps even cooked in coconut milk, as happens with the Creole dish *seré* and the Garifuna dish, *hudut*, a mixture of fish and plantains.

Because much of what's served in the restaurants of Belize's tourist towns is aimed squarely at American and European tastes, with pizza, pasta, hamburgers and steak sandwiches dominating the menus of many hotel restaurants, you need to go to local Belizean-orientated restaurants if you're looking to experience something out of the culinary norm. Local dishes to look out for include *panades* (a cornmeal turnover stuffed with beans, fish or meat and fried), *garnaches* (crisp corn tortillas topped with beans, cheese and salad) and **tamales** (also known as *bollos* or *dukunu*, a corn dough, sometimes stuffed with chicken, steamed in plantain leaves). Two particularly intriguing dishes you'll occasionally see chalked up on specials boards are **gibnut**, a rodent that apparently tastes like a cross between chicken and rabbit, and **cowfoot soup**, a gooey mixture of vegetables and (as the name suggests) cow's hoof. Cowfoot soup seems to fulfil the same purpose for Belizeans as kebabs do for British people, often eaten in the early hours of the morning after a night out. Perhaps, like a doner, it only becomes appealing after a certain number of beers. You may also see offered the meat and eggs of the green iguana (known locally as 'bamboo chicken') and turtle eggs, although as both species are endangered, these should be avoided.

Meat eaters generally do very well in Belize. Chicken is probably the most popular meat and is prepared in a number of ways, from the spicy Jamaican '**jerk**' style to *escabeche* – chicken served in an onion broth. If you don't eat meat or fish, you should still be able to get by without too much of a struggle. Most touristy restaurants will offer at least one **vegetarian** option (usually a burrito) and veggie-friendly pizzas or pasta dishes are quite easy to come by, unless you venture away from the main tourist spots. Almost all of Belize's towns have a range of **Chinese** restaurants and many also boast an **Indian** restaurant, which offer the best choice for vegetarians. And if all else fails, it's back to rice and beans, which can be spiced up with a dash of hot sauce. Indeed, **hot sauce** has a ubiquity matched only by rice and beans, with bottles of the stuff adorning virtually every fast-food counter and restaurant table in the country. Nine times out of ten the hot sauce will be from the Marie Sharp range (*see* p.179), though some establishments prefer her competitor 'Hot Mama's' or imported Caribbean varieties. Marie Sharp's rags to riches story has made her quite a celebrity in Belize and just about every gift shop stocks some of her range of sauces, jams and jellies. In fact Sharp's *habanaro* pepper hot sauce, which comes in varying heats from 'mild' to 'beware', has become the most popular souvenir with visitors to the country.

Drinks

All of the main US carbonated soft drinks – Coca Cola, Pepsi, Fanta etc. – are available throughout Belize, and tourist bars often sell imported beer and spirits, albeit for a considerable mark-up. Locally produced drinks are generally a good deal cheaper and much easier to find. These include fresh fruit juices, shakes (look out for the unusual, but not unpleasant tasting, seaweed shakes sold on street corners), rum and beer. There are a number of different **rums** available in Belize, some of which are Caribbean imports. The locally distilled One Barrel is widely agreed to be one of the more palatable brands, especially when served with coconut water and pineapple under the name 'Panty-Ripper', one of the most popular cocktails in the country's resorts.

While you can buy American beer in most supermarkets and some bars, the Belizean-brewed alternative, **Belikin**, is available absolutely everywhere, and is much more reasonably priced. There are several varieties: a regular lager, a premium lager (slightly pricier and sold mainly in resorts), Lighthouse lager and Belikin stout. Stout and regular are sold in the same bottles, which feature a crude depiction of the Temple of the Masonry Altars at the Mayan site of Altun Ha. Regular has a green bottle-top, stout a blue one. Some bars can offer draught Belikin, but usually your choice will be limited to bottles of regular and stout. You have to be 18 to drink in Belize. You may be asked for ID to prove your age if you look young.

Unfortunately, despite Belize growing a small amount of its own **coffee**, most of what's served in the country's restaurants – even in high-end resorts – tends to be rather weak and watery. Strangely, even though many hotel rooms provide coffee machines, they don't always supply coffee. And as ground coffee is not always available in the country's smaller villages, you might want to stock up in Belize City.

Eating Out

Belize is not yet a fast-food nation. The great multinational burger and fried chicken concerns have yet to make their presence felt here and, at the time of writing, there is just one international fast-food franchise in the entire country – a rather lonely branch of Subway in Belize City. Still, inexpensive, speedy snacks do make up a large part of the Belizean diet, with the Burger King role provided by street vendors and the small shed-like structures you'll see at the side of the road serving up simple snacks, such as *empanadas* and tacos, for a couple of dollars.

Other than this, Belize's **restaurant** scene can be divided into two main categories: those places aimed at locals, which tend to be simply decorated affairs offering a limited menu aimed at Belizean tastes; and those places aimed at tourists, which are usually a good deal swankier and turn out a range of international dishes. The latter are often more stylish, but can also be rather uninspired and generic. For a more authentic Belizean experience, you're best off dining at small, family-run places. To find a good one, don't bother trying to judge it by its exterior appearance – Belize's restaurants certainly aren't going to win any awards for style. Instead ask around for recommendations – a taxi driver or hotel receptionist should be able to help you – or just look out for the place that's doing the most business.

In Belize most people eat their largest meal of the day at midday – which is why most businesses shut down at this time – and, if you are keen to keep your food budget down and taste authentic Belizean dishes, it's advisable to do as the locals do, and get your table early. Not only will the food not have been sitting around for hours, but you'll also get a good deal more choice as some cafés and restaurants close after lunch time and do not open again till the next day. Others are only open for a limited time in the evening, from 6 till 8pm. Breakfast can usually be had any time after 7am, when eggs, sausages, bacon and beans with **fry jacks** (portions of fried flour dough) or buttered **johnny cakes** (savoury flour biscuits) will be on offer.

Belize is becoming ever more adept at servicing the needs of tourists and, unless you are somewhere particularly remote, you should usually be able to find somewhere open for an evening meal, at least six days a week. Remember many businesses, including most restaurants, are closed all day Sunday. And those that don't shut on Sundays (most typically, Chinese restaurants) tend to close instead on Mondays.

Travel

06

Getting There

By Air

The majority of visitors to Belize arrive on flights from the United States. This includes visitors from the UK, Europe and Australasia, who will usually have to connect via one of the US cities of Atlanta, Charlotte, Dallas, Houston or Miami. There is just one international airport in Belize, the Philip Goldson International Airport (t 225 2045 for flight information), which is located in Ladyville, 12 miles north of Belize City.

Air fares are cheapest during the low season of May–November, and at their most expensive in December–April, the high season, reaching a peak during the six-week holiday period either side of Christmas.

From the UK

At the time of writing, it is not possible to fly direct to Belize from the UK. However, a radar tower (the country's first) and a new longer runway capable of dealing with transatlantic aircraft are currently under construction at Philip Goldson International Airport. Direct flights from the UK and Europe will hopefully (but by no means definitely) be available from 2007.

The total travelling time from the UK can be as little as 12 hours and as much as 36 hours, depending on which part of the country you're coming from, stopover times and the number of connections you need to make. American Airlines offer flights via Dallas or Miami, Continental via Houston, and US Airways via Dallas or Houston. Fares range from £650 to £850, depending on the season. A slower, but cheaper alternative (reducing your total airfare by up to £200) can be to fly to Cancún, Mexico, and then get a bus the rest of the way (see p.62 for bus details). Discounts are generally more readily available on flights to Cancún than to the USA (though it depends on the time of year).

From Ireland

There are no direct flights from Ireland to Belize. You'll have to make it to the USA and connect from there. Aer Lingus offer flights from Dublin and Shannon to Boston, Chicago and New York, and from Dublin only to Los Angeles. Fares range from below €700 to over €1,000.

From the USA and Canada

Direct flights from the USA to Belize depart from Atlanta (Saturdays only with Delta), Charlotte (Saturdays and Sundays with US Airways), Dallas (daily with American Airlines), Houston (daily with Taca, Costa Rica's national carrier, and Continental) and Miami (daily with American Airlines). Flight fares start at around $400 from Atlanta and Houston, $500–600 from Charlotte, Dallas and Miami. Flying time is roughly 4hrs from Atlanta, 3hrs from Charlotte and Dallas, 2½hrs from Houston and 2hrs from Miami. To get to Belize from more outlying cities, such as Los Angeles and New York, you'll have to change flights at one of the airports listed above.

You cannot fly direct from Canada to Belize. You'll have to travel to the USA and connect from there.

From Australia and New Zealand

Qantas and Air New Zealand both offer services from Australia to Belize City via Los Angeles (and at least one other airport) from around Aus$3000.

By Sea

It's possible to reach Belize via water taxi from Honduras and Guatemala (but not Mexico). Boats from Puerto Cortés, Honduras, to Dangriga are run by Nesymein Neydy (t 522 0062) and leave on Mondays and Tuesdays at 9am. The journey takes around 3hrs and costs US$50. Gulf Cruza (t 202 4506/523 4045) run a service from Puerto Cortés, Honduras, to Placencia on Mondays at 10am, which takes 4hrs and costs US$50. From Guatemala, Requena's Water Taxi (t 722 2070) departs Puerto Barrios for Punta Gorda in southern Belize at 2pm daily. The journey

Exit Tax

Although there's no entry tax to Belize, do bear in mind when calculating your budget that you need to keep back US$35 to pay the exit tax, which applies to all tourists departing the country by air. This must be paid (when passing though to departures) either in cash (US dollars only) or by credit card (US cards only).

Airline Carriers

UK and Ireland

Aer Lingus, UK t 0870 876 5000, Ireland t 0818 365 000, www.aerlingus.com.

American Airlines, UK t 0845 778 9789, Ireland t (01) 602 0550, www.aa.com.

Continental, UK t 0845 607 6760, Ireland t 1-890 925 252, www.continental.com.

Taca (also known as Grupo Taca), UK t 0870 241 0340, www.taca.com.

US Airways, UK t 0845 600 3300, Ireland t 1-890 925 065, www.usairways.com.

USA and Canada

American Airlines, USA/Canada t 800 433 7300, www.aa.com.

Continental Airlines, USA/Canada t 1-800 231 0856, www.continental.com.

Delta Airlines, USA/Canada t 800 241 4141, www.delta.com.

Taca (also known as Grupo Taca), US t 1-800 400 8222, Canada t 1-800 722 82222, www.taca.com.

US Airways, USA/Canada t 800 622 1015, www.usairways.com.

Australia and New Zealand

Air New Zealand, Australia t 1-800 809 298, New Zealand t 0800 737 000, www.airnz.co.nz.

Qantas, Australia t (13) 1313, New Zealand t 0800 808 767, www.qantas.com.au.

Discounts, Special Deals and Online Travel Sites

The great online marketplace represents your best bet for finding a cheap flight to Belize, although to get the very best deals you'll have to be as flexible as possible with your dates, whilst at the same time being willing to accept the most rigidly applicable, non-refundable, non-alterable tickets going.

www.airbrokers.com
www.arrowtravel.com

www.cheapflights.co.uk
www.cheapflights.com
www.cheapflights.com.au
www.cheap-flight-finder.com
www.cheaptickets.com
www.ebookers.com
www.expedia.ca
www.expedia.co.uk
www.expedia.com
www.flightfareshop.co.uk
www.flights.com
www.flights.com.uk
www.flyaow.com
www.hotwire.com
www.kayak.com
www.lastminute.com
www.lastminute.com.au
www.lastminute.co.nz
www.moments-notice.com
www.opodo.co.uk
www.site59.com
www.skyauction.com
www.travelocity.ca
www.travelocity.co.uk
www.travelocity.com

Student and Youth Deals

There are a number of dedicated travel agents for students, who are entitled to significant discounts. Note that the term 'student' in this instance is taken to mean anyone under 26, or anyone under 32 in full-time education.

STA Travel:
UK: t 0870 163 0026, www.statravel.co.uk.
USA: t 800 781 4040, www.statravel.com.
Canada: t 888 427 5639, www.statravel.ca.
Australia: t 1300 733 035, www.statravel.com.au.
New Zealand: t 0508 782 872, www.statravel.co.nz.

Student Flights (UK), t 0870 499 4004, www.studentflight.co.uk.

Travel Cuts (US & Canada), USA t 1-800 592 2887, Canada t 1-866 246 9762, www.travelcuts.com.

Usit (Ireland), t (01) 602 1904, www.usit.ie.

takes just over 1hr and costs US$17.50. Boats from Livingston, Guatemala, also leave for Punta Gorda on Tuesdays and Fridays at 7am.

As with air travel, you will not be charged an entry tax when arriving in Belize by boat but you will be required to pay a **conservation fee** of US$3.75 when leaving (if leaving by boat). This can be paid in US or Belizean currency.

By Land

Car Formalities

If you wish to bring your car into Belize from Guatemala or Mexico, you will need to obtain a temporary importation permit. Permits are valid for one month (extensions can be acquired from the Customs Department, t 227 7092) and are secured at the point of entry upon the presentation of your passport, travel documents, proof of ownership (vehicle registration) and a Belizean motor insurance certificate (this can be purchased at the border).

It's not usual for car rental companies in Guatemala or Mexico to allow their vehicles over the border, but if you do get permission you will have to show the rental documents at the point of entry with your passport.

Via Mexico

There are two routes into Belize from Mexico if travelling by land. The first is via the La Unión (Mexico)/Blue Creek Village (Belize) crossing, to the southwest of Orange Walk Town. However, tourists seldom use this point of entry, unless they happen to be driving near the small village of La Unión, as the crossing lies several miles from the nearest highway (in either country). The Subteniente López (Mexico)/Santa Elena (Belize) border crossing is far more convenient. It's positioned at the northern end of the Northern Highway and just 12 miles south of the junction of the Mexican highways 186 and 307. This crossing is around 9 miles from the Belizean coastal town of Corozal and 7 miles from the Mexican city of Chetumal (the capital of Mexico's Quintana Roo state). Daily buses run from Chetumal to Belize City (US$10) stopping en route in Corozal (US$2) and Orange Walk Town (US$4).

When crossing the border you will be required to exit the bus to show your documents to immigration and make a declaration to customs. The journey from Chetumal to Corozal takes around an hour, including the stop at immigration and customs. The journey to Belize City takes a further 2½–3½hrs.

A cheap, simple, but fairly time-consuming route into Belize involves flying to Cancún in Mexico and then travelling by bus. Modern, air-conditioned buses leave around every 30–50 minutes, between 5am and midnight, for the 5–6hr journey to Chetumal, from where you can pick up a service to Belize City. Tickets cost a very reasonable US$20.

Via Guatemala

The Guatemala/Belize border crossing is 10 miles southwest of San Ignacio, near the

Land Departure Fees

When leaving Belize via land you must pay an exit tax of US$18.75, comprising a border processing fee of US$15 and a conservation fee of US$3.75, which can be paid either in Belizean or US currency.

village of Benque Viejo del Carmen, in Belize's Cayo district. The Guatemalan border town of Melchor de Mencos can be reached by bus from Flores, Guatemala, for about US$3. There are also buses, run by Línea Dorada, leaving at 5am and 7am from Flores to Belize City (taking around 4–5hrs) for US$17. Línea Dorada also provides a Guatemala City–Flores service, leaving at 10am and 9pm, which takes around 7–8hrs and costs US$30.

Entry Formalities

All visitors to Belize must present a valid passport upon arrival. The passport should be valid for at least 6 months beyond the start of your intended stay. In theory, all visitors are meant to be assessed upon arrival to make sure that they have a return ticket out of the country and adequate funds (judged as US$60 a day) for the proposed length of their stay (i.e. are not looking for work), but these enquiries are usually reserved for residents of other Central American countries, not tourists. Citizens of the UK, European Union, Australia, Canada, Hong Kong, Mexico, New Zealand, Norway, United States, Venezuela and CARICOM member states do not require visas to enter Belize and will be given a visitor's permit (stamped in your passport) valid for up to 30 days. If you wish to stay longer, extensions of entry are available for US$25/month, for up to 6 months, and for US$50/month thereafter. These can be obtained in Belize from the immigration office in the district you are staying in or from the Belize Immigration and Nationality Department in Belmopan (t 822 2423).

Citizens of countries not listed above will need to apply for a visa to enter Belize. Details can be found on the website of the Belize Tourism Board, www.travelbelize.org, or you can contact your nearest Belize embassy or consulate (www.belize.gov.bz/diplomats).

Travel Agents and Tour Operators

The number of foreign-based tour operators offering holidays to Belize is growing all the time, as the country becomes an increasingly popular tourist destination. While it's perfectly possible to plan every aspect of your holiday before you leave, it's just as easy to improvise your holiday once on Belizean soil using the country's domestic tour operators (see p.64).

UK-based Tour Operators

Condor Journeys and Adventures, t (01700) 841 318, *www.condorjourneys-adventures.com*. Tours include: a 7-day 'Reef and Rainforest Combo Tour', taking in Baron Creek Cave or Actun Tunichil Muknal, Caracol, Mountain Pine Ridge, Ambergris Caye, Hol Chan and Shark Ray Alley, and cave-tubing from £704 pp for two people. Also offer custom-made tours and a booking service for hotels in Ambergris Caye, Turneffe Atoll, South Water Caye and Placencia.

Explore!, t 0870 333 4001, *www.explore.co.uk*. Offer a 15-day 'Discover Belize' package, taking in Belize City, Community Baboon Sanctuary, Crooked Tree, a Lamanai river trip, Altun Ha, Placencia, Cockscomb Basin Wildlife Sanctuary, St Herman's Blue Hole National Park, San Ignacio, Xunantunich, Tikal and Caye Caulker, from £1,522 (including flights from London).

Journey Latin America, t (020) 8747 3108, *www.journeylatinamerica.co.uk*. Offer flights, tailor-made tours and a hotel booking service. Combination Belize, Guatemala and Mexico cruise and land-based expeditions also available.

Kumuka Worldwide, t 0800 389 2328, *www.kumuka.co.uk*. Offer a 13-day 'Reef and Rainforest Tour' in Belize, Mexico and Guatemala.

Last Frontiers, t (01296) 653 000, *www.lastfrontiers.com*. Specialize in themed tailor-made trips (themes include 'family', 'honeymoon', 'archaeology' and 'walking') throughout Belize.

North South Travel, t (01245) 608 291, *www.northsouthtravel.co.uk*. Small travel agent whose profits go to charitable projects in Africa, Asia and Latin America.

Reef and Rainforest Tours, t (01803) 866 965, *www.reefandrainforest.co.uk*. Tours include: 14-day 'Budget Tour', taking in Crooked Tree, Cayo District and Ambergris Caye from £1,636, including international flights; 15-day 'Incurable Romantics Tour' staying in luxury accommodation and taking in the Mountain Pine Ridge, Ambergris Caye, jungle trekking, horse-riding, wildlife-watching and canoeing, from

£2,398 including international flights. Specialized family tours are also available.

Responsible Travel, t 08700 052 836, *www.responsibletravel.com*. Travel agent that encourages responsible tourism on all trips, and works only with Belizean guides and locally owned accommodation. Tours include: 8-day 'Adventure Holiday', taking in Sittee River, Glover's Island, snorkelling, diving and kayaking; 8-day 'Sea Kayaking Holiday' based on Placencia and the cayes. Also two to three conservation, research and education projects.

South American Experience, t (020) 7976 5511, *www.southamericanexperience.co.uk*. A 14-day 'Adventure' tour, taking in the Mountain Pine Ridge, Caracol, Lamanai and Ambergris Caye, from £2,070. Tailor-made tours and Guatemala/Belize combination trips also available.

Trips Worldwide, t (0117) 311 4000, *www.tripsworldwide.co.uk*. Packages include: 15-night 'Highlights Trip', taking in Mountain Pine Ridge, Placencia, Orange Walk and the Cayo Lowlands, from £1,755 including international flights.

US-based Tour Operators

Adventures Abroad, t 1-800 665 3998, *www.adventures-abroad.com*. Offer both multi-country trips and Belize-only tours, including a 10-day 'Tour Belize' trip, taking in Belize City, Tikal (Guatemala), Crooked Tree, Altun Ha, Lamanai river trip, Belize Zoo, San Ignacio, Guanacaste Park, Cahal Pech, Caracol, Xunantunich and Caye Caulker, from US$2,027.

The Adventure Center, t 1-800 228 8747, *www.adventurecenter.com*. Offer both multi-country trips and Belize-only tours, including a 14-day 'Discover Belize Tour', taking in the Community Baboon Sanctuary, Crooked Tree, Lamanai river trip, Altun Ha, Placencia, San Ignacio, Xunantunich, Tikal and Caye Caulker, from US$1,590.

Back Roads, t 1-800 462 2848, *www.backroads.com*. Activity holiday specialist. Tours include: a 6-day 'Family Multisport Tour', taking in cycling, walking and snorkelling in Mountain Pine Ridge, Caracol, Placencia and the Maya village of San Antonio.

Ecosummer Expeditions, t 1-800 465 0102, *www.ecosummer.com*. A range of sea-kayaking tours including: 12-day 'Caves to Cayes Tour', visiting Placencia and nearby cayes, Cockscomb Basin Wildlife Sanctuary, Gales Point, Caves Branch, Cahal Pech, Belize Zoo, and Community Baboon Sanctuary, from US$1,799.

International Expeditions, t 1-800 633 4734, *www.internationalexpeditions.com*. Offer Belize and Guatemala combination tours.

Island Expeditions, t 1-800 452 3212, *www. islandexpeditions.com*. Watersports specialist. Tours include 10-day 'Coral Jaguar Expedition', taking in the reef, Dangriga and Cockscomb Basin Wildlife Sanctuary, from US$1,899.

Journeys International, t 1-800 255 8735, *www.journeys-intl.com*. Tours include: 8-day 'Belize Cayo and the Cayes for the Family Tour', taking in Belize Zoo, San Ignacio, Xunantunich, Mountain Pine Ridge, Tikal and South Water Caye, from US$2,395.

Kumuka Worldwide, t 1-800 517 0867, *www. kumuka.com*. Offer Belize, Guatemala and Mexico combination trips.

Slickrock Adventures, t 1-800 390 5715, *www.slickrock.com*. Belize specialist offering a range of adventure tours, including stays on their own private island and an 8-day 'Belize Adventure Week', taking in Actun Tunichil Muknal, Caves Branch, Xunantunich, Dangriga and Glover's Reef, from US$2,195.

Wilderness Travel, t 1-800 368 2794, *www. wildernesstravel.com*. 8-day 'Private Journey Tour', taking in Mountain Pine Ridge, Xunantunich, and Turneffe Islands, from US$3,195.

Belize-based Tour Operators

As Belize is a fairly small country, many of its tour operators are jack-of-all-trades sorts, offering a selection of some of the most popular activities (snorkelling, diving, horse-riding, kayaking, cave-tubing) and trips to all the major sites, both natural and archaeological, including: Caracol, Xunantunich, Mountain Pine Ridge, Belize Zoo, Altun Ha, Cahal Pech, Cockscomb Basin Wildlife Sanctuary, Community Baboon Sanctuary, Lamanai and Tikal. The following is a list of some of the country's better-known, and better-regarded operators.

Belize City & District:

Belize Shore Tours, t 223 4874, *cavetubing@ yahoo.com, www.ecotoursbelize.com* (*see p.100*).

Hugh Parkey's Belize Dive Connection, t 223 4526, *www.belizediving.com* (*see p.100*).

Jaguar Paw, t 820 2023, **f** 820 2024, *www. jaguarpaw.com* (*see p. 109*).

Sea Sports Belize, t 223 5505, *www.seasports belize.com* (*see p.100*).

S & L Travel and Tours, t 227 7593/227 5145, *www.sltravelbelize.com* (*see p.100*).

Orange Walk:

Jungle River Tours, t 302 2293 (*see p.207*).

Belmopan:

Roaring River Adventure Tours, t 820 2025, *www.rratoursbelize.com* (*see p.147*).

Ian Anderson's Caves Branch Adventure Company and Jungle Lodge, t 822 2800, *www.cavesbranch.com* (*see p.150*).

San Ignacio:

David's Adventure Tours, t 804 3674, *www. davidsadventuretours.com* (*see p.156*).

Mayawalk Tours, t 824 3070, *www.mayawalk. com* (*see p.156*).

Pacz Tours, t 804 2267, *www.pacztours.net* (*see p.156*).

Cayo Adventure, t 824 3246, *www.cayo adventure.com* (*see p.156*).

Incidentally, only Mayawalk and Pacz tours are registered to offer tours to the Actun Tunichil Muknal caves.

Placencia:

Aahsum Adventures, t 523 3159, *www.aahsum belize.com* (*see p.191*).

Joy Tours, t 523 3325, *www.belizewithjoy.com* (*see p.191*).

Ocean Motion, t 523 3363, *www.oceanmotion placencia.com* (*see p.192*).

SeaHorse Dive Shop, t 523 3166, *www. belizescuba.com* (*see p.192*).

Toadal Adventure, t 523 3207, *www.toadal adventure.com* (*see p.192*).

Ambergris Caye:

Grumpy and Happy, t 226 3420, *www.grumpy andhappy.com* (*see p.126*).

Tanisha Ecological Tours, t 226 2314, *www. tanishatours.com* (*see p.127*).

SEArious Adventures, t 226 4202 (*see p.127*).

SEAduced, t 226 2254 (*see p.127*).

Caye Caulker:

Tsunami Adventures, t 226 0462, *www. tsunamiadventures.com* (*see p.137*).

Dolphin Bay Travel and Tours, t 226 2351, *www.cayecaulker.org/dolphinbay* (*see p.137*).

Volunteer Projects

If you feel like contributing a little bit more to the country, there are plenty of volunteer projects available, enabling you to help out with conservation work or participate in community aid and education programmes. You'll normally be expected to commit to at least a few weeks of work, pay your own air fare and contribute towards the (usually pretty basic) food and lodging. Some organizations prefer volunteers with previous experience, and specific qualifications or skills, but many are happy to accept anyone who is keen to get involved.

Belize Audubon Society, *www.belizeaudobon society.com*. Volunteers contribute to the running and maintenance of the national parks and reserves managed by the society, the country's largest and most important private conservation group. A minimum of three months' work (one month for volunteers on marine projects) is requested.

Cornerstone Foundation, t 824 2373, *www. peacecorner.org/cornerstone.htm*. Based in San Ignacio, Cornerstone offer three- to six-month volunteer programmes on a range of projects – helping with HIV/AIDS education, promoting women's issues, environmental work etc. A contribution of US$1,155 for a three-month stay covers your lodging and one meal a day, and, of course, helps fund the work of the organization. You will be expected to put in a minimum 30-hour week.

Earthwatch, US/Canada t 1-800 776 0188, UK t (0186) 531 8838, Australia t 3-9682 6828, *www. earthwatch.org*. Volunteers have the opportunity to join scientific research teams carrying out field studies in rainforest ecology, marine science, archaeology and wildlife conservation. Trips can cost US$700–4,000, which covers food, accommodation, onsite travel and equipment. Expeditions are usually a set 9 or 14 days.

Elderhostel, US t 1-800 454 578, *www.elder hostel.org*. Offer one- and two-week programmes for over-55s in association with the Oceanic Society Expeditions (*see* p.141).

Global Vision International, UK t 0870 608 8898, US t 1-888 653 6028, *www.gvi.co.uk*. Offer volunteers a variety of conservation, research and education projects in a number of locations in Belize. Placements are for a minimum of two months and cost UK£1,395/US$2,580.

Plenty Belize, *www.plenty.org*. An NGO based in Punta Gorda that takes on a small number of volunteers each year to help with its local, community-orientated projects.

ProWorld Service Corps, t 824 2003, *www. proworldsc.org*. Offer a range of in-depth programmes on health care, education, the environment, women's rights, construction, journalism, arts, technology and business.

Teachers for a Better Belize, *www.twc.org/belize*. A non-profit organization that sends primary school teachers to the Toledo district to take part in workshops to train Belizean teachers.

Trekforce Expedition, *www.trekforce.org.uk*. Offer two-month expeditions (£2,590) consisting of a period of jungle training followed by a project taking in anything from building and infrastructure maintenance to tree planting and data collection. The expedition can be extended to three months to include a Spanish course in Guatemala, or to five months to include both the Spanish course and a two-month teaching placement in a Belizean village.

Getting Around

By Air

Flying is not just the fastest and most efficient way to get from town to town, it also has the added advantage of giving travellers a glorious elevated perspective of the country, offering beautiful bird's-eye views of the forest and sea below.

Belize's domestic air connections are provided by two airlines, **Maya Island Air** (US t 1-800 523 1247, Belize t 226 2435, *www. mayaislandair.com*) and **Tropic Air** (US t 1-800 422 3435, Belize t 226 2012, *www.tropicair.com*). Both of these offer regular scheduled flights in small propeller-powered planes along two short-hop multi-destination routes: Belize City– Caye Caulker (CUK)–San Pedro (SPR)–Corozal (CZH); and Belize City– Dangriga (DGA)– Placencia (PLJ)–Punta Gorda (PND). These routes start at either Philip Goldson International Airport (BZE) or the Belize Municipal Airstrip (TZA). Bear in mind that single air fares from the international airport can cost up to US$25 more than those from the municipal. If you are travelling with a group, it may be more economical to share a taxi to the municipal airstrip than to connect through the Philip Goldson. Fares from the international/municipal airstrip are as follows: Caye Caulker, US$54/US$30; San Pedro, US$54/US$30; Corozal, US$94.50/US$70.50; Dangriga, US$54.50/US$35.50; Placencia, US$81/US$68.50; Punta Gorda, US$103/US$88.

These short, frequent flights are used rather like pricier versions of buses by their regular passengers. There is no real need to book ahead – just turn up and purchase a ticket, although it is possible to reserve or book seats online or by telephone. As most of the 'airports' outside the capital consist of little more than a small dirt runway and the airline offices, don't get there too long before your flight is scheduled to leave, as your time will be more comfortably spent elsewhere.

In addition to offering domestic connections, both Maya Island and Tropic Air offer a regular service between the international airport and Flores, Guatemala (US$103.50 each way) for speedy access to the Mayan site of Tikal.

By Boat

While getting to the cayes by aeroplane is very quick, it's by no means cheap (or indeed often as convenient) as the scheduled water taxis operating out of Belize City. There are several services, the most commonly used being the **Caye Caulker Water Taxi Association** (t 223 5752/226 0992, *www.cayecaulker watertaxi.com*), which operates several boats a day from its terminal by the Swing Bridge out to San Pedro (Ambergris Caye) via Caye Caulker. The same route is also served by **Thunderbolt** (t 226 2904) and **Triple J** (t 207 7777). *See* p.120 for more details on all. Thunderbolt also offer a daily service from San Pedro to Corozal (with a stop en route at Sarteneja). Another mainland destination that benefits from a regular boat service is Placencia. Here the **Hokie Pokie Water Taxi** (t 523 2376) speeds passengers across the lagoon from Independence Creek, dropping them near the centre of the village.

By Bus

With no railway, Belize's bus network represents the main form of terrestrial public transport. It's a fairly extensive (if not entirely comprehensive) network taking in most of the country's major towns and villages. Belmopan and Belize City are the main hubs for bus travel and pretty much every tourist destination can be reached from these two cities. Regular buses run along the country's four main highways, with the Northern Highway and Western Highway bearing the majority of the traffic.

As good as the bus coverage is to destinations on these highways, some of the villages and attractions lying off the main routes can only be reached via slow, rather intermittent local services (operating according to a timetable of perhaps one day, and none on Sundays). Some are not served by public transport at all.

Much of the country's bus fleet is made up of old, noisy converted US school buses that offer little room for people let alone luggage, and can get very crowded. A few of the more expensive express services have air conditioning. Most buses will stop anywhere en route to drop off or pick up passengers, though designated 'express' buses will only stop at certain points in the journey.

Until recently most of the country's bus routes were served by just one company, **Novelo's**, who bought out almost all of their rivals over a period of a couple of years. Unfortunately, their plans to establish a long-lived bus route monopoly proved somewhat over-optimistic, and in late 2005 they folded. At the time of going to print the Belize Transport Board and the Government of Belize had not yet arranged permanent replacements for the gaps left by Novelo's abrupt demise. Bus companies in possession of temporary permits are instead operating their own services, albeit keeping as close to the original schedules and routes as possible, so as to minimize disruption. Notwithstanding the current confusion, exploring Belize by bus remains one of the easiest, cheapest and most convenient ways of getting around the country. Hopefully, by the time you read this, normal service will have been resumed on most routes.

Finally, it should be said that, while the majority of Belizeans are honest and helpful, theft does unfortunately still take place from time to time on the region's buses. Keep an eagle eye on your luggage at all times, and if the conductor takes it from you to store, make sure you are waiting for it when it's unloaded.

By Car

Belize has four highways: the Northern Highway, which runs from Belize City, past Corozal, to the Mexican border; the Western Highway, which heads from Belize City, through San Ignacio, to the Guatemalan border; the Hummingbird Highway, which runs from Belmopan to Dangriga connecting the Western Highway with the Southern Highway; and the Southern Highway, which starts just east of Dangriga and continues south down to Punta Gorda. Everywhere you

Tips for Driving in Belize

• Big and bulky is best. Unless you're planning on doing all your driving on the four main highways, you will need a 4WD, especially during the wet season (June–Oct). Many of Belize's tourist attractions, including most of its Maya sites, all of the Mountain Pine Ridge area and even the tourist hot spot of Placencia, are accessible only by crude dirt tracks. Many lodges – including some of the country's very fanciest places – also lack paved access. As a consequence, many of the country's hire companies deal only in 4WDs. A Daihatsu Terios or a Suzuki Jimny, the standard budget 4WD cars, are fine for most conditions and routes, although you might want something a little sturdier, and with a touch more ground clearance, when the rains start coming down.

• Drive defensively. Despite the many and various hazards of their roads, the country's high road-accident rate, and the numerous billboards urging drivers to reduce their speed, many Belizeans continue to drive as if it's coming up to the end of the movie and they only have four minutes left to save the world. You should drive extremely cautiously at all times.

• Avoid driving at night. Most stretches of highway, aside from the short sections passing through the centre of towns, are entirely unlit and boast a whole host of bumps and dips that are difficult enough to see during daylight hours, let alone in the pitch dark. Remember, it's the tropics, so daylight comes to an abrupt end around 6–6.30pm throughout the year. Plan to be off the road well before then.

• Watch your speed. Speed limits are 55mph (90kmph) on highways, and 40mph (65kmph) or 25mph (40kmph) in towns and villages. These should be signposted, although they're

often not. Be aware that, while speed limits are posted in miles per hour, the speedometers of many Belizean vehicles are calibrated in kilometres. Do watch your speed. Highways pass right through the centre of a number of towns and villages, where you'll often see groups of schoolchildren wandering along the road.

• Carry a phrase book. Although Belize is officially an English-speaking country, it's not uncommon to come across Belizeans who can speak only Spanish, especially away from the main tourist trail. If you are planning on driving in the far north or west (i.e. the main Spanish-speaking areas), it's a good idea to take a phrase book with you just in case.

• Pay attention. You'll need your wits about you, not just to avoid any hazards, but simply to work out where you're going. Signposting in much of the country is generally quite good – certainly when compared with some other Central American countries – but it can still be quite easy to miss a turning if you don't keep an eye on the mileage signs. Ideally you should travel with a companion who is a good map-reader (and, for preference, fluent in Spanish).

• Don't get ripped off. Car crime is, as everywhere, common here. However, almost all problems can be avoided if you follow the same common-sense rules you would anywhere.

– Keep doors locked and windows rolled up when driving through town.

– Never stop for anyone other than a policeman or another official person.

– Don't pick up hitchhikers.

– Don't leave your valuables on display.

– Don't leave your vehicle parked in the street overnight.

– If you think you're being followed, drive to nearest busy, well-lit area and call the police.

need to go is either on or off (sometimes quite a way off) one of these main roads, all of which are paved and generally quite well maintained. There's very little traffic outside central Belize City. You will still need to exercise caution, however, as what traffic there is can often be travelling at quite a speed (or practically no speed). Remember these are 'highways' in name only. Most are in fact narrow roads with just one lane in each direction and limited overtaking opportunities. Indeed, each highway passes through the centre of a number of towns and villages. As a consequence, urban sections of highway are lined with speed bumps designed to get

you to cut your speed. There are three types of bump: small rounded bumps, large rounded bumps and very large, exhaust-destroying square-edged pedestrian crossings (which also serve as informal bus stops, hence all the people you'll see standing beside them, but making no attempt to cross the road). In theory, all are painted with bright yellow stripes and have signs placed 100 yards in front warning you of their presence. In practice, many are completely unmarked and rather well camouflaged. If driving through a town, drop your speed, whether you can see speed bumps up ahead or not. Other dangers and distractions to look out for include pick-up trucks packed with workers barrelling along the road (overtake carefully), schoolchildren (many very young and unaccompanied by adults) wandering or even playing along the side of the road, and dogs, goats and coatimundi darting out in front of your vehicle. Traffic accidents are the number one killer in Belize (240 dead, 1,478 injured in the past 10 years), so always stay alert and take extra care when it's raining. Downpours can be fierce, quickly slicking up the road surface and spinning vehicles off the road with alarming regularity.

If sticking exclusively to the highways, most of Belize can be covered relatively quickly by car, with San Ignacio in the west and Corozal in the north both lying less than two hours from Belize City. Once off the highways, however, things get a little bit more tricky and a whole lot more time-consuming. Roads to some of the country's more outlying attractions are unpaved and often in very bad condition. Some are little more than badly rutted, potholed dirt tracks that quickly become impassable in the rainy season. It's always advisable to ask at your hotel about the status of a particular road before setting out, particularly if it's been raining heavily. And make sure you have a full tank of petrol and a spare tyre. As in the USA, you drive on the right-hand side. Seat belts are compulsory; you can be issued with a small fine if caught not wearing one.

Notwithstanding the problems (and the price, see 'Car Rental' below), driving still represents the most flexible way of getting around Belize, allowing you to devise your own schedule, with no timetables to adhere to. You just need to bear in mind a few tips before you begin (see box on p.67).

Car Rental

Renting a car in Belize is a relatively straightforward process. Tourists need only show their passport, a valid photo driving licence from their home country and an internationally accepted credit card (i.e. Visa or Mastercard) in order to hire a car for the duration of their visitor's permit. The credit card will need to have enough credit to cover both the full cost of the hire period and the excess (or deductible, typically US$750) due if the vehicle is damaged beyond repair.

Car Rental Firms

Avis, Poinsettia Road, Ladyville, t 205 2629, *www.avis.com*
Budget, Mile 2, Northern Highway, t 223 2435, *www.budget-belize.com*
Crystal, Mile 4, Northern Highway, t 223 1600, *www.crystal-belize.com*
Euphrates, 143 Euphrates Ave/Zeitown St, Belize City, t 227 5752, *www.ears.bz*
Jabiru, 5576 Princess Margaret Drive, Belize City, t 224 4680, *www.jabiruautorental.bz*
Pancho's, 5747 Lizarraga Ave, Belize City, t 224 5554, *www.panchosrentalbelize.com*
Hertz/Safari, 11A Cork St, Belize City, t 223 0886, *www.hertz.com*
Thrifty, corner Faber Rd and Central American Blvd, Belize City, t 207 1271, *www.thrifty.com*
Vista, 798 Vista Del Mar, Belize City, t 225 2292, *www.vistarentalsbelize.co.*

Car hire in Belize is a tad expensive, and that's putting it mildly. With hire rates from US$85 per day and insurance (a necessity) around $15 per day, you're looking at a total hire cost of around $600 a week, which is pretty expensive by US or European standards. The price of petrol isn't particularly cheap either (although it's still cheaper than in the UK), averaging at around US$45 for a full tank for a standard low-end 4WD. However, if you plan to see a lot of the country, you may still find it a cheaper alternative to taking a series of separate tours, particularly if you are travelling in a group or with your family.

Unsurprisingly, as it's the entry point for the vast majority of visitors, Belize City is home to most of the country's car rental firms, with numerous offices located both at the airport and downtown. As with renting anywhere, you should make sure that an official note has been made of any damage – which on a rental pool 4WD that's spent the last few years bumping and banging its way around Belize's jungle roads is liable to include a whole host of minor bumps and scratches – before you sign the contract. Your rental firm will probably hand over the car with a full tank of petrol and will expect it to be returned in the same state. Most rental cars have manual gear shifts. If you want to drive an automatic, you'll need to make a request well in advance.

Practical A–Z

07

Active Belize

Belize is a place to get active, at least some of the time. Though many people see the country in tropical getaway terms – as a place to sunbathe, order cocktails and not much else – an increasing number of visitors come to undertake some of the variety of activities the country has to offer, chief among them exploring the country's barrier reef. Most tourists take at least one snorkelling trip during their vacation and many also go scuba diving. Other activities on offer include kayaking, windsurfing, parasailing, sailing, caving, river-tubing and horse-riding. All are available throughout the year, even if most can be pursued most comfortably in the dry season. Tour operators are thick on the ground in all of the country's major tourist hot spots and many lodges and hotels also offer a range of activities.

Caving

Western Belize's limestone landscape is absolutely riddled with caves. Years of water erosion have produced a labyrinthine system of subterranean tunnels stretching into the earth for many miles, filled with gnarly stalactites and stalagmites. Many of the larger caves contain relics left behind by the Maya, who considered them to be sacred – literally gateways to the underworld – and performed religious ceremonies there. Because of the need to preserve these Mayan relics, and the danger of letting people explore on their own, many caves can only be visited in the company of an official guide. Some of best include **Actun Tunichil Muknal** (see p.151) and **Barton Creek Cave** (see p.152), to which a full tour, including transport and lunch, will cost around US$80. Caves you can explore on your own include **St Herman's Cave** (see p.150) and the **Río Frío Cave** (see p.169). San Ignacio is the country's main base for cave exploration, with all of the town's tour operators offering trips (see p.156). See also p.152 for the Mayan view of caves.

Diving and Snorkelling

Belize is one of world's premier diving locations, welcoming hard-core enthusiasts throughout the year come to explore its 180-mile barrier reef and collection of atolls and cayes, which together provide home to a myriad assortment of marine life. Although the country does boast a number of very challenging dive spots, it's also one of the best places for less experienced swimmers to learn how to snorkel. Its waters are warm, predominantly calm – particularly on the sheltered side of the reef – and, best of all, clear, offering great visibility. Furthermore there's a whole tourist infrastructure in place dedicated to getting people out in the ocean with a pair of flippers on their feet. The main coastal resorts – San Pedro on Ambergris Caye, Caye Caulker and Placencia – all have dozens of places hiring out snorkelling gear, offering snorkelling and diving tours, and providing diving training. You can take a four-day PADI Open Water Certification course for around $300. However, if you don't want to give up four precious vacation days getting fully qualified, you can opt instead for the one-day introductory course, which will teach you the basics of scuba diving – in order to see if it's something you want to take further – for around US$75.

The top spots for inexperienced snorkellers are **Hol Chan** and **Shark Ray Alley** (see pp.125–6), where, if you go as part of an official tour, a guide will use food to lure a great smorgasbord of fish – often including nurse sharks, rays and grouper – into viewing range. And if you don't fancy going on an organized tour, there are also a few places where you can go snorkelling on your own, just off the northern cayes, where the reef lies less than a mile off shore. Simply hire a kayak and snorkelling gear – many hotels lend them out to their guests free of charge – paddle out to one of the permanent buoys just off the reef, tie up your kayak and get exploring. You can also snorkel independently at the **Split** on Caye Caulker (see p.136). However, if you are going to do this, make sure you respect the integrity of the reef (see p.35 for tips on reef safety).

Most other sites are accessible only by boat, which usually means taking an official tour (or hiring your own boat, see 'Sailing', below). For more experienced divers, **Lighthouse Reef** and its famous **Blue Hole** are probably the main draws (see pp.141–2).

Fishing

Belize's superabundance of fish life seems to attract an almost equally large number of fishermen (that's not being sexist, they are always men) intent on hooking them out of the water. In fact, it's something of a wonder there are any left.

Fly-fishing trips are offered to the country's coastal mangroves and tidal flats, which provide fertile grounds for snook, tarpon bonefish and barracuda, while Hemingway-esque **sports-fishing** tours out onto the open ocean on the hunt for big game – sailfish and marlin – are also offered by many of the country's coastal tour operators out of Ambergris Caye (see p.126), Caye Caulker (see p.137), Hopkins and Placencia, though these can be pricey – upwards of $750 a day in some instances. Most fishing trips involve the catch and release method, so as to preserve stocks, although a number of specimens are caught as trophies each year.

There's no official season, but December to April is generally considered the best time to fish. It's also possible to go river and lagoon fishing on the mainland, with the Sibun and Belize Rivers generally regarded as offering the best fishing opportunities.

Hiking

Hiking the country's jungle trails on the hunt for wildlife is, of course, one of the most popular activities in all Belize. See pp.40–8 for more information and tips on wildlife-watching.

Horse-riding

Cayo district – particularly the area around San Ignacio and the Pine Ridge Forest Reserve – has a number of stables offering horse-riding trips, which represent one of the best ways to explore a large portion of the region's hilly difficult terrain in a single day.

Some of the best include the **Banana Bank Lodge** (p.149), **Blancaneaux Resort** (p.169), the **Lodge** at Chaa Creek (p.162), **Windy Hill Resort** (p.157) and **duPlooys'** (p.162). Prices start from US$25 per hour, rising to $65 and above for a full day in the saddle.

Kayaking

Available both off the coast and inland, kayaking is another hugely popular activity. On the northern cayes, it's often combined with snorkelling and offers a great way of seeing some marine wildlife without the hassle (and expense) of an organized tour (see 'Snorkelling', above). Many of the hotels on Ambergris Caye, Caye Caulker and Placencia – the main resort areas – provide kayaks for their guests to use free of charge. Otherwise, there are plenty of places where you can rent them out, for US$15–30 per day. It's a reasonably safe activity, especially if undertaken in the calm waters sheltered by the reef, although you should still exercise a good degree of caution, particularly if heading further out to sea. Always wear a life vest – again these are usually provided as standard by hotels.

It's also possible to explore the country's inland waterways via canoe, with many tour operators offering paddling trips along the Macal and Mopan rivers near San Ignacio. One of the most atmospheric kayaking trips involves exploring the river flowing through the stalactite- and stalagmite-adorned **Barton Creek Cave** (see pp.152–3).

River- and Cave-tubing

This requires a little explanation. River-tubing describes the practice of sitting in a huge inflated tyre inner tube and either paddling or allowing yourself to be floated down a river. Cave-tubing is more or less the same thing, it's just done in a river that flows through a cave. It's become a hugely popular activity in recent years, with almost all of the country's tour operators now offering trips, usually in conjunction with a visit to another attraction – e.g. Xunantanich and cave-tubing, Belize Zoo and cave-tubing.

The country's gently flowing rivers (outside of the rainy season, at least) provide the ideal conditions for the sport, and it's very easy to learn. In fact, you could perhaps see it as a sort of stabilizer version of canoeing. The most popular destinations include the **Caves Branch River**, where most tours are led by Ian Anderson' Adventure Company (see p.150–1), and **Barton Creek Cave** (see p.152–3). Trips can cost from as little as US$20, and as much as $95, depending on where you are coming from, who you are coming with, and how much you do.

Sailing

Sailing, kayaking's big brother, is growing in popularity all the time. The main centres at which to pursue it are Ambergris Caye, Caye Caulker and Placencia, where organized sailing tours are offered out into the Caribbean Sea, taking in a variety of itineraries, including wildlife-watching – you can visit a community of manatees at Swallow Caye (see p.136) – fishing, snorkelling and visits to some of the reef's uninhabited islands, perhaps for a spot of lunch and sunbathing. Sunset and moonlight cruises are also offered. And if you want to devise your own itinerary, you can hire a boat to do a little impromptu exploring of your own. **Belize Sailing Charters** (t 523 3138, *www.belize-sailing-charters.com*) and **Nepenthe Charters** (t 600 2302, *www.sailing-belize.com*) offer a range of craft and choices – both skippered and bareboat. Expect to pay from US$975 for a three-day cruise. Belize's calm coastal waters provide good conditions for novices, although the heavy motorboat traffic around here will take some careful negotiation.

Windsurfing and Parasailing

Windsurfing is possible in a number of locations across the country, including the northern cayes and off the coast of Hopkins, where the waters are generally calm – in fact, they can sometimes be a bit too calm if the wind drops. Board rental starts at around US$30 per day, with lessons from $40 an hour. Keep a careful lookout for motorboats which are extremely common in the country's coastal waters. For something a little more intense (or if the motorboat traffic gets too heavy), you might want to try parasailing, whereby you are attached to a parachute and lifted into the air on the back of a motorboat. **Fido's Fun Sports** (t 226 3513, *www.belizeparasailing.com*) in San Pedro – it occupies the same pier as the Island Ferry stop – is one of the main operators.

Climate and When to Go

Belize occupies a subtropical location 16–18.5° north of the equator. The climate here can generally be characterized as hot throughout the country throughout the year. Temperatures range from 10°C (50°F) to 35°C (95°F) with an average mean temperature of 26°C (86°F). Though most of the country consists of lowlands of a similar elevation, which enjoy largely similar weather patterns, what topography there is does provide a degree of climatic differentiation. The summits of the Maya Mountains, which rise to around 1,000m (3,300ft) in the country's southwest, can often be quite chilly, while the offshore cayes, which frequently endure baking conditions, benefit from cooling sea breezes. The south, much of which is blanketed in thick broadleaf jungle, is the country's wettest region, receiving over 170 inches (432cm) of rain annually, compared with around 50 inches (127cm) in the dryer north.

Belize enjoys a distinct two-season year: a dry season from December to April, which also corresponds to the peak tourism months when you can expect to meet the greatest number of fellow visitors and pay the most expensive prices, particularly around the public holidays of Christmas and Easter; and a wet season from May to November. The former is probably the best time to go. Although the country will be more crowded, its low overall population density – combined with the fact that Belize has yet to become a major mass-tourism destination – means that it rarely feels overwhelmingly so. In addition, you will manage to avoid both the worst of the mosquito swarms, which traditionally happen in August when the winds are at their stillest, and, more importantly, the hurricane season, which runs from June to November. Also, some of the unpaved roads in the south of the country can become impassable once the rains really start to come down.

If you do come in the rainy season, expect regular torrential – albeit often short-lived – downpours throughout the country, which do at least serve to spruce up the vegetation and give everything a lush, green look.

Hurricanes

Hurricanes, always a worry in this locale, are becoming an increasing concern as the frequency and ferocity of the region's storms seem to have gone up a notch in recent years. 2005 was the worst hurricane season on record, principally because the region's seas achieved the hottest temperatures on record (the main cause of hurricanes) – up to 30°C (86°F) in certain instances. Thankfully, most of the hugely destructive hurricanes of the past few years have either just skirted Belize or missed it entirely. In fact, Belize generally doesn't see that many hurricanes making landfall – certainly nothing like the number the US does, but then it's a much smaller country.

The last big one to hit was Hurricane Iris in 2001, whose 150mph winds tore into the southern half of the country, causing plenty of damage to buildings in the Toledo district, but thankfully very little loss of life. Historically, the country has not always been so lucky. Belize City was hit by two major hurricanes in the 20th century, the first of which, in 1931, killed an estimated 10% of the city's population, while the second, Hurricane Hattie in 1961, led to the city being shorn of its capital status and the building of a replacement, Belmopan, in the centre of the country (*see* p.145).

These days, safety procedures throughout Belize are generally pretty good, which is why Hurricane Iris didn't cause as much devastation as might have been the case. The region's weather patterns are carefully monitored and warnings issued early. If travelling in the hurricane season, be sure to keep a close eye on the weather reports, and be prepared to change your plans at a moment's notice. The coast and cayes are, as you might expect, the areas most at risk. At the first sign of a serious hurricane brewing, people staying on the cayes are usually evacuated to the mainland. And that's the best advice for you too. Get yourself as far west as you can as soon as you can. All Belizean towns, even the smallest, have hurricane shelters.

The hurricane season runs from June to November, although the worst storms tend to hit from September onwards.

Crime and Safety

Belize has a much lower crime rate than most other Central American countries. However, the advice on crime does tend to change depending on what part of the country you're travelling to. On the cayes and

Safety Tips

• Make and bring with you photocopies of all your important documents – passport, airline tickets, traveller's cheques etc. When travelling with the real things, keep the photocopies in a separate part of your luggage to where you store the originals.
• Don't keep all your money in one place; divide it into separate stashes.
• When walking around, keep your documents and money in a waterproof money belt tucked beneath your waistband. It can be a bit uncomfortable, but it's not nearly as uncomfortable as having all your documents stolen.
• In major towns, try to rely on credit cards (which can be cancelled) as much as possible.
• Don't carry your bag or rucksack over one shoulder. Always use both straps or, if you're using a single strap bag, loop the strap over your head.
• Don't display ostentatious wealth. Keep your camera hidden away unless you're actually using it.

• Don't walk around unfamiliar areas of town on your own after dark. Try to find out which are the dodgy areas and steer clear. If you don't know where the dodgy areas are, stick to the busy main streets.
• Try to look as least like a tourist as possible. Act confidently and stride purposefully, as if you know exactly where you're going and precisely what you're doing (even if you're completely lost). If you need to check your bearings on a map in an unfamiliar town, try and do so inside a shop or café rather than on a street corner.
• And finally, if you are mugged, make no attempt to keep hold of your valuables. Give the thieves what they want with the minimum of fuss. The vast majority of hold-ups are non-violent. Don't do anything to unnecessarily provoke your assailant.
• One more thing. Don't commit a crime yourself. Belize police have a reputation, for – how to put this – not being the most gentle of custodians, and they can hold somebody without charge for up to 48hrs.

What to Do If the Worst Happens

If it's an emergency, call **t** 911 for the police, or **t** 90 for medical assistance or the fire brigade. If it's not (or no longer) an emergency, but you've been the victim of a crime, the police still need to be informed; call **t** 224 4646. The chances of anything being recovered are, of course, slim, but you'll need to make an official report for insurance purposes.

Make sure you bring the relevant phone numbers with you if need to cancel credit cards, have airline tickets re-issued, etc. If you lose your passport (or have it stolen), you'll need to contact the relevant embassy or consulate, see pp.75–6, who should also be able to help contact friends and family in the event of something serious taking place.

in Placencia, the main tourist hot spots, things are on the whole pretty safe. Crime levels are low and very few street robberies take place. A bit of minor pickpocketing is probably the worse you can expect. The situation is a touch more tricky in Belize City, albeit by no means as bad as its reputation suggests. Despite what some Internet bloggers will tell you, Belize City is not a hotbed of crime. But crimes do take place here. Those most likely to affect tourists are (again) pickpocketing, bag-snatching, robberies from (mainly budget) hotel rooms and, if walking on your own away from the main tourist trail after dark, perhaps even mugging. However, so long as you take the same common-sense precautions you would anywhere, you should be fine (see above for safety tips). For more on safety in Belize City, see p.96.

A more worrying development has been a spate of armed robberies in the west of the country, which have seen gangs of Guatemalans (or what are believed to be Guatemalans) coming across the border and deliberately targeting hotels and tour buses full of tourists. This has led to an increased police presence and a general upping of the security level in the area – particularly in the Pine Ridge Reserve where the majority of these hold-ups have occurred – which, it is hoped, should put an end to the problem. Check with your hotel before you arrive for the latest update on the situation.

'What You Looking For?'

Belize City has quite high unemployment levels and, as you walk around the city, you will no doubt pass groups of men hanging around on street corners with nothing better to do than to try and engage you in conversation. Mostly, that's all it is, a way of passing the time – or a way of trying to cadge some dollars or sell some marijuana – rather than anything more sinister. Of course, there are certain things you can do that will make an approach more likely and which you should probably avoid – looking at a map is definitely one of them. This will almost inevitably prompt a cry of 'what you looking for?' from someone. A polite 'just looking around' will probably end the conversation, or will at least get your questioner to reveal their intentions – offering a tour, asking for money or recommending a relative's restaurant. A common ruse with the city's beggars is to find out where you're from, sing your home country's praises and then ask for money. What you give is up to you, although it goes without saying that you should try not to appear too wealthy – with dollar bills practically spilling out of your wallet – as this will only serve to increase the level of attention you receive.

The best advice is to be polite and keep walking. If you're worried about the motives of your interrogator, be non-committal.

Drugs

Despite the regularity with which marijuana will be offered to you for sale in the main tourist areas, particularly Belize City, and the openness with which it is often smoked, possession of the drug is still officially illegal in Belize. Although people found holding small amounts are rarely prosecuted, being caught holding a sizable stash could, in theory, land you with a hefty fine or perhaps even a jail sentence. Steer clear.

Women Travellers

Women may be singled out for special attention, especially if wearing skimpy clothing, although this is rarely anything worse than one of the country's would-be casanovas trying to attract your attention with a complimentary whistle. As everywhere, these ostentatious demonstrations of admiration are usually done less for your benefit than for the benefit of the whistler's associates.

Studious, haughty indifference is the best response. Treat all unwanted attention the same way you would anywhere. Be polite but firm with your refusals, and keep walking.

Rapes and sexual assaults do happen in Belize, but no more frequently than anywhere else. Simply take the same precautions you would in any country. Don't walk alone through unfamiliar areas, particularly late at night. Don't use unlicensed taxis. Don't hitchhike. If in a bar, never leave your drink unattended or unwatched for even a short while, as it's been known for them to be spiked with 'date rape' drugs such as Rohypnol and scopolamine.

Disabled Travellers

The situation for disabled travellers in Belize is not as good as it should be – in fact far from it. Visitors with mobility difficulties do come to Belize. However, the number of places they can access easily – especially without assistance – is extremely limited.

Of course, it's understood that many of the country's more remote attractions – its jungles, mountains and Mayan ruins – do, by their very nature, pose serious problems for anyone with mobility difficulties. What's

---

Disability Organizations

In Belize
Special Tours Belize, 72 Western Highway, San Ignacio, Cayo District, t 600 4284, *www.speciatoursbelize.com*. Tour operator catering to needs of travellers with disabilities.

In the USA
Accessible Journeys, 35 West Sellers Avenue, Ridley Park, PA 19078, t 800 846 4537, *www.disabilitytravel.com*.

Mobility International, PO Box 10767, Eugene, Oregon 97440, t (541) 343 1284, *www.miusa.org*.

In the UK
Disability Now, 6 Markets Road, London N7, t (020) 7619 7323, *www.disabilitynow.org.uk*.

Radar, 12 City Forum, 250 City Rd, London EC1V 8AF, t (020) 7250 3222, *www.radar.org.uk*.

---

less understandable is the attitude of the government, who have yet to pass legislation requiring new businesses to provide wheelchair access. Things are left instead to the whim of the business owners – some do, some don't. Many (in fact most) hotels and restaurants still do not have ramps. Those that do include some of big resort-style hotels in Belize City, Ambergris Caye and Placencia.

If you have mobility difficulties, your best bet would be to get in touch with one of the official bodies below who can provide expert detailed advice.

Electricity

Belize's electric current is supplied at 110v AC at 60Hz. The country's outlets take US-style flat-pronged, two-pin plugs. Note, if travelling from Europe or the UK, that adapters can be very difficult to track down in Belize. The Ace Hardware Store on Albert Street in Belize City sells Europe-to-US adapters, but not UK-to-US ones. You'd be better off bringing your own.

Embassies and Consulates

Australia and New Zealand do not operate embassies in Belize. Instead, citizens from these countries should contact their respective embassies in neighbouring Mexico, who deal with all Belize-related enquiries (Aus: t 0052 55 1101 2200, *www.mexico.embassy. gov.au*; NZ: t 0052 55 5283 9460, *kiwimexico@ prodigy.net.mx*).

Canadian Honorary Consul, 80 Princess Margaret Drive, Belize City, t 223 1060, *cdncon.bze@btl.net*.

UK High Commision, Embassy Square, Belmopan, t 822 2146, *www. britishhighbze.com*.

US Embassy, 29 Gabourel Lane, Belize City (due to move to Belmopan 2007), t 227 7161, *http://belize.usembassy.gov*.

In the UK

Belize High Commission, Third Floor, 45 Crawford Pl, London W1H 4LP, t (020) 7723 3603, *bzhc-lon@btconnect.com* (open Mon–Fri 10–1).

In the USA

Consulate General of Belize, Korean Trade Center, Park Mile Plaza, 4801 Wilshire Blvd, Suite 250, Los Angeles, CA 90010, t (323) 469 7343, *belizeconsul@earthlink.net* (*open Mon–Thurs 9–5, Fri 9–4.30*).

Festivals, Events and National Holidays

All businesses close for the duration of a public holiday. Hotel accommodation can also be scarce during major holidays and events, particularly Easter and Christmas, which see the biggest disruption to services with most bus services not running. If travelling at these times, you'll need to book your room early. Do note, when making arrangements, that if a particular national holiday falls on a Sunday, it is will be observed instead on the succeeding Monday.

Gay Belize

Homosexuality has been legal here since 1988. Nonetheless, because of widespread lingering prejudice, gay Belize barely exists.

Calendar of Events and National Holidays

1 Jan New Year's Day – National Holiday.

Feb/March Ambergris Caye Carnival. Week-long celebration of over-indulgence prior to the beginning of Lent, with parades, dances and lots of eating and drinking.

9 March Baron Bliss Day – National Holiday. Baron Henry Edward Ernest Victor Bliss was the country's greatest benefactor. Upon his death in 1926, he left his entire multi-million pound fortune to the Belizean people to be used for improving projects. However, in order to access the money, the Belizeans had to accept a few preconditions, one of which was to have a special day each year set aside for sailing and fishing. The day of the Baron's death is now commemorated each year with a ceremony at the lighthouse in Belize City beneath which he is buried, followed by a boating regatta, plus various events around the country (*see p.97* for more information on the Baron).

Easter Good Friday and Easter are both national holidays. Easter is strictly observed throughout the country and is the event which will probably cause the most difficulties for travellers, as businesses and bus services shut down pretty much for the duration.

1 May Labour Day – National Holiday.

25 May Commonwealth Day – National Holiday.

26 June El Día de San Pedro. Popular, energetic local festival celebrating the town's patron saint, St Peter.

10 September National Day – National Holiday. This holiday commemorates the Battle of St George's Caye in 1798 when British loggers (and their slaves) made their final victorious stand against the Spanish fleet, thereby paving the way for the country to be incorporated into the British Empire. Festivities are centred mainly on Belize City, where there are parades, performances of music, food stalls and religious services (*see p.26* for more on the battle).

21 September Independence Day – National Holiday. Just as the battle that brought Belize into the British imperial fold warrants its own festivities (*see above, National Day*), so the moment Belize finally wrested itself from the imperial grip is also celebrated – albeit with a bit more fervour, just a few days later. In fact, the two events together provide an excuse for around a week and half of general merry-making. Most major towns lay on fairs, bands and food stalls.

12 October Columbus Day – National Holiday.

19 November Garinuga (Garifuna) Settlement Day. Every year, for one whole week, the country's main Garifuna communities – including Punta Gorda, Hopkins, and Dangriga – celebrate the arrival of the very first Garifuna settlers in Belize, an event which is believed to have taken place on this day in 1823. Celebrations are intense and lively and attract visitors from all over the country (and beyond). If visiting one of these communities at this time, expect re-enactments of that first landing, dancing, drinking, parades, music (including plenty of Punta Rock, the Garifuna's most celebrated and successful musical style) and a whole lot of drumming. For more information, see the **National Garifuna Council of Belize** website, *www.ngcbelize.org* (*see also p.175*).

25 December Christmas Day – National Holiday. As in many countries, Christmas in Belize is traditionally a family time – a time to decorate your house and have home-cooked meals. Most businesses shut over the Christmas period.

26 December Boxing Day – National Holiday.

There is no visible gay scene, and no openly gay bars, discos, hotels or tour operators. That said, gay visitors are generally tolerated, and while macho Caribbean-style discrimination does take place, this is usually little worse than a bit of name calling ('batty boy' is a commonly used insult). The situation is certainly better than in nearby Jamaica, where gay people are regularly attacked.

The Belizeans' famously easy-going character means that most people exhibit a commendable 'live and let live' attitude – indeed, a gay cruise ship denied entry to the Cayman Islands in 1998 was allowed to dock here instead, the event passing off without incident. Still, don't expect to be taking part in any Gay Pride marches during your time here. While gay travellers will probably be welcomed in most places (certainly most tourist-orientated places), you should refrain from indulging in public displays of affection.

Further Resources

Planet Out, *www.planetout.com*. Gay travel site.

Purple Roofs, *www.purpleroofs.com*. Worldwide accommodation listing service for gays and lesbians: B&Bs, inns, guesthouses, hotels and tour operators.

Undersea Expeditions, t 1 800 669 0310, *www.underseax.com*. Gay and lesbian dive travel company.

Geography

Belize occupies a narrow strip of subtropical land on the eastern side of the Central American isthmus, bordered to the north by Mexico, to the west and south by Guatemala, and to east by the Caribbean Sea. Indeed, Belize covers as much aquatic territory as it does terrestrial.

Offshore lie a 180-mile-long coral reef, three atolls (ring-shaped formations of coral surrounding a lagoon) and over 450 small islands, known as cayes, that represent the uppermost parts of a great limestone ridge, which also forms much of Mexico's Yucatán peninsula. The largest of these cayes support vegetation and communities of wildlife (and people), the smaller ones tend to be barren outcrops.

Mainland Belize is a truly tiny place; under 200 miles long and less than 70 miles wide (and that's at its widest point), producing a grand total area of 8,866 square miles (22,963 sq km). Most of country is made up of lowlands and is pretty flat, the major exception being the great granite Maya Mountains, which take up much of the southwest of the country and ascend to elevations of over 3,500ft (1,000m). Belize's western half generally offers the most spectacular scenery, with dozen of limestone caves and great swathes of pine forest. In fact, an estimated 70% of the country is still blanketed in forest, much of it primary broadleaf forest. This is at its thickest in the southern half of the country, which enjoys a wetter, more humid climate than the rest of Belize.

Health

Belize may be in the tropics (or more accurately the subtropics) – thus conjuring up images of terrible exotic diseases, deadly insects burrowing their way beneath your skin to remain undetected for years (by which time they've grown several metres long) and fearsome jungle-dwelling creatures – but it's really a pretty safe place. Very few travellers encounter any health problems at all during their trip.

Obviously precautions still need to be taken, both before you leave – making sure you take out the necessary travel insurance and get the recommended inoculations – and once you're there – avoiding contaminated food and drink, staying out of the sun and evading the attentions of the ever-present mosquitoes, particularly in the wetter, more humid southern half of the country.

Insurance

It's vital that you take out travel insurance before your trip. This should cover, at a bare minimum, cancellation due to illness, travel delays, accidents, lost luggage, lost passports, lost or stolen belongings, personal liability, legal expenses, emergency flights and medical cover. The latter is, of course, the most important part of any policy. You need to establish whether your policy will pay out as and when you require treatment or (the more common option) only when you return home, in which case you'll have to pay your medical bills up front and claim the money back later – so be sure to keep hold of all the relevant paperwork. However, if you're particularly concerned – Belize's medical provision is by no means a world leader – it should be possible to arrange a policy whereby you can be flown out of the country to receive medical treatment elsewhere (i.e. in the USA), although this can be rather costly (albeit by no means as costly as paying up front for a significant medical procedure).

Inoculations and Vaccines

There are no inoculation requirements to enter Belize, unless you're coming from a country harbouring yellow fever, such as Columbia, in which case you'll need to present a current, valid certificate of inoculation. It is recommended, however, that you have inoculations (or boosters) against hepatitis A and B, typhoid, polio and tetanus, although you should note that none of these is a major concern. You'll need to get your jabs done a few weeks in advance for them to be effective. It's also worth taking a course of antimalarials (see below for details).

Food and Drink Dangers

As is the case with most trips, the ailment you're most likely to succumb to in Belize is an upset stomach, which is as likely to be caused by a change of digestive scenery – as your stomach gets used to the new diet – as from contamination.

Though Belize's drinking water is 'officially safe', you're probably better off relying on bottled water, which is available throughout the country. If camping, sterilize any water drawn from outdoor sources by boiling it (for at least 5 minutes) or treating it with chemical purifiers, even if you've taken your supply from a clear running stream. Canned and bottled drinks, including the ubiquitous Belikin beer, are safe to drink.

Most infections are in fact caused, not by infected drinking water, but by unhygienically prepared food, although standards of hygiene are pretty good throughout the country, particularly in those restaurants aimed at tourists. Always wash and peel fresh fruit and vegetables. When eating out, stick to hot meals. Don't drink milk or eat any dairy product you suspect may not have been pasteurized.

If you do get diarrhoea, the most important thing is to keep drinking. Most of the pain you feel is the result of lost fluid, so you need to replenish constantly, ideally with a rehydration solution to replace some of the lost minerals, packets of which can be picked up at most pharmacies. Ideally, you should bring your own supply, as the last thing you want to do when you've got diarrhoea is go searching for a pharmacy. Don't use anything to aid constipation as this may prevent your body from expelling the bacteria causing the problems and may prolong your symptoms. When you're feeling a bit stronger, you can begin to eat light, easily digestible food, but make sure you're fully recovered before eating out again.

Occasionally the ingestion of contaminated food or water can lead to development of something more serious, such as amoebic dysentery or even hepatitis A. Seek medical help if your diarrhoea continues for more than three days, if your stools are bloody, if you develop a prolonged fever, or if you have constant severe stomach pains.

Sun Dangers

Being near the equator, Belize gets a lot of sunshine. The country enjoys average temperatures of 26°C (86°F), rising to over 35°C (95°F) at the height of the dry season. Stay out of direct sunlight as much as possible, especially around midday when the ultraviolet rays will be at their fiercest. Use a strong sunscreen – at least factor 15 – wear a wide-brimmed hat and drink plenty of water. Try to avoid getting sunburnt. Not only will it be extremely unpleasant, but it could lead to something worse, such heatstroke or, if you're fair skinned, perhaps even skin cancer, cases of which are increasing by the year. If you do get heatstroke, the advice is pretty much the same as for diarrhoea. Drink plenty of fluids including, for preference, a rehydration solution.

Insect Bites and Insect-borne Diseases

Unfortunately the nagging discomfort of insect bites is pretty much guaranteed, unless you're very lucky – or extraordinarily careful – and somehow manage to keep your entire body either swaddled in insect repellent or within a hole-less mosquito net for the entire duration of your trip.

Mosquitoes are present in all lowland areas. You'll find the greatest concentrations in wet, swampy areas, as the blood-sucking beasts breed in bodies of still (often stagnant) water. Pretty much anything – a puddle, a water butt, even an old oil can – can provide a home to a colony. August, when the country's winds are at their calmest, tends to see the largest swarms. Ankle-biting sand-flies – also known as chiggers or 'no-see-ums' because of their diminutive size – are common to most beaches, and you should also watch out for ticks in the jungle.

Protect yourself by covering up as much of yourself as is comfortably possible. If trekking through forest, this means long trousers and sleeves. Wear proper hiking boots, not sandals. Use a strong insect repellent on all areas of exposed skin and keep reapplying according to the maker's instructions – typically every 5–6 hours for a solution containing 35% DEET. However, be careful not to apply DEET-based repellent to cuts or areas of sensitive skin. Insect repellents based on natural ingredients can also be effective, tend to be kinder to your skin and smell nicer, but do have to be reapplied more regularly – perhaps every couple of hours. One of the best is Rainforest Remedies insect repellent, which is produced by a San Ignacio-based firm and is widely available in the west of the country. Take special care at dusk when insects are at their most active. If possible, bring your own mosquito net, which you should ideally tuck under your mattress at night. Many hotels will supply them as a matter of course (and will have screened windows), but these may have holes. The mosquitoes will still get you, of course, but hopefully not in such great numbers. And remember, the more you scratch, the longer it will take for them to heal.

If a tick attaches itself to you – a distinct possibility if you go walking through the jungle in short sleeves and shorts (it's happened to me) – you'll have to get it out using tweezers. Grasp firmly and pull directly away from the body (do not twist) ensuring that all of the tick is removed.

Dengue Fever

It happens very rarely, but sometimes an insect bite can lead to something a good deal more serious than an itchy leg. Dengue fever, a viral disease present in Belize, is transmitted by the aedes mosquito. If contracted, the virus usually produces nothing worse than flu-like symptoms – a fever, aches, a rash and vomiting – at least on the first infection. Unfortunately, a second infection can be much more severe and in some instances can even result in death, although this is usually only true of young children or the very old. Still, it's a worry, not so much for the likelihood of you catching it – it's pretty rare with just a few dozen cases reported each year – but because there is no vaccine and no cure, so there's not a great deal you can do once you've got it, other than take plenty of fluids and ride it out.

Malaria

Malaria, which as everyone knows is spread by mosquitoes, is still present in all Central American countries. However, Belize sees very few cases each year. Symptoms include headaches, muscle pains, severe fevers, alternating periods of feeling very hot and extremely cold, shaking, and, occasionally in severe cases, hallucinations and coma.

The country's wetter, swampier regions – particularly the southern half of the country – are the most prone to outbreaks, principally because they have the largest numbers of mosquitoes.

There is no cure for malaria, but there are preventative measures you can take. Belize's malarial strain can be effectively combated by a simple course of chloroquine, which involves taking a couple of tablets once a week on the same day. You need to start the course two weeks before arriving in the country for it to be effective. Remember, no prophylactic is entirely foolproof, and you should still use plenty of insect repellent to give yourself added protection.

Chagas' Disease

This is a very uncommon ailment, which usually only affects people living (or staying) in very poor areas. It's transmitted to humans by cone-nose bugs (also known as 'assassin bugs', or by the deceptively sweet name of 'kissing bugs') which live in the untreated walls and roofs of simple indigenous adobe houses, from where they fall onto their victims, biting them and feeding on their blood. The bug passes on the disease, not by the bite itself – which while irritating is harmless – but by the singularly unpleasant practice of subsequently defecating on the wound. Symptoms include a severe fever and swollen glands, but these usually pass relatively quickly. However, as with malaria, and some other remissionary diseases, Chaga's is often not gone for good, but may return later (sometimes decades later) in a much more virulent form, which in severe cases may even result in death. There is no cure. However, it's extremely rare for it to be contracted by tourists and can be prevented by the simple expedient of sleeping beneath a mosquito net.

HIV/AIDS

It's not a huge problem (yet), but, as everywhere, it is a concern. The same worldwide rules apply. If you're going to have sex with a stranger, use a condom. Do not share hypodermic needles.

Rabies

Contracting rabies is a possibility – the disease is present in the country – but an extremely remote one. Only a handful of cases have been reported in the past couple of decades (and none since 1989). There is a vaccine you can take, but, as it involves an intense, unpleasant procedure involving three injections, and must be begun a month in advance of your trip, it's only recommended for people who are going to be directly handling animals – such as volunteers on conservation projects.

Animal Nasties

Belize does have large numbers of big black scorpions, which look absolutely deadly but are in practice just a bit annoying – especially as they often behave in stereotypical fashion, hiding themselves in shoes and items of discarded clothing. Always shake out your garments thoroughly before putting them on if staying in a rural area. A scorpion sting is apparently no worse than a wasp or bee sting, which should come as some comfort, unless you happen to be allergic to wasp and bee stings. If you are, you might want to consider bringing injectable adrenaline (*epinephrine*) or an Epipen.

Belize is also home to a number of species of tarantula, but these are rarely seen and by no means as deadly as their legend would suggest – again, think bee sting level (*see* p.48 for more information).

Poisonous snakes are the most dangerous land animals Belize has to offer. The bite of the country's two most venomous species – the coral snake and the fer-de-lance – can kill. Still, there's no need to be unduly alarmed. Most visitors to Belize do not encounter a single snake (deadly or otherwise) during their time in the country. Just be sure to take special care when walking through dense undergrowth or grassland, particularly at dawn or dusk, when snakes are most likely to be active. And always wear closed hiking boots or shoes, never sandals, if walking in an area where there could possibly be snakes (for more information on snakes, *see* p.46).

If bitten, get yourself to hospital as soon as possible. Ideally, you should provide the medical staff with a description (or even a positive identification) of the snake so that the correct antivenin can be administered.

Marine Animal Nasties

It's not just on land that you have to worry about what's got its beady eye on you. There are plenty of dangerous critters out at sea as well. That said, you're unlikely to encounter anything in the major league of scary, such as a large shark – whale sharks excepted, but they're totally harmless, feeding only on plankton. Small nurse sharks and rays are much more common, but pose little threat.

First Aid

You should bring a first-aid kit with you in order to be able to deal with any minor medical ailments that might crop up. This should contain:

General all-purpose antibiotics
Aloe gel (for sunburn)
Anti-inflammatory drugs (such as ibuprofen)
Antiseptic cream or spray
Bandages and gauze
Condoms
DEET-based insect repellent
Iodine tablets (for purifying water)
Painkillers (aspirin, paracetamol)
Penknife
Plasters
Rehydration salts
Safety pins
Scissors
Sterile syringes and needles
Steroid cream (for rashes)
Sunscreen
Thermometer
Tweezers

In fact, out on the reef the main danger is posed not by what's coming to get you, but by what you might accidentally touch, such as a heavily armoured black sea urchin whose spines can easily penetrate the skin and are poisonous (but not fatal). They are easy to spot, however, popping out of holes in the coral like great gothic pin cushions. Stay alert and avoid. If pranged, remove the spine and disinfect the wound as quickly as possible. And if you can't get the spine out, seek medical attention. Don't go sticking your hand into any hand-sized holes in the coral, as these may well house moray eels who will let you know you're not welcome by trying to bite a large chunk out of you.

Remember, out on the reef, you have to be as wary of damaging the coral as you are of anything damaging you. For tips on reef safety, *see* p.35.

The Botfly

Like the Wizard of Oz, the botfly has a public image way out of proportion to its true stature. The number of people who've heard gruesome tales of botfly infestations is always way in excess of the number of people who've actually had botfly infestations. But then, with this particular beastie, it's the tale that's the thing. It's the gruesomeness of what the botfly does – gleefully retold by generations of travellers – that has spread its fame.

It all starts with the mother botfly, who has developed a rather ingenious method for finding a suitable environment in which her young can grow. Once pregnant, the mother botfly captures a mosquito and lays her eggs on its body. When the mosquito subsequently lands on a prey animal to feed, the eggs, alerted by the warmth of the animal, hatch, and the larvae drop onto the prey animal – which can include a person – burrow under the skin and set up home.

To start with, a botfly larval infestation looks much like a mosquito bite. The trouble is, it doesn't heal, and as the larva grows it will start to move in a rather unpleasant David Cronenberg sort of a way (which can hurt). Left to its own devices, the larva will continue to grow for up to 6 weeks, by which time it will be around 1½ins long (3.8cm), whereupon it will exit its human host, drop to the ground and pupate into an adult fly. The good news is, the botfly isn't actually dangerous. If you suspect you have a botfly larva growing within you, there are various ways to deal with it, all based on the fact that, in order to survive, the larva has to maintain an airway through your skin. Block up the airway with a blob of Vaseline, and the larva soon suffocates and dies, but as it remains within your body it will still have to be removed (i.e. squeezed out).

Another tried and tested method is to draw it out by offering it something even tastier than human flesh – cow flesh. Place a piece of steak over the bite and, so the theory goes, the larva will come out of its own accord, tempted by the delicious beefy smell, and will transfer itself to the steak, which can then be thrown away, and your wound

Hospitals in Belize

Belize Medical Associates, 5791 St Thomas St, Belize City, **t** 223 0302, *www.belizemedical.com*. Well-equipped private hospital.

Universal Health Services, corner of Blue Marlin and Chancellor Aves, West Landivar, Belize City, **t** 223 7870, *www.universalhealthbelize.com*.

La Loma Luz Hospital, San Ignacio, **t** 804 2985.

treated with antiseptic. In practice, you should probably seek out medical assistance as soon as possible, and be sure to tell the doctor what you think it is, as misdiagnoses are common.

Hospitals and Medical Provision in Belize

Ambulance t 90

Belize's medical provision is rather limited. But then it does have a very small population. There are very few doctors in the entire country, and many communities are not served by a hospital at all.

As you'd expect, Belize City offers the widest range of medical facilities (*see* p.81). And, if you are going to fall ill, this is probably the best place to do it. For your own peace of mind, you should probably take out adequate travel insurance (*see* p.77).

Pharmacies

Most Belizean towns have at least one well-stocked pharmacy, selling a wide range of drugs and medications – in theory anyway. In practice, the supply of certain drugs often runs out and may not be regularly replaced. Be sure to bring any prescription medicines you need from home, as you will not be able to rely on getting them here. You should also make sure you have a letter from your doctor detailing your medical needs in case you have to explain your tablets to the authorities.

And if you do need to get hold of a certain drug when in the country, it's worth learning its correct scientific name, as this is more likely to be stocked than a specific brand-name drug.

Maps

Don't count on picking up maps once in the country, as the tourist board does not hand them out as a matter of course. Instead, you'll probably be redirected to the Angelus Press Bookstore in Belize City. Try to get hold of a good, up-to-date country-wide map before you arrive. One of best and easiest to use is the 'International Travel Map 1: 250,000', which also has an inset map of Belize City.

That said, if you do arrive map-less, it shouldn't be a disaster. Less than 200 miles

Map Shops

In the UK

Stanfords, 12–14 Long Acre, London, WC2 9LP, **t** (020) 7836 1321, *www.stanfords.co.uk*.
Travel Bookshop, 13 Blenheim Crescent, London W11 2EE, **t** (020) 7229 5260, *www.thetravelbook shop.co.uk*.

In the USA

Distant Lands, 56 South Raymond Ave, Pasadena, CA 91105, **t** 800 310 3220, *www.distantlands.com*.
Longitude Books, Suite 1206, 115 West 30th Street, New York, NY 1001, **t** 800 342 2164, *www.longitudebooks.com*.

long and 70 miles wide, there isn't really enough of Belize to get seriously lost in. The country has only four main highways, which together take you through most of the country's major towns.

You should be able to get around more or less okay for a day or two simply by asking directions – so long as you don't attempt any off-roading. However, your journey will of course be much improved by knowing where you're going and what to expect.

For a few pointers, you could pick up Emory King's *Driver's Guide to Beautiful Belize*, available from the Angelus Press, which provides route maps to the entire country.

Money and Banks

Belize's currency is the Belizean dollar (BZ$), which is divided into 100 cents (c). It's tied to the US dollar at a fixed rate of US$1=BZ$2. Coins come in denominations of 1c, 5c, 10c, 25c, 50c and BZ$1. Notes come in denominations of BZ$1, BS$2, BZ$5, 1 BZ$10, BZ$20, BZ$50 and BZ$100. Incidentally, the lady whose portrait graces all Belizean notes and coins is the British Queen, Elizabeth II. Even though Belize became independent from the British Empire in 1981, the British Queen is still the official head of state. It's a very flattering likeness, which seems not to have been updated since the 1950s (unlike the poor old ageing Queen on British bank notes).

US dollars are effectively used as a second currency in Belize, accepted pretty much everywhere, although you will always be given your change in Belizean dollars.

Remember to check whether the quoted price for a particular service is in US or Belizean dollars, as mistaking one for the other can make a big dent in your finances.

ATMs are available in all the main urban centres – Belize City, Belmopan, Corozal, Dangriga, Orange Walk, Punta Gorda, San Ignacio and San Pedro – although only Belize Bank machines accept international cards on the Plus or Cirrus networks. Other banks accept only domestic cards.

Internationally recognized credit cards (Visa and Mastercard) are accepted by larger, internationally orientated businesses – car rental companies, airlines, upmarket hotels, resorts etc. – and the number of smaller places that accept them is growing.

You can change money in all banks, although for the best exchange rate it's best to bring US dollars with you, rather than try and change any other currency.

Opening Times

Belize's opening hours are by no means totally synchronized. Many shops and businesses of the same type open and close at very different times. The one constant, however, is that on Sundays most things – businesses, shops, even most restaurants – are shut, the main exceptions being the country's tourist attractions, including its Mayan sites. As a general rule of thumb expect shops to be open 9am–12 noon and 1pm–5pm, although some may open earlier and shut later. Lunch is usually strictly observed. Half-day opening on Saturday is common. Banks are only open Mon–Fri 8.30am–3pm (sometimes till 4pm on Fri).

Post, Email and Internet

All of Belize's major towns – including Belize City, Belmopan, Corozal, Dangriga, Orange Walk, Placencia, San Ignacio and San Pedro – have a post office, although many smaller ones do not. It costs very little to send a postcard or a small letter from Belize: US$0.30 to the US, US$0.40 to Europe. If you want something to arrive quickly, send it from Belize City, as things can take quite a while to be despatched from more rural areas.

You can receive post and parcels in Belize via the General Delivery (or poste restante) method, whereby the post office will hold the mail for you until you come to collect it, although this is probably only a good idea at major branches, such as the main one in Belize City. You'll have to show your passport to claim your mail. Make sure that the sender addresses the envelope with your name exactly as it appears on your passport (and that it's marked 'General Delivery') or it may not be handed over.

All of the country's major towns can also provide Internet access. The level and rate of access are improving all the time, as more Internet cafés open, and slow dial-up connections are replaced by speedy broadband ones. Wi Fi connections are also becoming increasingly common. Expect access from around US$2–3 per hour in an Internet café, more in a hotel.

Shopping and Crafts

The first thing you'll probably notice about the Belize shopping scene is just how un-westernized it is, with no international chain stores and very few recognizable brand names on display. Belize City has a few department stores and San Pedro a number of fashion boutiques aimed at western tastes, but most of the shops here tend to be small scale and locally orientated. Aside from the Tourism Village in Belize City, which is a special shopping area that's been set up to service cruise liner passengers (see p.95), there are no major malls or shopping centres in the country.

However, it's not just the shops that are rather limited in scope. You won't find as wide a range of arts and crafts on sale here as you will in some other Central American countries either. Those items that are worth hunting out include: wooden carvings of the country's famous animals – jaguars, sharks, manatees, lobsters – available in all the main tourist areas; woven baskets and slate carvings sold at the various Mayan sites in the south; traditional wood and leather Garifuna drums, available from the workshops of Dangriga; and Mennonite furniture.

The latter is available throughout the country. In fact, as you drive around, you'll often pass groups of Mennonites selling their distinctive wooden wares from the side of the road – traditionalists from a horse and buggy, progressives from the back of a lorry. The most commonly purchased items are small low-set reclining chairs (see p.31 for more on the Mennonites).

However, according to customs reports, the most popular souvenir of all with visitors to Belize, uncovered in luggage more times than any other items, are bottles of Marie Sharp's hot sauce. If you decide to follow suit, be sure to pack yours carefully – it really is about the last thing you want breaking in among your clothes. For more information on Marie Sharp, see p.179.

A word of caution – avoid buying any souvenirs that utilize animal products, particularly anything made from coral or turtle shells, anything made from rare hardwoods (such as mahogany or purple heart) and any archaeological artefacts, the sale of which is strictly prohibited.

See the relevant area chapters for more details on shopping opportunities.

Telephones

Belize's domestic landline phone network is operated by BTL, 'Belize Telecommunications Ltd' (www.btl.net). The cheapest way to make an international call from Belize is to purchase a BTL pre-paid phone card for use in a BTL public pay phone. The cards, which come in denominations from US$1 to US$25, are available in convenience stores and gas stations throughout the country. Simply dial the number printed on the card, enter the card's individual pin number (which you reveal by scratching the back of the card) and then follow the automated prompts to make your call.

Many US mobile (cell) phones can be used in Belize, as can other international GSM phones. Contact your network provider for more information. For visitors from the UK, Europe or Australasia, whose phones may not work here, it is possible to hire a mobile phone at Philip Goldson International Airport (t 225 4162, btlport@btl.net). This is certainly a more convenient option than constantly hunting down phone booths, particularly if you're doing a lot of travelling about, but it's not cheap – rates start at around US$6 per day, plus a $150–200 credit-card deposit – and coverage is by no means total throughout the country.

To call Belize from abroad, dial 00 and then the country code, 501, followed by the local phone number. There are no area codes in Belize. All phone numbers have seven numbers, which must be dialled in full wherever you are in the country.

To call abroad from Belize, dial 00 and then the country code (UK 44; Ireland 353; USA and Canada 1; Australia 61; New Zealand 64), then dial the number, omitting the first zero.

Time

Belize occupies the same time zone as the central United States (US Central Time), six hours behind Greenwich Mean Time.

Tipping

It's welcome but in most instances not expected. Tipping is certainly not a mainstay of the Belizean service economy, as it is in certain other countries, notably the US. You should only venture an extra gratuity if you feel the service genuinely merited it.

Tipping hotel porters and maids around $1 a day is standard. And you might want to round the bill of a good meal up by 10% (though there's no need to round up the bill of a bad meal). However, do first make sure that a service charge hasn't automatically been levied, a common practice in many of the more up-market touristy restaurants.

Tourist Offices and Information

The Belize Tourism Board's main tourist information office is located at mile 3.5 on the Northern Highway, in the New Horizon Investment Building, a 10-minute taxi ride north of Belize City (t 1-800 624 0686, 223 1913/1910, www.belizetourism.org). It also operates a small desk at Philip Goldson International Airport, as well as regional offices at Corozal (p.216), Placencia (p.191) and Punta Gorda (p.198). The Ministry of Tourism in

Belmopan can also provide information on the country's attractions (*see* p.147), as can the Belize Tourism Industry Association, the public face of a group of tourism businesses, which maintains a small office in Belize City (*see* p.99). Information on the northern cayes is generally provided principally by locally run initiatives, such as *www.ambergriscaye.com* and *www.gocayecaulker.com*.

There are no Belize tourist information centres in the UK or USA.

Where to Stay

The number of places to stay in Belize keeps rising by the year, as tourism to the country continues to increase. The country's main tourist hot spots – such as Ambergris Caye and, in particular, Placencia – are currently seeing huge amounts of development, with scores of new hotels and condominium complexes being created. While most of these new places are aimed at the moderate and luxury end of the market, there's still plenty of choice at the lower end of the spectrum, with the country particularly well provided with traditional family-run guesthouses. Where Belize is less strong is in its provision of really low-cost, backpacker-orientated accommodation, with very few hostels or camp sites. However, some budget places do have dorms and some will let you pitch a tent in their grounds.

Prices, Facilities and Booking

In general, you should expect accommodation prices to be a fair bit higher than in neighbouring Central American countries. Certainly, if backpacking your way around, you'll have to up your budget a fair bit from the rock bottom Mexico-Guatemala level of US$5 per day. In Belize, US$10–15 will get you something as basic as you can comfortably deal with – probably consisting of little more than a small room, access to a shared bathroom and cold water. For a decent level of comfort – i.e. a private bath, hot water and perhaps even complimentary breakfast – you're realistically looking at a daily budget of US$20–40. Above this, the standard of accommodation and level of facilities continue to rise till you hit the upper echelons of the grand lodges and resorts, the

Accommodation Price Categories

Prices refer to an average double room with bath/shower in high season:

luxury	$$$$$	US$120 and above
expensive	$$$$	US$80–119
moderate	$$$	US$40–79
inexpensive	$$	US$26–39
budget	$	US$25 and under

sort of places that come with their own stretches of jungle, riding schools, spas and museums. It's also possible to rent apartments and condos for long stays, particularly in the main visitor destinations of Ambergris Caye, Caye Caulker and Placencia.

Prices are at their highest around the public holidays of Christmas and Easter, when pre-booking is advised. It's also a good idea to book your room in advance during the high season, December–April, when there will generally be more pressure on rooms. Bargains are more readily available in the low season, particularly at high-end places. Remember that the posted room rates often don't include the 9% hotel room tax.

In the past few years, it's become much easier to reserve in advance via the Internet or email. Some places require you to place a deposit using a credit card. Some even ask that you pay the full amount of your intended stay in advance. Be sure to check carefully what's being requested before committing yourself. It goes without saying that you shouldn't provide your credit card details unless the website is using a secure server with a valid safety certificate. If possible, bring a print-out of your confirmation email with you as proof of your reservation.

Types of Accommodation

Most of the terms in the Belize accommodation lexicon should be pretty self-explanatory – it's an English-speaking country after all – although there are a couple of words that might require further clarification. The first is 'cabanas', which is essentially a catch-all term referring to any freestanding structure (or group of free-standing structures), be it made in the traditional style with wooden walls and a thatched roof, or out of concrete with a tin roof. The level of facilities is no guide. Cabanas are available in all price categories throughout the country.

The second term, 'lodge', is generally taken to mean any large accommodation in a rural location, although it's usually used to describe something rather up market. Within this group is the subsection, 'ecolodges', which are places that make a point of promoting themselves as environmentally friendly. Many are – maintaining stretches of forest, using sustainable energy sources, helping to preserve habitats – but you shouldn't necessarily take everything at face value. The prefix 'eco' is often used as much as a marketing slogan as a statement of conservational intent. If you're concerned about the potential environmental impact of your visit, be sure to check your proposed lodge's 'ecological' credentials more closely.

The final term, 'resort', refers mainly to large generic, purpose-built, very well equipped (but less distinctly Belizean) projects aimed at the US package market. These are principally found in the main tourist hot spots of Ambergris Caye and Placencia and tend to aim for a tropical island getaway sort of a feel. They tend to be less concerned with promoting themselves as 'eco' as being seen as 'luxurious' and 'fun'. In fact resort construction is becoming a major conservational worry in Belize, as these places tend to eat up vast supplies of resources and create vast amounts of waste, which the country's limited infrastructure struggles to cope with.

The Local Alternative

Rather than stay in official hotel or hostel accommodation, another option is to opt for a homestay – actually living with a Belizean family in a domestic house. Several Creole, Maya and Garifuna communities offer homestays, including at the Monkey Bay Wildlife Sanctuary (*see* p.108), Gales Point (*see* p.110) and the Community Baboon Sanctuary (*see* p.111). This can be a great way to learn more about the country from the people who know it best, giving you something more than the usual tourist experience.

In a similar vein, it's also possible to stay in the purpose-built guesthouses of several Maya and Garifuna villages in the south of country, represented by the Toledo Eco-tourism Association, whereby your meals, tours and entertainment are provided by local villagers (*see* pp.201–2).

Belize City and District

Streets lined with elegantly faded clapboard houses, restaurants serving up spicy creole cooking, a breezy Caribbean shoreline, friendly, welcoming locals – there's much about Belize City to attract and enchant the visitor, although the chances are that these will not be the first things you hear about the place. The city gets a lot of bad press. You need only do a quick Internet search to uncover a seemingly endless litany of abuse. There are two principal complaints – that the city is a hotbed of crime, and that it's dilapidated and ugly. Neither is (entirely) true. While Belize City does have a problem with (mostly petty) crime and parts of it are rather run-down, the same could be said about many cities.

08

Don't miss

⭐ **Belize's rich history**
Museum of Belize **p.97**

⭐ **Jaguar and puma sightings**
Belize Zoo **p.106**

⭐ **Manatee-watching**
Gales Point **p.109**

⭐ **Howler monkeys**
Community Baboon Sanctuary **p.111**

⭐ **Mayan temples**
Altun Ha **p.112**

See map overleaf

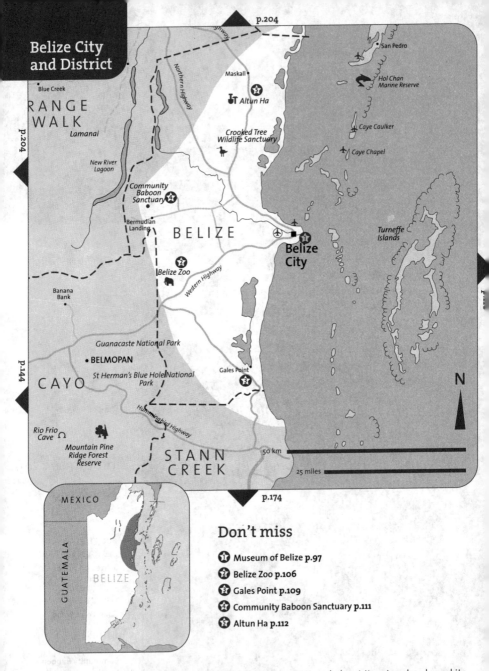

p.204

p.204

p.144

p.174

San Pedro

Hol Chan Marine Reserve

Maskall

Altun Ha

Crooked Tree Wildlife Sanctuary

Caye Caulker

Caye Chapel

Blue Creek

ORANGE WALK

Lamanai

New River Lagoon

Community Baboon Sanctuary

Bermudian Landing

BELIZE

Turneffe Islands

Belize City

Belize Zoo

Western Highway

Banana Bank

Guanacaste National Park

BELMOPAN

St Herman's Blue Hole National Park

Gales Point

CAYO

Hummingbird Highway

Rio Frio Cave

Mountain Pine Ridge Forest Reserve

STANN CREEK

50 km

25 miles

N

Northern Highway

MEXICO

GUATEMALA

BELIZE

Don't miss

- ⭐ Museum of Belize **p.97**
- ⭐ Belize Zoo **p.106**
- ⭐ Gales Point **p.109**
- ⭐ Community Baboon Sanctuary **p.111**
- ⭐ Altun Ha **p.112**

There's certainly nothing exceptional about its crime levels and its streets feel much less intimidating than many other Central American cities. Unfortunately, at some point in the past, Belize acquired a reputation for being 'dangerous', and, regardless of how many people pass through its confines each year unmolested –

i.e. the vast majority of them – it seems that reputation is going to continue to stick.

So, while it's understandable to approach your time in the city with a measure of foreboding, it's worth pointing out that the city's seedier areas lie well off the main tourist trail, and most problems can easily be avoided by employing the same common-sense rules you would anywhere – don't display ostentatious wealth, don't walk around unfamiliar areas of town on your own after dark, etc.

Spend a few hours exploring its streets and you'll soon discover that the city's vibe is more friendly than threatening. It's certainly Belize's liveliest, most energetic and most crowded urban centre, its 70,000 inhabitants accounting for around one quarter of the country's total population. Though no longer the country's capital (Belmopan took over that title in 1970), it is still by far the largest city in Belize, as well as the cultural and commercial centre of the country. It also provides a convenient base from which to explore some of the region's major attractions, including Belize Zoo, the Mayan ruins of Altun Ha, and, of course, the nearby cayes and barrier reef, which are the country's main tourist draw.

Despite its national importance, there's still something charmingly low-key about Belize City. But then, by international standards, this 'city' is really little bigger than a mid-size town. It's certainly no hi-tech metropolis, rather a higgledy-piggledy agglomeration of clapboard and concrete houses set amid tropical greenery. Many buildings sit on small stilts, a consequence of having been built on reclaimed swampland, and most of its roads are potholed and uneven. It may not be pristine – some of it is very ramshackle – but much of it is very pretty, with an aesthetic more Caribbean than American. Indeed, the city's appearance is largely the result of local, not international, tastes. You won't see much in the way of western, brand-name street furniture here, with hand-painted signs, local stores and creole restaurants taking the place of the billboards, chain stores and American fast-food restaurants that clutter the sightlines of so many other cities. Though Belize City has suffered a good deal of hurricane damage over the years, several grand colonial-era structures survive, their elegant pastel-hued confines now often as not home to hotels, restaurants and embassies.

It's a small and compact place, filled with cars and people, but a relatively easy one to get around, with everything of interest lying a short distance from the city's main landmark, the Swing Bridge, which spans Haulover Creek just inland of where it connects with the Caribbean Sea. You can easily walk the entire tourist trail – which, in truth, comprises just a handful of formal attractions – in 45 minutes. And if you like what you see, and have managed keep hold of your valuables, get online and post a report. Try and get the city's reputation moving in the right direction.

Belize City

History

It has been claimed that Belize City was built on a foundation of coral pieces, logwood chips and rum bottles, which were used to fill in the swampy ground bordering Haulover Creek by the area's first inhabitants, British pirates. These pirates had long been using the islands of the barrier reef as impromptu bases from which to launch attacks on Spanish ships carrying booty across the Atlantic when, in the 1650s, a few decided to try their hand at something a bit more legitimate. The country's first permanent settlements, of which Belize City was one, were established as bases for the export of logwood, a valuable commodity at the time from which a blue-purple clothing dye could be extracted.

Soon, the Baymen, as the ex-pirates called themselves (because they operated out of the Bay of Honduras), had a thriving business on their hands, which they oversaw from their main base on St George's Caye. At that time, Belize City was considered the lesser settlement, principally because it was home to the African slaves who actually performed the hazardous task of cutting the trees. Incidentally, it is from these slaves that the majority of the country's Creole population is descended.

Unfortunately for the Baymen, their erstwhile enemies, the Spanish, took exception to their actions, principally because they believed it to be no less illegal (if slightly less aggressive) than their former piracy. It was Spain's contention that the entire Central American mainland, including Belize, belonged to Spain. To prove their point, Spanish forces attacked the British settlers several times throughout the 18th century, forcing them to abandon their settlements on at least four occasions. Each time, however, the settlers returned, rebuilt and restarted their business, which by the late 18th century also included the export of mahogany.

Formal attempts were made to address the situation with Spain and Britain signing a number of treaties. The final one, in 1786, gave the Baymen the right to cut wood in the area, but not to perform any other form of agriculture, set up government or form an army. It was a compromise that satisfied nobody, and so it came as little surprise when, in 1798, the Spanish launched a major attack on the Baymen determined to settle the matter once and for all. They did, although not in the way they were hoping. The Baymen's forces, bolstered by British Navy troops and their own slaves, roundly defeated the Spanish in the Battle of St George's Caye. It proved to be the turning point in the conflict, with Spain relinquishing her claim to sovereignty (and, indeed, most of her American territories) soon after.

Getting to Belize City

By Air

Most visitors to Belize arrive at Philip Goldson International Airport (**t** 225 2045 for flight information), 12m north of Belize City in Ladyville. The arrivals hall is very small with passport control, a tour desk, the baggage carousel and customs all located just a few feet apart, although it's due for a revamp once the current runway expansion programme is complete (tentatively scheduled for early 2007). Porters hover eagerly just the other side of customs, ready to carry your bags the short distance to the taxi rank (roughly 20yds away). As they get paid a mandatory US$1 per piece of luggage carried, be sure to keep hold of your bags if you don't want to pay.

Getting into town is a pretty straightforward if rather expensive process. **Taxis** line up just outside the exit, although you'll probably be intercepted by a driver way before you reach the front of the rank. Check for the green licence plate indicating that it is an official taxi and agree upon a price before you get in, as the taxis don't have meters. A ride to the city centre should cost around US$25 and take around 30 mins. There is an alternative, budget route into town, although it is a good deal more convoluted. As there's no direct bus service, you'll have to walk for a mile to the Northern Highway and then flag down a bus heading into the city.

Departure tax: There is a departure tax payable by all foreign nationals exiting the country by air. This currently stands at US$35, which must be paid either in cash (US dollars only) or with an American credit card as you pass passport control. You can change **currency** at a small branch of the Belize Bank, at the exit to the arrivals hall (*open 8.30–1 and 2–4*).

By Bus

Most of the city's main bus terminals are located along West Collet Canal Street, around a mile from the city centre, a rather run-down area, which can be pretty intimidating at night. If arriving after dark, and pick-up has not been arranged, it's a good idea to take a taxi to your hotel. This should cost around US$3–4.

Getting around Belize City

On Foot

Its pavements are often narrow, uneven, congested and bordered by large storm drains. Indeed, some streets don't have pavements at all. And yet Belize City is still a place best explored on foot, being small, compact and largely flat. In any case, the lack of a bus service and the difficulty of driving do rather narrow your options. You'll have to exercise a degree of caution, however. Traffic flow is heavy throughout daytime hours, particularly around the Swing Bridge, and there is a distinct lack of pedestrian crossings. However, drivers are reasonably tolerant of the foibles of disorientated pedestrians and heavy congestion means they're rarely travelling at much of a speed. Your disorientation shouldn't last for long. The streets south of the creek adhere to a sort of rough and readily understandable grid pattern. And, while those to the north have a more higgledy-piggledy arrangement, the city's small size means that its layout should quickly become familiar.

By Taxi

At night, for safety's sake, it's probably best to switch to travelling by taxi. Official ones can be identified by their green licence plates. You shouldn't have any problem in locating one but, if you do, you can usually find them waiting outside the city's larger hotels, particularly the Radisson and the Princess. Expect to pay US$4/5 for a journey anywhere within the city. As taxis do not have meters, always agree on a price beforehand.

By Car

Owing to a whole host of difficulties – hectic traffic, narrow streets, misleading one-way systems, a lack of secure parking spaces – not to mention the city's reduced, easily walkable dimensions, driving around the city centre is not recommended. Still, if you're determined, be sure to drive slowly and carefully and remember to lock your vehicle. Don't leave anything of value on display within it. There are few parking restrictions, and spaces are usually easy to find along the streets. If you struggle, however, there are public bays on Marine Parade opposite the Radisson and on Barrack Road near the Princess Hotel.

By Bus and Guided Tours

There are no bus services within the city itself, only from the city's bus terminals to the country's other destinations. Short tours of the city's main sites on road-trains (US$28 for 1hr) or horse-drawn carriages (US$55 for 2hrs) are offered by **Calypso Trains** (**t** 223 5365) out of the Tourism Village when the cruise ships are in.

Getting away from Belize City

By Air

Domestic flights to destinations around the country – including Caye Caulker, San Pedro, Dangriga, Placencia and Punta Gorda – leave from both Philip Goldson International Airport and the Belize City Municipal Airport, which is located around a mile from downtown. There are also regular flights to Flores in Guatemala (often used for visits to Tikal). **Tropic Air** (t 226 2012) and **Maya Island Air** (t 223 1140) are the main domestic carriers (for more information, *see* p.65). A taxi to the municipal airstrip will cost around US$4. There is no bus service.

By Bus

Novelo's (t 207 4924, 207 7146 or 227 3929, *novelo@btl.net*), the country's largest bus company, who have in recent years bought out many of their smaller rivals (but *see* p.66), operate daily services to Belmopan, Corozal, Dangriga, Orange Walk, Placencia, San Ignacio and Punta Gorda from their terminal on West Collet Canal Street. **James Bus** also operate daily services to Belmopan, Dangriga and Punta Gorda. Their station is located in front of the petrol station on Vernon Street.

International services to Mexico and Guatemala depart from in front of the Water Taxi Terminal, by the Swing Bridge.

By Boat

Owned and operated by the Tourism Board, the **Caye Caulker Water Taxi Association** (t 223 5752 or 226 0992, *ccwatertaxi@btl.net, www.cayecaulkerwatertaxi.com*) operates services out of its covered terminal at the foot of the Swing Bridge (North Front Street). Taxis run daily to and from San Pedro (Ambergris Caye) stopping at Caye Caulker on the way. Stops at Caye Chapel or Long Caye are also available on request – enquire when buying your ticket and alert the captain when boarding. Boats leave for Caye Caulker and San Pedro at 8am, 9am, 10.30am, 12 noon, 1.30pm, 3pm, 4.30pm and 5.30pm (the last goes to Caye Caulker only) with an additional service at 5pm on Fri, weekends and holidays. The journey to Caye Caulker takes around 45mins and costs US$10 single, US$17.50 return. For San Pedro, it will take around 1hr 20mins and cost US$15 single, US$27.50 return. Ideally, you should purchase your ticket at least an hour before the boat is scheduled to depart to be sure of getting a seat (the boats are pretty small). Bring a waterproof coat if it looks like rain, as some of the boats are not covered. Otherwise, you may find that your only protection against a tropical downpour is a thin tarpaulin. Charters and snorkel tours are also available; ask in the terminal.

A couple of rival private firms also operate similar services. **Triple J** (t 207 7777) runs water taxis to Caye Caulker (US$ 7.50 one way, US$12.50 return) and San Pedro (US$10 one way, US$20 return) from their pier on the Southern Foreshore. Boats leave at 8am, 10.30am, 12 noon, 3pm and 4.30pm. **Thunderbolt** (t 226 2904) also operates a twice-daily service for the same prices as Triple J. Boats leave from the north side of the creek, just east of the church.

By Car

Although driving around the city centre is not recommended (*see* 'Getting around Belize City'), it does make a good way of exploring the rest of the country. And, if you hire your car at the international airport – where most of the rental offices are located – you should be able to avoid the city centre altogether. Two highways connect with Belize City: the Northern Highway, which leads up to the Mexican border; and the Western Highway which runs all the way to Guatemala, passing through Belmopan and San Ignacio on the way. Both can be accessed from the airport without having to backtrack to the city.

For more information on renting a car, *see* p.68.

Now free from foreign interference, Belize City had the chance to expand significantly, which it did throughout the early 19th century as more and more British settlers arrived, although the British government itself showed no great interest in the country, not even bothering to officially incorporate it into the British Empire until 1871, when it was rechristened British Honduras. As the country's largest urban centre, Belize City was the obvious choice for capital, a title it would hold until 1970 when it was replaced by Belmopan, a decision prompted by the events of 1961 when a devastating hurricane-induced tidal wave destroyed much of the coastal city. The authorities, fearing that the city might never recover, decided to relocate the capital inland, away from the worst excesses of the weather. In fact, Belize was soon rebuilt and thriving again, while the purpose-built Belmopan, the new capital, never quite took off in the way that had been hoped, with most of Belize City's population (including, tellingly, most civil servants and government staff) remaining where they were. It may no longer be the official top city, but Belize City is still regarded by many as the country's true capital.

Belize City

The Swing Bridge and the North Side

Being a rather compact city and quite simple to navigate, the city's attractions are best visited as part of a walking tour, beginning, inevitably at the **Swing Bridge**, the city's most celebrated landmark. In fact, it's so 'celebrated' that you could be forgiven for feeling a twinge of disappointment upon first catching sight of it, as it is rather small (around 50m long) and not particularly spectacular, comprising an unremarkable span of concrete and riveted steel painted green and yellow. Still, having been built way back in 1922 in Liverpool, England, it can boast the proud claim of being the oldest functioning swing bridge in the world. If you're lucky (and the traffic attempting to cross the river rather less so), you may spot it being manually 'swung' – a process which involves the combined exertion of four men (who use poles to turn a central capstan), impedes access across the river for around 20 minutes and generally causes quite a commotion. The bridge swings around its central axis until it points parallel to the shore, allowing ships to pass either side. Contrary to tourist board pronouncements, this does not occur every day, but only if there are boats trying to get through, although it does always happen at the same time of day – 5.30am and/or 5.30pm Monday–Saturday.

Orientation

The city is divided into northern and southern sides by Haulover Creek (so named because cattle were once 'hauled over' by ropes), the last stretch of the Belize River before it reaches the Caribbean Sea to the east. The two sides are connected by the famous **Swing Bridge**, the city's chief landmark, next to the north foot of which sits a building containing the **Maritime Museum** and the main **water taxi terminal** for trips out to the cayes.

North of the Swing Bridge is the Fort George area, the city's most up-market neighbourhood and the location of the **Tourism Village**, the **Baron Bliss Memorial**, the **Museum of Belize** and most of the city's swankier hotels and restaurants.

South of the Swing Bridge is the city's main commercial district, which leads down to two of the city's other major sites, the **House of Culture** and **St John's Cathedral**.

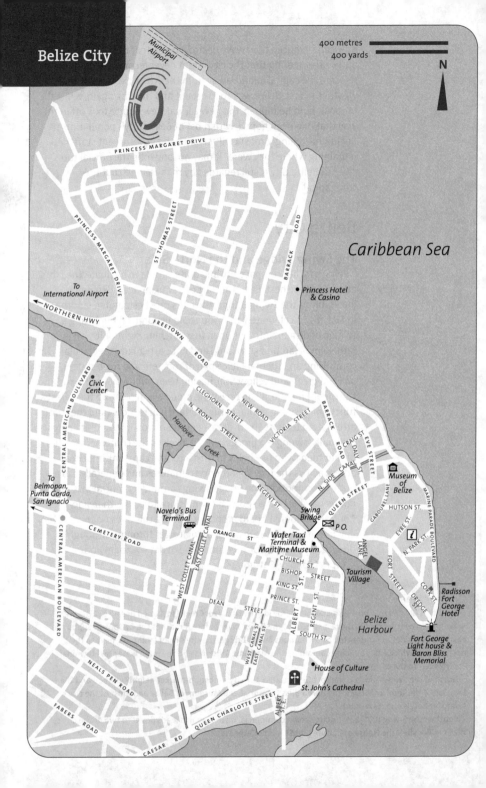

Maritime Museum and Coastal Zone Museum
t 203 1969; open Mon–Sat 8–5.30; adm US$4, for entry to both museums

Just east of the bridge's north side, on North Front Street, sits a large wooden building that started life as a customs house, became a fire station for a while, and is now home to the city's main Water Taxi Terminal (*see* p.92), as well as the **Maritime Museum and Coastal Zone Museum**, two rather well-put-together collections spread over a couple of floors. The downstairs Coastal Zone has displays relating to the country's abundant marine life, the highlight being a scale model of the barrier reef; while the upstairs Maritime Museum focuses on the Belizeans' own relationship with the seas – from pirates to cruise ships. While perhaps not worth a dedicated trip, it's a nice way to spend an hour if you're killing time until the next water taxi turns up next door.

The Image Factory
91 N Front St, t 223 4151, www. imagefactory.bz; open Mon–Fri 9–6.30 (closed for lunch 12– 1.30pm), Sat 9–12; adm free/ donations welcomed)

Continuing east along North Front Street, you pass on your right the **Image Factory**, a cheery gallery showcasing Belizean handicrafts, with an attached bookshop and art store.

Further east, past City Hall where North Front Street turns into Fort Street, and stretching for several hundred metres along the riverside, is the city's heavily guarded **Tourism Village**, a large shopping centre built in the early part of this century to cater (almost exclusively, not to say rather controversially, *see* box) to the ever-growing cruise liner trade. In 2005, nearly a million people visited the city on cruises. Because the village's opening times are arranged to coincide with the arrival of a liner, the appearance of the area can change dramatically depending on when you visit. When a ship is in town, this whole part of town is absolutely buzzing with activity, not just within the village itself, but on the street outside, which will be awash with vendors trying to sell their wares (be it food, souvenirs or a tour) to those few cruise liner passengers who do choose to leave

Tourism Village

The idea of creating a special area to provide up-market services to the growing number of people who visit the city on cruises was generally welcomed when first mooted in the early part of the century. However, the resulting 'Tourism Village' on the waterfront near the mouth of Haulover Creek has been the source of no little controversy. Many have complained that the village, far from acting as a gateway to the city, passing on the benefits of the cruise liner trade to the community at large, as was originally hoped, has instead become a separate, self-serving enclave. It certainly doesn't show a particularly welcoming face to the town, set back behind high fences with its entry points patrolled by burly security guards. Indeed, the village has received a lot criticism over its access policy. Although entry to the village is officially supposed to be open to anyone, foreigner or Belizean alike, in possession of a valid form of photographic ID, there have been numerous reports of locals being denied access. Likewise, some of those operating the cruises have been accused of warning their passengers not to venture out of the village's confines into the 'unsafe' city – unless as part of an official guided tour, of course.

Some of the village's defenders have claimed that, without adequate safety procedures in place, the village wouldn't attract half the custom it does, considering the city's unsavoury reputation. Furthermore, they claim that the city's businesses do benefit from the small proportion of visitors who choose to leave the village's confines to explore the city, as shown by the hordes of traders who congregate around the exits when the boats come in. Still, despite its obvious success, and whatever additional trade it may have brought, it's left a sour taste in the mouths of many.

Safety

It's fair to say that Belize City has a bit of a reputation for being unsafe. This is not entirely undeserved, although it is rather exaggerated. Street crime and robberies do take place here – the various signs advertising the sale of burglar bars are confirmation enough of that – and you certainly wouldn't want to do much walking away from the main tourist areas after dark. But the situation is not nearly as bad as some sources would have you believe. Just use the same common-sense rules and care you would in any unfamiliar city and you should be okay. Stick to the busy main streets and keep all valuables out of sight. At night, it's probably a good idea to get a taxi to and from your destination (and after a bellyful of Belikin and *bocas*, you probably won't feel much like walking anyway). The presence of the baseball-cap-wearing Tourist Police (**t** 227 2222), a small force who patrol the city centre and Fort George area (i.e. the main tourist trail) looking after the welfare of the city's visitors, should give you a further measure of reassurance.

To be honest, you're much more likely to encounter low-level hassle – begging, offers of drugs, etc. – than serious crime. Women may be singled out for special attention, especially if wearing skimpy clothing, although this is rarely anything worse than one of the town's would-be casanovas trying to attract your attention with a shout of 'hello sexy'. Treat all unwanted attention the same way you would anywhere. Be polite but firm with your refusals, and keep walking.

Finally, it's worth mentioning that, despite the regularity with which marijuana will be offered to you for sale as you make your way around the city, possession of the drug is officially illegal in Belize. Being caught holding could, in theory, land you with a hefty fine or perhaps even a jail sentence. Steer clear.

---

the village's confines during their hours ashore. At other times, the street can be empty and almost eerily quiet. The village (when open) can be visited by non-cruise tourists, although you'll have to show a form of photographic ID in order to obtain a visitor's pass.

Belize Audubon Society
t 5004 4918, www. belizeaudubon.org; open 8.30–4.30

Past the Tourism Village, on the other side of the road, is the **Belize Audubon Society**, a prominent NGO involved in the running of a number of reserves around the country (including Crooked Tree, Guanacaste National Park, St Herman's Blue Hole National Park and the Shipstern Nature Reserve). It can provide information on the reserves and operates a small nature-themed gift shop. From here, the road follows the shoreline, curving around a promontory of land before heading north, and changing its name to Marine Parade. At the tip of the promontory, opposite a small park, lies the tomb of the city's most famous benefactor, **Baron Bliss**, which sits beneath a small, specially commissioned red and white **lighthouse** (*see* box on p.97). The walk from here north along Marine Parade is one of the most pleasant the city has to offer, particularly on hot days when sea breezes can take the edge off the unrelenting sun, and pelicans and frigate birds glide overhead. A well-maintained pavement (it's not really wide enough to be considered an esplanade) takes you past some of the town's grandest buildings and hotels. Look out for **Memorial Park** on your left, which was laid out to commemorate the country's war dead; here you'll find the National Handicrafts Centre (*see* p.101) and the Belize Tourism Association Industry Office (*see* p.99). From the seafront you should also be able to see if a cruise liner is in town. The liners don't actually dock in Belize City itself, but rather anchor off shore from where small skiffs ferry groups of cruisers to the Tourism Village. Marine Parade has been widened and extended in the past few years, and now runs over a stretch of reclaimed land (protected by a new sea wall) connecting with the junction of Craig Street, Eve Street and Barrack Road.

From here, Barrack Road heads north along the shore to the Princess Hotel (site of the city's only cinema, bowling alley and casino) and the slightly scrubby BTL Park beyond. Eve Street, meanwhile, heads south back towards the town. A side road off Eve Street, Gaol Lane (actually marked on the sign as 'Goal Lane') heads east to Gabourel Lane, where you'll find the city's latest cultural offering, the rather fine **Museum of Belize**, which opened in 2002 in the city's former prison (which only released its last inmates in 1993). Aiming to give an entire overview of the history of the country, the museum boasts an interesting collection of Mayan artefacts (including a replica of the jade head of the Sun God found at Altun Ha, see p.113) as well as a wealth of historical documents and photographs, not to mention an impressive (and slightly scary) collection of mounted Belizean insects. And, to give you an idea of what the building used to be like, there's also a restored prison cell.

*⓫ **Museum of Belize***
t 223 4524; open Mon–Fri 9–5; adm US$5

Further down Gabourel Lane, more or less opposite its junction with Queen Street, is the heavily guarded **US Embassy**, a lovely colonial-era building that was originally built in 1866 in New England, before being dismantled and shipped to Belize for reassembly. This embassy is actually due to close in a year or so

08 Belize City and District | Belize City

Baron Bliss

Belize City's greatest benefactor was a mysterious character, and there is still much about his life that remains unexplained, not least what motivated him to leave his vast fortune to a country on whose soil he never set foot. What is known is that he was an Englishman, born Henry Edward Ernest Victor Barretts on 16 February 1869 in Buckingham; that he was an engineer by profession and that he was married. What is slightly less well understood is how he acquired his wealth (nearly $2 million by the time he died), how he came by the title of Baron Bliss (an obscure Portuguese title) and how he came to be paralysed and confined to a wheelchair at the age of 42. Or, indeed, why he then chose to leave his wife and take to the seas aboard his ship, 'The Sea King', in order to start a new life in the Caribbean.

It is known that following sojourns in the Bahamas, Trinidad and Jamaica, he dropped anchor just outside Belize City, and that less than two months after that he was dead. In that time, however, it seems he developed an inordinate fondness for the country. Certainly nothing else can explain his decision to bequeath to Belize his entire estate.

Once he knew his time was drawing to a close, he invited the country's Attorney General aboard his ship to whom he laid out a long list of stipulations detailing exactly what the money could and could not be used for. Some of it was to be used for his burial arrangements, it being the Baron's wish to be buried in Belize City next to a lighthouse. Unfortunately, the city didn't have a lighthouse at that time, so he was temporarily laid to rest in Memorial Park, while a 50ft/15m structure was erected in his honour on the southern tip of the Fort George District. His granite tomb can now be seen at its foot.

Of more use to the Belizeans was the Baron's decision to grant them access in perpetuity to the interest (and only the interest) on his banked wealth for the purpose of 'improving' projects. It has paid for numerous improvements to the city in the years since, including a school of nursing and (just recently) the Bliss Centre for the Performing Arts. The day of the Baron's death, 9 March, is a national holiday, Baron Bliss Day, celebrated with parties and a regatta.

once its replacement, currently under construction in Belmopan, is complete (there's no word as yet on whether it's to be returned to New England). From here, head southwest down Queen Street, past the Police Station and the Angelus Press bookstore, and back to the Swing Bridge.

The South Side

Seemingly always packed with people and generally always bustling with life, the area just south of the Swing Bridge is the city's main commercial district (in terms of commerce directed at native Belizeans rather than tourists), the first evidence of which lies just east of the bridge in the shape of the Commercial Centre, a rather gloomy market hall. From here, two roads head south. Take the one to the left (or east), Regent Street, which leads to the city's rather pretty green-and-white, colonial-style **Supreme Court Building**, the third such building to have been erected on this site. The original was demolished in 1878, the second destroyed by fire in 1918, while the third was completed in 1926 and has so far managed to survive unscathed. Its uppermost dome-capped clock tower was erected in memory of former governor, William Hart Bennett, who tragically died during the 1918 fire.

South of here, Regent Street connects with Bishop Street, at the eastern end of which, overlooking the river, you'll find the **Bliss Centre for the Performing Arts**, the city's main arts venue, which was built a few years ago with money provided by the ongoing Bliss legacy (see p.97).

Bliss Centre for the Performing Arts
t 227 2110

Back on Regent Street, the next site of interest comes at its southern end in the shape of the **House of Culture**. This wonderfully grand wooden building, set in attractive neatly tended gardens, was, until the 1970s (when the capital was moved inland to Belmopan), the home and office of the country's Governor General. Today, in these post-colonial times, it plays host to a number of 'artistic' events (exhibitions, recitals, concerts, seminars, music classes) and contains an exhibition of colonial-era government finery – silverware, glassware, furniture – much of it dating back to the 18th century.

House of Culture
t 227 3050; open Mon–Fri 8.30–4.30; adm US$5

Almost directly across from the House of Culture is **St John's Cathedral**, the oldest Anglican cathedral in Central America (1812). The method and manner of its construction – built by slaves, from bricks brought over from England as ships' ballast – perhaps explains its rather boxy, functional aesthetic. The interior is, however, worth a few minutes' perusal, containing a statue depicting the 'dove of peace' and some memorial plaques of the church's first parishioners. The cathedral entrance actually lies on Albert Street, the road running parallel to Regent Street to the west. Just south of here is **Yarborough Cemetery**, the first public cemetery

St John's Cathedral
t 227 2137; open Mon–Fri 8.30–5; adm free, although a contribution is requested

in Belize (there was obviously quite some demand; it was full by 1896), which stands on the threshold of 'Eboe Town', a slave settlement in the 18th and early 19th centuries. Overlooking the park is a rather garishly painted statue of Isiah Emmanuel Morter, the 'Coconut King of Belize', who upon his death in 1924 left his substantial fortune to the Belizean chapter of the UNIA (United Negro Improvement Association).

Albert Street, which runs north from here up to the Swing Bridge, is the city's main shopping street. Its northern end, in particular, is lined with clothing boutiques, hardware stores and food shops (including a couple of supermarkets). Its side streets are also home to a number of shops, including several record stores. The northern end of Albert Street is also where you'll find the rather small **Battlefield Park**, once the site of pre-Independence political rallies, but rather down-at-heel these days. Despite the best intentions of a recent 'Art in Motion' project which saw the park's benches decorated with colourful paintings, it's still a pretty unappealing place, with the tramps (of whom there are several) getting more benefit from the newly prettified seating than anyone else.

Tourist Information in Belize City

Previously located in the Central Bank building behind the Museum of Belize, the country's main tourist information office has recently been moved to the much less convenient location of mile 3.5 on the Northern Highway, in the New Horizon Investment Building, a 10min taxi ride away. Within the city, information is still available from the smaller **Belize Tourism Industry Association** office. They stock a range of leaflets on attractions both in the city and around the country, but unfortunately cannot provide city maps. You'll be directed instead to the Angelus Press bookstore (*see* listings below). Incidentally, the office is located on the upper floor – use the outside steps on the left of the building.

There's also a small tourist desk at the airport, between passport control and the baggage carousel, which can provide a few leaflets as well as copies of the free local tourist papers.

(i) **Belize Tourism Industry Association**
10 North Park St,
t 223 3507; open
Mon–Fri 8.30–4.30

Services in Belize City

Banks: Alliance Bank, 106 Princess Margaret Drive, **t** 223 6783; Atlantic Bank, Freetown Rd, **t** 227 7124; Barclay's Bank, Albert St, **t** 227 7211; Belize Bank, 60 Market Square, **t** 227 7132 (operates a 24hr ATM); Scotia Bank, Albert St, **t** 227 7027. There's also a 24hr cash machine at the junction of Albert and Regent St.

Books: Angelus Press, 10 Queen St, **t** 223 5777; The Book Centre, 4 Church St, **t** 223 7457. Both stock a range of stationery, educational titles and books by local authors, as well as a few guides and maps.

Hospitals: Karl Heusner Memorial Hospital, Princess Margaret Drive, **t** 223 1564; Belize Medical Associates, 5791 St Thomas St, **t** 223 3837 (*www.belize medical.com*). Both operate a 24hr service.

Internet: Mail Boxes Etc, North Front St (from 13 Bz cents per minute);

BTL Office: 1 Church St; Turton Library, Front St (both from US$2 per hour).

Library: Turton Library, Front St, **t** 227 3401 (*open Mon–Fri 9–6*).

Pharmacies: Brodies, Regent St, **t** 227 7070 ext 266; Central Drug Store,

18 Albert St, t 227 3200; Generic Pharmacy, 168 North Front St East, t 203 3440.

Police: The Belize City Police Station (t 227 2210) is the large yellow and green building about halfway down Queen St (opposite New Road). The Tourism Police can be contacted on t 227 2222.

Post office: The main post office is located on the corner of Queen and Front St. Other smaller branches can be found on Queen St and Queens Square.

Scooter rental: Let's Ride, Barrack Rd, t 203 1021.

Supermarkets: Brodies, Regent St, t 227 7070.

Tour Operators in Belize City

There are numerous tour operators in Belize City offering tours of the city, to the nearby cayes (snorkelling and diving trips available) and to sites and destinations around the country, including Belize Zoo, Altun Ha, Lamanai and Crooked Tree. Competition for custom can be fierce when the cruise ship passengers are in town, with the street outside the Tourism Village becoming packed with guides, all excitedly offering their services and proclaiming the value of their deals. If you plan to organize a tour in this way, do ask to see the guide's BTB licence. It might also be a good idea to check the prices first with one of the companies listed below, so as to get an idea of how much you should expect to pay.

Belize Shore Tours, t 223 4874, *cavetubing@yahoo.com, www.ecotours belize.com*. Offers 5hr snorkelling trips to Shark Ray Alley and Caye Caulker; cave tubing at Cave's Branch River (5hrs, US$60); as well as a range of combination sightseeing tours: Belize City and Altun Ha (4½ hrs, US$45); Belize City and Belize Zoo (4½hrs, US$45) and boat tours to Lamanai (6½hrs, US$75 inc. lunch).

Hugh Parkey's Belize Dive Connection, t 223 4526, *hugh@belizediving.com, www.belizediving.com*. Operates from the Radisson Fort George Dock and offers snorkelling/diving trips to the barrier reef (US$65/90) and Turneffe Atoll (US$90/140) and the Blue Hole (US$100/175). All trips include a stop at Swallow Caye to see (but not swim with) the manatees. The price includes hire of all the necessary equipment, park entry fees, lunch, drinks and VAT.

Sea Sports Belize, 83 North Front St, t 223 5505, *info@seasportsbelize.com, www.seasportsbelize.com*. Offers snorkelling/diving trips to the barrier reef (US$87.50/109), Turneffe Atoll (US$109/163) and the Blue Hole (US$136/190) as well as deep-sea fishing (5–6hrs, US$708.50), reef fishing (5–6hrs, US$545), river fishing (3–5hrs, US$381.50) and trips to Swallow Caye to see the manatees (US$54.50).

S & L Travel and Tours, 91 North Front St, t 227 7593/227 5145, *info@ sltravel belize.com* or *sltravel@btl.net*, *www. sltravelbelize.com*. Custom-designed tours taking in everything from visits to Maya sites and river trips to cave-tubing, bird-watching and diving.

Shopping and Markets in Belize City

Even though this is the most populated urban area in Belize, the shopping is still pretty low-key. Shops are mostly small and primarily geared towards local, not international tastes. You'll find no big-name chains or fashion houses here.

There are two main shopping areas. The first lies just south of the Swing Bridge, and encompasses much of Albert Street and Regent Street (not quite as glitzy as its London namesake), plus their connecting tributaries. The shops here cater primarily to Belizean needs – clothing boutiques, supermarkets, electrical stores etc. There are also a number of record shops on the side streets, often as not blaring out booming reggae. The atmosphere in this district tends to be much less intense and in-your-face commercial than at the other main area, which comprises the section of Front Street between the Water Taxi Terminal and the Tourism Village (plus the Tourism Village itself), and which is aimed primarily at cruise ship passengers.

There are also several markets and stores dotted around the city (*see* below) where local craftspeople can sell their handiwork (carvings of local animals – sharks, manatees, lobsters – are popular) in slightly more relaxed surroundings. A few places, such as the Handicraft Centre and Image Factory, have a close relationship with the artisans who make the products, ensuring them a fair return on their efforts.

Ace Hardware Store, Albert St. Admittedly, visiting a hardware store is not usually at the top of most people's vacation to-do lists, but this store provides a handy pit stop for Europeans who have forgotten their American electrical adapters. You can also pick up a torch here if you are planning on staying at a jungle lodge or visiting some of the country's numerous cave systems.

Commercial Centre, Albert St, **t** 227 2117. Built on the site of an old market, this cavernous shopping hall lies just southeast of the Swing Bridge. The ground floor houses a small food market as well as a few jewellery shops and souvenir stalls, and there are a couple of businesses upstairs. It can be a bit hit-and-miss – bustling, colourful and intense when in full swing, rather grimy and deserted-looking at other times. On some days only a few stalls bother setting up.

Farmer's Market, Roger's Stadium, occurs every Tues, Fri and Sat, 5am–12.30pm. Great place to stock up on all manner of tropical fruit and vegetables, or just to have an early morn-ing wander and observe the hustle and bustle.

Image Factory Gift Shop & Gallery, North Front St, **t** 223 4151. Gallery store selling local art, crafts and books (*see* p.95).

Mirab, on the corner of Fort and Dredge St. Large, air-conditioned department store with a reasonable range of homewares, electrical items, gifts and clothing. Bags must be checked in at the front of the store, before you begin your browsing.

National Handicraft Centre, 2 South Park St, **t** 223 3636 (*open Mon–Fri 8–5,*

Sat 8–4). A great source of souvenirs, this pale pink building on the edge of the memorial park houses a large range of arts and crafts including carvings, jewellery, furniture and Mayan baskets and textiles, all made by local craftspeople.

Sing's, Albert St. A large, colourful store that stocks a large collection of cheerful knick-knacks, T-shirts and souvenirs.

Tourism Village, Fort St. The most controversial (*see* p.95) addition to the city's list of attractions, the Tourism Village certainly provides the biggest range of shopping choices (for foreigners, if not locals), with dozens of businesses filling its securely gated waterfront confines, selling duty-free alcohol and perfume, jewellery (there's a large diamond concern), jade vases as well as Belizean souvenirs – Mayan fabrics, wooden carvings etc. Be warned, despite its 'duty-free' status, prices here are a touch high (but then, it is selling to a largely captive market) and, because it only opens when a cruise ship is in town, can be rather noisy and chaotic (particularly on the street by the entrance, outside the village proper) with stallholders and tour operators eagerly competing for the few available hours' worth of tourist dollars. Non-cruise tourists can visit the village, but will have to show photographic ID in order to obtain a visitor's pass.

Spectator Sports in Belize City

Football matches, as well as other major sporting events, can be seen at weekends at the Marion Jones Sports Complex (near the municipal airstrip). The smaller Roger's Stadium also holds various lower key sports events. Call the National Sports Council, **t** 227 2051, for schedules.

Where to Stay in Belize City

Considering it's not exactly the country's main tourist destination, Belize City's hotels can be surprisingly expensive when compared to those in the country's more popular locales. However, rather than go seeking out a bargain, you should, for safety's sake, probably stick to the hotels listed below. And you should certainly avoid staying off the main tourist trail. In general, the more up-market hotels are located in or around the Fort George district to the north of the river, whereas the budget lodgings can be found on the south side.

Luxury ($$$$$)–Expensive ($$$$)

The Belize Biltmore Plaza, Mile 3.5 Northern Highway, **t** US 1-800 780 7234, **t** 223 2302, **f** 223 2302, *www.belize biltmore.com* (US$95). The Biltmore, a 10min taxi ride north of the city centre, has all the facilities you would expect from a chain – a swimming pool, a fitness centre, a tour desk and a gift shop, as well as a popular restaurant and bar (no need to head back into town if you're looking for nightlife). Its 75 rooms (split into Standard, Premier and Deluxe categories) surround an attractive courtyard and are well equipped, featuring dataports, but rather generic.

Chateau Caribbean, 6 Marine Parade, **t** 223 0800, **f** 223 0900, *www.chateau caribbean.com* (US$89). The colonial-style building is very pretty, and the hotel enjoys a great location next to the Memorial Park overlooking the seafront. Unfortunately, the rooms themselves are in dire need of updating. Your best bet is to opt for one of the suites, which have balconies looking out to sea. The restaurant and bar here also have good views, although the food has had varying reports. Incidentally, the hotel provided one of the location for the 1980s film, *Dogs of War*.

The Great House, 13 Cork St, **t** 233 3400, **f** 233 3444, *www.greathousebelize.com* (US$140). Overlooking the seafront, this beautiful wooden colonial house was built in 1927. Formerly a family home, it now boasts 12 spacious and attractive rooms, all with cable TV, coffee makers and refrigerators. Verandas at the front and back of the house offer good views, and additional services include a tour desk, car rental, wireless Internet access and a very popular seafood restaurant, the Smokey Mermaid (*see* p.104).

★ The Great House >

The Princess Hotel and Casino, Barrack Rd, **t** US 888 896 7855, **t** 223 2670, **f** 233 2663, *www.princess belize.com* (US$140). This large 181-room resort-style hotel is absolutely crammed with facilities – a bowling alley, a cinema, a casino, an Olympic-size swimming pool with Jacuzzi, a children's pool and fitness centre, plus a couple of restaurants and bars. The décor is rather unimaginative and, in some of the public areas, a bit tatty, but all the rooms are large and have sea views (though you will have to pay for a suite if you want a balcony as well). Its location and size (not to mention the high level of security) make the hotel feel rather detached and removed from the rest of the city. Whether you consider this to be a good thing or a bad thing depends on your opinion of the city itself.

Radisson Fort George Hotel & Marina, 2 Marine Parade, **t** US 800 333 3333, **t** 223 3333, **f** 227 3820, *www.radisson. com/belizecitybz* (US$179–189). This, the most expensive hotel in Belize City, has 102 large well-appointed, if rather generic rooms, all with a/c, cable TV and coffee makers. Those on the top floor of the 'Club Tower' have great sea views (and are the most expensive). Aimed squarely at the tastes of its principally American clientele, it's got plenty of amenities – a gym, a shop, two swimming pools, two restaurants, two bars and a café – but little in the way of character.

Moderate ($$$)

The Bakadeer Inn, 74 Cleghorn, **t/f** 223 0659, *www.bakadeerinn.com* (US$50). Located on a quiet street near Haulover Creek, this inn offers basic (but clean) rooms, all with private bathrooms, cable TV and fans. There is also a small courtyard and a lounge area where you can get to know your fellow hotel guests.

Coningsby Inn, 76 Regent St, **t** 227 1566, **f** 227 3726, *coningsby_inn@btl.net* (US$55). This attractive bright white-and-red building has 10 good-sized, secure rooms, all with private bathrooms, TV and a/c, plus an attractive communal balcony and restaurant (where breakfast is served).

D'Nest Inn, 475 Cedar St, Belama, **t** 223 5416, *www.dnestinn.com* (US$60/70). Located in a residential area 3m from downtown Belize City, this stunning little Caribbean inn offers three beautiful rooms furnished with antiques. The rooms are named after the birds that nest in their pretty English-style garden. You can choose from the Dove Nest, which has a hand-carved king-sized bed; the Hummingbird Nest, which has a queen-size four-poster bed (both US$70); or Kiskadee Nest, which has just a standard size (albeit antique) four-poster bed (US$60). All three rooms have a/c, cable TV, Internet connection and private baths.

Embassy Hotel, International Airport, t 225 3333/4444, *www.embassyhotel belize.com* (US$49). It may not be the prettiest hotel in the city, but it's certainly handy for the airport, which lies just across the parking lot. Rooms are reasonably sized and pleasantly, if unimaginatively, furnished. Self-catering one-bedroom apartments are also available for US$300 a month, and the hotel can arrange good deals on car rentals.

Hotel Mopan, 55 Regent St, t 227 7351, f 227 5383, *www.hotelmopan.com* (US$45). This popular and friendly family-run establishment offers 15 comfortable non-smoking rooms, all with private bathrooms, cable TV and fan (a/c is available for an extra US$10). They also have two Internet stations, wireless access and a tour company that can arrange visits to nearby conservation and Maya sites.

Villa Boscardi, 6045 Manatee Drive, Buttonwood Bay, t/f 223 1691, *www.villaboscardi.com* (US$70). Situated in a safe residential area on the outskirts of town, this lovely little B&B offers six comfortable, attractively decorated rooms, all with cable TV, private bathrooms and a/c. The price includes a tasty cooked breakfast.

Inexpensive ($$)–Budget ($)
Belcove Hotel, 9 Regent St West, t 227 3054, f 227 5248, *www.belcove.com* (US$25/32). This charming little hotel lies just on the cusp of dodginess, where the main tourist trail turns into something slightly less welcoming. It's perfectly safe, however, with its front door monitored throughout the night. The staff are extremely friendly and helpful, and the rooms, though simple, are clean and pretty good value.

Budget ones come with fans and a choice of shared or private baths, while de luxe rooms (around US$45 for a double) have cable TV, a/c and private bathrooms. There's also a nice riverfront balcony on the second floor, where you can enjoy a cold beer and watch the comings and goings on the nearby Swing Bridge.

Freddie's Guest House, 86 Eve St, t 223 3851, *freddies@btl.net* (US$25). Situated on a quiet and pleasant residential street north of the bridge, Freddie's has three clean and peaceful basement rooms. Two of the rooms share a bathroom while the other has its own private bathroom.

Isabel's Guest House, 3 Albert St, t 207 3139, f 227 1582, *pmelhado@hotmail.com* (US$25). This small, funky little guesthouse is situated opposite the south end of the Swing Bridge, next to the Central Drug Store. All the rooms are clean and spacious with private bathrooms and fans. Some overlook the bridge. With the constant rumble of the traffic outside, it's not the most peaceful of locations, but it does offer good value for money.

Seaside Guest House, 3 Prince St, t 227 8330, f 227 1689, *www.seasidebelize.com* (US$30). Popular with backpackers (book ahead), this friendly (and safe) little place offers four-bed dorms (US$12) as well as single and double rooms with shared bathrooms. The rooms are a bit small, but are perfectly adequate if you're prepared to rough it for a few days. And if you want a bit more space, there's a peaceful veranda overlooking the Caribbean Sea. Reasonably priced meals and drinks are available, including vegetarian options.

Eating Out in Belize City

It's not exactly a gastronomic oasis, but these days there's a pretty varied selection of cuisine available in Belize City, with a few foreign choices (Indian, Chinese, Jamaican) and a good selection of seafood augmenting the staple Belizean fare of rice and beans. If you're on a tight budget (or are after something quick), you can pick up *empanadas*, tacos, burgers and other

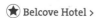
Belcove Hotel >

snacks very cheaply from vendors in small shed-like structures at the side of the street. Otherwise, try **Anne's Pastries** on Albert Street for decent cakes or **Scoop's** ice-cream parlour on Eve Street. Vegetarians should head for **Mama Chen's** on Eve Street (t 223 4568), which serves reasonable Taiwanese veggie cuisine.

Most of the more up-market places are located in hotels and tend to charge rather inflated prices for what is often pretty ordinary 'international' fare – burgers, Caesar salads, pizzas, steaks etc. Much better value is offered by smaller places aimed at the local population (and charging local prices). And, if you've got a hankering for an additive fix, Belize City is home to the country's only US fast-food franchise, a rather lonely branch of Subway, on Freetown Rd near the Flag Monument.

Restaurants

Smokey Mermaid, 13 Cork St, t 223 4759. One of the city's top gourmet choices, this pleasant restaurant situated in the Great House Hotel's inner courtyard is open from breakfast (around US$22) until late. The menu changes daily but usually features plenty of seafood (including lobster, in season), plus a few pasta and meat choices (such as lamb chops with rosemary). Three courses with drinks will come to a not insubstantial US$50, but the food is very good.

St George's Dining Room/Baymen's Tavern, at the Radisson, Marine Parade. Sat amid its air-conned, piped music surrounds, this can feel a bit like a land-based cruise ship. The overpriced menu certainly seems to have had trouble settling on a single port of call, taking in pizzas (US$10–18), Thai noodle soup (US$5.25), burgers (US$7.25) and steak and kidney pie (US$9), but unfortunately no local dishes. It's all a bit generically lacklustre, but safe, cosy and familiar.

Harbour View >

Harbour View, Fort St, t 223 6420. This maritime-themed restaurant (which translates as nautical maps on the tables and waitresses dressed in sailor-suit-style uniforms) is the city's most romantic dining spot, particularly at night when the outside balcony provides good views of the sun setting

over the city. It's also got a pretty decent kitchen, turning out a rather refined menu of snapper, lobster (in season) and steaks, as well as quality wines and spirits. Main courses cost around US$10–12.

Jambel Jerk Pit, King St, t 227 6080. It may not look like much – a handful of tile tables spread around a small café-like dining room, adorned with Jamaican flags and pictures of reggae stars (and in which a TV stands permanently switched on in the corner), but this serves some of the city's best food, including its highly recommended spicy jerk chicken and shrimp. There are a few more tables in the adjoining outside courtyard. Nothing costs much more than US$6.

Sumathi, Barrack Rd, t 223 1172. The town's best Indian restaurant serves up a pretty decent (and pretty authentic-tasting) selection of biryanis, tandooris and seafood specials, as well as a good range of vegetarian dishes. It's located about 15 mins from the city centre – you can use the walk along the seafront past the Princess Hotel to work up an appetite.

Cheap Eats and Belizean

Big Daddy's Diner, 2nd Floor, Commercial Centre, Albert St, t 227 0932. Something of a local institution, this cafeteria-style eatery located upstairs in the Commercial Centre serves up filling breakfasts, burgers and buffet lunches for a pretty reasonable US$2–4.

Dit's Restaurant, 50 King St, t 227 3330. Cheap, cheerful and always busy, this local favourite on the south side of the creek serves all the usual rice and beans dishes (around US$3) plus corn cakes (*garnaches*), tamales and sticky pastries and cakes.

E&C Restaurant, Albert St. A locally orientated place at the southern end of town serving inexpensive regional specialties (such as cow-foot soup), as well as American dishes – burritos, burgers etc.

Macy's, 18 Bishop St, t 207 3419. Popular and long-established, this creole restaurant serves up some rather unusual dishes – such as iguana, gibnut and armadillo – along with staples like chicken and rice, and meatballs. The menu changes daily so you should be able to find something that appeals (or appalls) for around US$3–6.

Marlin's Restaurant and Bar, 11 Regent St West. Enjoy generous portions of simply cooked fish and seafood at this riverside location next to the Belcove Hotel. Pretty empty early in the week, it tends to fill up at weekends (with both Belizeans and tourists).

⭐ Nerie's >

Nerie's, corner of Queen and Daly St, t 223 4028. Spanning two floors, this is a very popular choice, always buzzing with locals at lunch time who come to fill up on cow-foot soup, gibnut stew or (for the less adventurous) chicken with rice and beans. As it's aimed primarily at Belizeans, it's pretty reasonably priced, with most dishes coming in at under US$5. The seafood comes quite highly recommended.

Cafés

Le Petit Café, Cork St (next to Great House Hotel). Owned by the Radisson Hotel, this small café is a good place to stop off for coffee, sandwiches, home-made cakes and filled croissants to enjoy in its shady little courtyard.

Moonclusters Coffee House, Daly St. This side-street coffee bar makes a good pit stop as you wander your way around the city, offering an extensive range of hot and cold drinks, from espressos to fruit smoothies.

Arts, Entertainment and Nightlife in Belize City

The main source of culture in the city is the **Bliss Centre for the Performing Arts**, on the Southern Foreshore just south of the Swing Bridge, which opened a few years ago. It stages a year-round repertoire of concerts and theatrical performances. Call t 227 2458 for the latest schedule. Occasional concerts are also put on at the **House of Culture** on Regent St (*see* p.98).

Otherwise, the city boasts little in the way of formal entertainment attractions. It has just one cinema, one bowling alley and one casino; all of which, handily enough, are located at the **Princess Hotel** (t 223 7162, *www. princessbelize.com*). The cinema has

two screens showing the latest inter-national releases every night at 6pm and 9pm, with an additional afternoon matinée at weekends at 3.30pm. The bowling alley (which also has pool tables and arcade games) is open seven days a week, 11am–11pm, while the large casino has all the usual gaming tables, plus all the usual distractions to keep you gambling – live shows, a free buffet etc. It's open daily from noon till 4am.

The situation is a lot less clear cut when it comes to **nightlife**. Belize City party people are a fickle lot and it's almost impossible to tell where's going to be hot and where's not from one week to another. The only thing you can count on is that Friday night is *the* night to go out and most of the action, for locals and tourists alike, occurs in and around the bars of the top hotels.

Most hotel bars operate daily reduced-price happy hours, and several offer free bar food (typically *bocas* – fried appetizers). Some also stage live music. Your best bet is to ask around for details of the latest place to be seen. Your hotel staff or taxi driver may be able to point you in the right direction. The following should provide a starting point on your quest for a good night out.

The Belize Biltmore Plaza Hotel has two bars: the **Palm Court Bar**, which operates a happy hour 5pm–7pm (two local drinks for the price of one) every night; and the **Biltmore Bar**, which hosts live music on Thursdays (6.30pm–10.30pm) and Saturdays (6pm–9pm). The Radisson's **Baymen's Tavern** (the bar of the St George's Dining Room) also operates a daily happy hour 6pm–9pm and puts on live music nightly (although this tends to take the form of a lone guitarist, with accompanying drum machine, playing easy listening classics). The **Vogue Bar** at the Princess Hotel has a DJ Thurs–Sat 9pm–2am.

The **Eden** nightclub and **Caesar's**, both at the northern end of Barrack Road, are aimed more at locals, blaring out classic dance hits into the early hours of the morning. The more centrally located **Copa Cabana Club**, on the corner of Daly St and Queen St, has a more Latin-influenced vibe.

Around Belize City

Along the Western Highway

Old Belize Cultural and Historical Centre

Old Belize Cultural
and Historical
Centre
*Mile 5 Western
Highway, t 222 4286,
f 222 4199,
www.oldbelize.com;
open Tues–Sat 8–4,
Sun and Mon 10–4;
adm US$15*

Just 15 minutes' drive from Belize City and a popular day excursion with cruise passengers, this aims to give its visitors a neat, bite-sized overview of the country's history through a mixture of exhibits, recreations and dioramas. Your tour begins in prehistoric times with a small section of replica rainforest (complete with artificial water-fall and real butterflies), before heading off through a reconstructed Maya village, a Garifuna home, and past dioramas showing dye being extracted from logwood in the 1700s (the business that drew the first European settlers to Belize), sugar-making in the 1800s, chicle harvesting for chewing-gum production at the turn of the 20th century, and a Belize City street scene from the early 1900s. It's pretty interesting stuff and, considering it only takes around 45 minutes to get round, surprisingly informative. While the idea of reconstructions may seem a little cheesy, it's all very well done and does provide a handy snapshot into the country's past.

The museum lies next to the coast, and the property also contains an artificial stretch of white sand, 'Cucumber Beach' where you can sunbathe and hire canoes and rafts. There's also a reasonable restaurant, **Sibun Bite Bar and Grill**, selling burgers, salads, grilled fish and meat dishes as well as rice and beans.

Sibun Bite Bar
and Grill
*open Sun–Thurs 11–9,
Fri/Sat 11–10*

Gran's Farm

Gran's Farm
*Mile 14.25 Western
Highway, t 227 0406,
f 225 6216, www.
gransfarmbelize.com;
open Tues–Sun 9–5;
adm US$15*

Another mainstay of the cruise circuit, and thus more geared up for large groups than individual travellers, this large tropical fruit farm offers tours through its orchards and botanical gardens, canoeing on its creek and swimming in its pool (in fact, your ticket officially entitles you to three tours, swimming and 'lounging', so make sure you get your money's worth of lying around). There's also a gift shop and restaurant. It can get pretty busy if there's a cruise ship in town.

Belize Zoo

⭐ Belize Zoo
*Mile 29 Western
Highway, t 220 8004,
f 220 8010, www.
belizezoo.org; open
daily 8–5; adm US$8*

Everyone goes to Belize in the hope of getting that prize photo of one of the country's superstar animals – a tapir, a puma or perhaps even a jaguar – in the wild. Unfortunately, unless you're very intrepid, very patient and, most of all, incredibly lucky, the chances are pretty slim. Still, there's no need to let your roll of film go entirely to waste. At Belize Zoo, you'll find all the animals on any visitor's must-get photo-list, including jaguars, ocelots, toucans, crocodiles and much more. Frame them from the right angle and your subjects will give

Getting on to the Western Highway

By Car

To get on to the Western Highway from Belize City centre, take Orange Street, which becomes Cemetery Road, which in turn becomes the Western Highway just past the gas station and roundabout. If picking your car up from the airport, it's possible to connect with the Western Highway without backtracking to the city. Simply follow the road out of the airport till you reach a T-junction with a Shell gas station on your left. Turn left, and follow the road until you reach a police checkpoint. Take the left just before the checkpoint and follow the road all the way till you get to a roundabout. Turn right and you're on the Western Highway (or left if you want the Old Belize Centre). All of the sights listed on pp.104–6 are on this well-maintained road. Just look out for the signs and keep an eye on the mileage.

By Bus

Catch any bus heading west to Belmopan or San Ignacio. **Novelo's Buses** (t 207 2025) run to San Ignacio around every half-hour from early morning to 9pm (but see p.66). They can be caught at the main station on West Collet Canal St. Simply ask the driver to be dropped outside your destination.

---

every impression of having been 'caught in the wild' (and, once you're home, who's to know?).

Established in 1983 as a refuge for just 17 animals that had been used in a documentary and had become too tame to be sent back out into the wild, the zoo is now home to over 100 native animals. Today, the main aim of the zoo is to educate locals (and tourists) about Belize's wildlife and environment and, in so doing, help protect them for future generations. It still acts as a sanctuary, however, taking in injured animals as well as wild animals that people have attempted to tame (unsuccessfully) as pets. Where possible, these animals are rehabilitated and released back into the wild.

Don't be put off by the 'zoo' tag. This is no purpose-built city-style menagerie with faux 'natural' environments created for an assortment of alien creatures. Because all of the zoo's inhabitants are Belizean, creating the enclosures here has largely been a matter of separating up sections of forest. Nonetheless, with just 29 acres of land to play with, some of the animals have been luckier with their allocations of space than others. The tapirs and monkeys seem quite well provided for, while, perhaps inevitably, the birds of prey and big cats (particularly the jaguars and pumas) seem rather cramped.

As most tours (which, if a cruise is in, can constitute hordes of people) arrive in the middle of the day, the best time to visit is early morning or late afternoon. If you come in early April, you may be able to time your trip to coincide with the birthday celebrations of one of the zoo's tapirs called April, an event held on the first Friday of the month. This is particularly popular with children, as are the jolly signs outside the enclosures rendered in creole rhyming couplets ('I'm Scotty the Tapir, I'm handsome no true, But better step back, Cause I might pee on you').

The zoo relies entirely on entrance fees, donations and sponsorships for its survival, receiving no government funding. If you would like to make a contribution towards its upkeep, there are several membership programmes available, such as their 'adopt an animal' scheme, the details of which are available on their website.

Tropical Education Centre

Tropical Education Centre
Mile 29 Western Highway, t 220 8003, f 220 8010, www.belizezoo.org

The Tropical Education Centre, the research wing of Belize Zoo, is located across the highway from the zoo entrance, and encompasses a further 84 acres of unspoilt savannah and forest. Here, unlike the zoo, the animals – which include numerous species of resident and migratory birds – roam and fly free. Extremely popular with bird-watchers, it offers a range of activities and events including hiking tours, lectures, canoeing and, best of all, nocturnal zoo tours (US$10).

You can even stay the night at (in ascending level of comfort): its dormitory (US$17); forest cabana ($32.50); or VIP guesthouse ($35). Advance booking necessary. Camping is also permitted for US$6 per person.

Monkey Bay Wildlife Sanctuary

Monkey Bay Wildlife Sanctuary
Mile 31.5 Western Highway, t 820 3032, f 822 3361, mbay@btl.net, www. monkeybaybelize.com

This private nature reserve is actually split into two sections: the Monkey Bay Wildlife Sanctuary itself, which comprises over 1,000 acres of tropical forest and savannah, bordering the Sibun River; and the further 2,250 acres of the **Monkey Bay National Park** just over the river. It's a diverse environment, home to an equally diverse collection of wildlife, including tapir, jaguars, Morelet's crocodiles, over 250 bird species and, of course, the eponymous black howler monkeys (who had actually died out in the area and have only been reintroduced in the past few years). The sanctuary offers a compre-hensive range of tours, varying from short(ish) 3-hour trips to several days' worth of hiking (recommended for serious hikers only).

Once your legs finally tire from tramping up and down the various trails, head to the river where you can go swimming or canoeing. Keep a lookout for green iguanas, which can often be spotted on the river banks. The **Monkey Bay Iguana Project**, started in August 2004, has overseen a captive breeding programme of these scaly (and increasingly rare) beasts, which are released into the grounds once they reach a year old.

As well as tourists, Monkey Bay welcomes visits from students, researchers and scientists who come to take advantage of its wide-ranging facilities, which include a comprehensive natural history library, a team of knowledgeable guides, and a field research station. The sanctuary also offers a number of **accommodation** options, including tent hire (you can also pitch your own for US$5), dormitories (US$7.50 per bunk) and, if you really want to immerse yourself in the local culture, homestays, which involve staying with a host family in a rural Maya and Garinagu/Garifuna village.

Where to Stay and Eat on the Western Highway

★ Jaguar Paw >

Jaguar Paw, Mile 37 Western Highway, t US 1-888-77-JUNGLE, t 820 2023, f 820 2024, *www.jaguarpaw.com* ($$$$$; US$185). Set on 200 acres of land by the Caves Branch River, this resort offers a great range of adventure tours, as well as some fairly luxurious accommodation. It is named after one of the most famous leaders in Mayan history, and has 16 individually (not to say slightly randomly) themed rooms – African, English, Wild West, etc. – some of which have a good deal more style and work a lot better than others, but all are comfortable and well equipped with private baths and a/c. There's also a decent restaurant/bar and a swimming pool. The grounds are vast, containing a butterfly farm, an aviary, areas of jungle (with marked trails) and three water-cut caves, which can be explored by boat. Other activities on offer include zip-lining (US$55), rappelling (US$45) and rock-climbing (US$45).

Cheers, Mile 31.25 Western Highway, t 822 8014, f 820 2062, *www.cheers restaurant.com* (*open Mon–Sat 6am–8.30pm, Sun 7–7*). A long-time tourist favourite (as shown by the ceiling festooned with the signed T-shirts of past patrons), this open-side road-side diner serves up both a varied selection of American dishes (burritos, burgers) as well as plenty of Belizean choices (it's almost equally popular with locals). There are also cabanas for rent with king- (US$60) or queen- (US$55) sized beds available. All rooms have private showers and TVs. Air conditioning is US$15 extra.

JB's Watering Hole, Mile 32 Western Highway, t 820 2071, f 820 2125, *www.jb-belize.com*. Slightly more up-market than Cheers, JB's restaurant and bar, which is located less than a mile down the road from its rival, offers traditional Belizean dishes, interspersed with the odd inter-national offering (including mixed grills and even fish and chips). It also has a cabana to rent, although more (and a swimming pool) are currently under construction.

To the South

Gales Point

⚑ Gales Point

Gales Point is a friendly creole village spread along a narrow peninsula protruding into a large lake, the Southern Lagoon, which lies between Belize City and Dangriga. Just over two miles long and less than ¼ mile wide, this elongated community is made up principally of farmers and fishermen who, in recent years, have begun supplementing their traditional incomes with tourist-related activities – operating tours and opening restaurants and hotels.

Tourists are drawn to the area principally because of its abundant wildlife, which includes rare jabiru storks, crocodiles and hawksbill turtles which nest on the lagoon beaches. The main attraction, however, is the area's population of West Indian **manatees**, a sort of huge, slow-moving aquatic mammal, which are found in the Southern Lagoon in larger numbers than anywhere else in the Caribbean. Manatees are known locally by several different names. Some call them, rather floridly, sirenians, because it is believed that sailors once mistook these great lumpy beasts for the beautiful Sirens of Greek myth. Others, slightly more prosaically, refer to them as sea-cows, because they look a bit bovine. Your chances of spotting

Getting to Gales Point

By Car

The little road up to Gales Point lies off of the partially paved Coastal Highway (also known as the Manatee Highway), which links the Western Highway (at mile 30, between Belize Zoo and Monkey Bay) to the Hummingbird Highway. The turn-off to the village is about 23 miles along the Coastal Highway, if driving from Belize City, or 15 miles from the Hummingbird junction if coming from Dangriga.

By Bus

Belize City/Dangriga buses travel along the Coastal Highway at least once a day. However, they don't always go to Gales Point, so you may have to walk the last 2 miles in, or hitch a ride. Check with the driver.

one are actually pretty good – there are quite a few of them (drawn to the area by the lagoon's copious supplies of turtle grass, their favourite food), they're very large (the very largest weigh over 880lbs/400kg) and they have to rise to the surface every few minutes to breathe. Furthermore, there's now a whole tourist infrastructure in place dedicated to getting you up close and personal with the great mammals, with numerous operators offering trips. However, if you don't want to pay the US$40 tour price, you can just hire a canoe (for around a quarter of the cost) and go and see what you can find. Look for the noses popping out over the surface. They are fairly inquisitive animals, and you may find them swimming right up to your boat, so long as you stay still and quiet.

Turtle-spotting takes a little more effort and a degree more expense. Hawksbills only visit the area's beaches to lay between May and October, and then only at night. And, as these beaches form part of a protected area, you will have to join an official turtle-watching tour (around US$50) if you're hoping to see them in procreatic action.

Additional attractions in the area include the **Ben Loman cave** to the north, which is full of gnarly stalagmite formations, and the **village drum school**, where you can learn to play, tune and make a traditional drum. For more details contact Emmett Young or Randolph (Boombay) Andrewin on *methos_drums@hotmail.com* or *www.maroondrumschool.com, or* call **t** 603 6051.

Where to Stay and Eat in Gales Point

There are several options for budget travellers. The very cheapest, and most culturally intriguing, are **homestays**. For around US$5–7.50 a night, you can get a room in a local villager's house and a fascinating glimpse into creole culture (although no guarantee of running water). Deborah Callender at the **Orchid Café** (**t** 614 5621) in the village can provide details on this and other types of accommodation, as well as general information about the area. The **Methos Coconut Campground** has space for a number of tents (US$5) as well as a small guesthouse (run by the same people as the drum school above, **t** 603 6051 (US$25, shared bathroom only). **Gentle's Cool Spot** (**t** 221 2031) also has rooms and a decent restaurant/bar, where you can try the local speciality – cashew wine. Other B&Bs include **Ionie's** (**t** 220 8066) and

★ Manatee
Lodge >

Bridget Smith's (t 603 9914), both of which offer pretty basic, but perfectly adequate accommodation.

Manatee Lodge, t US 1-877 462 6283, t 220 8040, www.manateelodge.com ($$$$; US$85). At the other end of the scale from most of the village accommodation is this rather grand lodge overlooking the lagoon. The rooms are large and nicely decorated with painted murals. All have private bathrooms. Guests have free use of the lodge's canoes and sailing boats. Just be sure to bring a pair of binoculars to enjoy the ample wildlife-spotting opportunities. There is a wide range of tours on offer, including trips out onto the lagoon, and good hearty Belizean meals are served in the restaurant. It's a relaxing spot, ideal for watching the sunset over the Maya Mountains whilst lounging in a hammock, or for having a swim in the surrounding shallow waters.

Along the Northern Highway

Community Baboon Sanctuary

✪ Community
Baboon Sanctuary
Bermudian Landing,
t 220 2181, www.
howlermonkeys.org;
open daily 8–5;
adm US$5

The baboons at this sanctuary are not the famous red-bottomed creatures of the African plains, but **black howler monkeys**, which are known colloquially (if a touch misleadingly) as 'baboons' in Belize. The black howler is one of six species of howler found in Central America. While populations of the other five are relatively healthy across the region, black howlers have had their numbers severely reduced in recent years through a combination of hunting (for food) and the destruction of their native forests. Today, they are found in only a few isolated pockets of northern Guatemala, southern Mexico and, most significantly, Belize, where the greatest efforts are being made towards their conservation.

The sanctuary was founded in 1985 by Dr Robert Horwich and Fallet Young (who is the current manager) to help preserve the monkey's rapidly dwindling habitat. To this end, they worked in conjunction with 12 neighbouring landowners. Such has been the scheme's success (and the persuasive powers of its founders) that today the sanctuary comprises over 20 square miles, encompassing the territory of over 180 landowners, all of whom have set aside areas of forest for the monkeys (as well as the area's other wild flora and fauna) to live in. Thanks to their efforts, the howler population,

Where to Stay and Eat in Bermudian Landing

There are quite a few options within the sanctuary. **Homestays** are available in all of the villages within the sanctuary (prices and facilities vary); **camping** is available at the visitor centre (US$5 per person) and there are also a couple of basic lodges (*see* below). Information and reservations for all can be made through the Community Baboon Sanctuary (t 220 2181, *info@howlermonkeys.org*).

Nature Resort, next to visitor centre, t 610 1378, f 822 3930, *naturer@btl.net*. Owned by the family of the one of the sanctuary's founding members (Fallet Young), this has eight pleasant, rustic cabanas. Basic ones (US$27) have shared bathrooms, while the more de luxe versions (US$35) come with private bathrooms, fridges and coffee makers.

Getting to Bermudian Landing

By car: The village of Bermudian Landing is located around 26m west of Belize City. If driving, follow the Northern Highway, past Ladyville, until mile 13, then turn left to Burrell Boom. The sanctuary is a further 13m along this road.

By bus: Russell's bus company operates services to Bermudian Landing from Belize City at 12.15pm and 4.30pm weekdays and noon, and 1pm and 4.30 on Sat. Slightly inconveniently, return buses only operate early in the morning, making a one-day round-trip impossible. Alternatively, you can book a taxi in Belize City to take you there and back, or go on one of the numerous organized tours out of the city.

down to just a couple of dozen individuals a few years ago, now numbers over 2,000.

The centre of the sanctuary is the village of **Bermudian Landing**, where you'll find a small **museum** – which has information and displays on all of the animals and birds that inhabit the sanctuary – and a **visitor centre**, which also serves as a community meeting place. There are also a number of places to stay, eat and buy local crafts, all of which helps to support the sanctuary.

The admission price includes a guided 45- to 60-minute **tour** of the Bermudian Landing area, during which time you'll hopefully get to see some of the famously noisy creatures (*see also* p.43) chomping on the leafs of their favourite sapodilla trees (although you're just as likely to see them asleep). For the best viewing opportunities, try to come either very early or late in the day when the monkeys are at their most active. If you wish to stay longer, you'll have to do it in the company of an official guide (and pay extra), as the forests are private property (not to mention very easy to get lost in). Nocturnal hikes into the forests are available for US$10, as are night-time crocodile-spotting trips (US$30), canoeing (US$50 for a two-person canoe), bird-watching expeditions and local village tours, all of which can be organized at the visitor centre.

Altun Ha

⭐ **Altun Ha**
open 9–5; adm US$2.50

First, the name. Altun Ha is certainly a Mayan name, albeit perhaps of a more recent vintage than might be supposed, having been coined in 1964, the year archaeological work began on the site (which itself was only discovered in the late 1950s, during the construction of the Northern Highway). Altun Ha is simply a direct translation (into Yucatec Maya) of the name of the nearby village, 'Rockstone Pond'.

Evidence suggests that this area was settled from around 200 BC right up until the 10th century AD, or the end of the Late Classic Maya period. At its peak, in the 3rd century AD, as many as 10,000 people may have lived in and around this area. The settlement's proximity to the sea, as well as the large amount of jade and obsidian found here (both of which do not occur naturally in Belize) have led scholars to conclude that this was a major trading centre. The

Getting to Altun Ha

Unless you are going with an organized tour, the easiest way to get to Altun Ha is by **car**. Take the Northern Highway from Belize City for about 19 miles until the road divides. Follow the sign for Altun Ha to the right along the rather narrow and bumpy Old Northern Highway for another 10½ miles, and then turn left at the signpost for the site. It's around another 2 miles from here. The site welcomes a good number of tours throughout the day, so go early morning or late afternoon if you want to explore in peace.

If you want to take public transport, a **taxi** is probably your best bet. To get there by **bus** you need to catch the 1pm service from Belize City to Maskall village and get dropped by the turn-off for the site, from where you'll have to walk the final 2 miles.

presence of jade also suggests that the site played a significant religious role. The Maya regarded jade as the most precious of all materials. It could be worn and used only by people of great importance, such as religious leaders.

Today, the site is a grassy affair consisting of two central plazas surrounded by an assortment of buildings. Upon entering the site, you come first to Plaza A, where a burial chamber, known as the **Temple of the Green Tomb**, was found, filled with all manner of artefacts, including jade jewellery, stingray spines (used in blood-letting rituals) and even a paper-book (unfortunately, largely destroyed by the humidity). Further south, Plaza B is the location of the largest and most impressive temple, the **Temple of the Masonry Altars**, a rather crude depiction of which adorns Belikin beer bottles. This structure was expanded many times during Altun Ha's exist-ence; on each occasion a new temple, complete with altar, was built around the last. No fewer than seven tombs have been found here, the oldest of which (and the last to be uncovered) contained the settlement's most magnificent treasure, a 6in-/15cm-high **carved jade head of Kinich Ahau** (the Sun God) discovered lying over the right wrist of the remains of (probably) a high priest. Weighing nearly 10lbs/4.5kg, this is one of the largest examples of Mayan jade carving ever discovered. Unfortunately, this stunning piece is now locked away in a bank vault in Belize City. However, a fibreglass replica can be seen in the Museum of Belize (see p.97). To get an idea of what it looks like, take a look at the top left-hand corner of any Belizean banknote, where there's a small representation. Other items found within the same tomb include pottery, flints and fragments of jaguar pelt (probably used to cover the body).

Considering the history of Altun Ha, it's actually quite remarkable that any of these finds were uncovered at all. Following the settlement's ultimate abandonment, it was attacked and looted and the vast majority of buildings and tombs now lie empty.

On-site services include a refreshment stand, toilets and a visitor's centre, all of which are situated next to the car park, where you'll usually find a few tour guides hanging around offering half-hour tours for around US$10.

Where to Stay and Eat at Altun Ha

★ Marubu
Resort >

Marubu Resort, Mile 40.5, Old Northern Highway, Maskall village, **t** 225 5555, **f** 225 5506, *www.maruba-spa.com* ($$$$$; US$200). This ultra-refined, ultra-exclusive spa resort occupies its own 1,000-acre private jungle reserve. The rooms are supremely luxurious and the spa facilities almost as extensive as the grounds, encompassing everything from body wraps and mud therapy to Japanese hot tubs. Other amenities include a top-class restaurant, a bar, a swimming pool and a gym. A vast range of tours, including treks through the resort's own grounds, are offered. Wedding and honeymoon packages are also available.

Pueblo Escondido, Mile 30.5 Old Northern Highway, Luckystrike/Rock- stone Pond, **t** 614 1458, *www. pueblo-escondido.net* ($$$; US$40). This ecofriendly farm has a campground (US$20 or US$25 with breakfast), complete with fire hearth and bathroom facilities, as well a collection of wooden, thatched 'Tapesco' huts (a traditional style of shelter, originally designed for farmers working out on the fields, US$40). Meals, fishing and horse-riding are available. The farm is also open for day visits (US$10) when non-guests can wander (or cycle) along its various trails and orchards, and enjoy its lovely 'observation garden'.

Mayan Wells Restaurant, about 1½ miles from the ruins, **t** 221 2039. Popular restaurant near the ruins dishing up the usual Belizean fare for around US$5 a plate. There is also a camp site here with shower facilities.

Crooked Tree

Founded over 300 years ago, the small fishing community of Crooked Tree is one of the oldest villages in Belize. For much of its existence, the village lay far removed from the mainstream of Belizean society. Occupying an island in a network of creeks and lagoons, it was only connected to the mainland in 1984 via the creation of a 3-mile causeway. Prior to that, the only way to access the village had been by boat.

Today, it's been well and truly discovered, not least by bird-watchers, who come to spot the area's super abundance of wildfowl, which include jabiru storks, egrets and over 200 other species which visit the wetlands throughout the year. Bird numbers are at their highest during the dry season, when falling water levels and shrinking pools makes fish easy prey.

If you plan to visit, you may want to consider dropping in on the Cashew Festival held on the first weekend in May, when the harvest of the area's main crop is celebrated with live music and an abundance of food and drink – wine, jam, cake, juice and pastries all made from (you guessed it) cashews.

Did you know that there's a good deal more to the cashew plant than just its nuts? It's actually a surprisingly versatile crop. The nutshell, bark, root and gum all have commercial value, and each nut grows on top of a large, edible pear (it takes a lot of cashew trees to fill a single bag of nuts), which is used in local cooking. The pears are incredibly juicy – a bit like eating a bag of tangy custard.

Getting to Crooked Tree

The turn-off to Crooked Tree is on the left-hand side of the Northern Highway at Mile 33, if travelling north from Belize City, or 25 miles south of Orange Walk. Buses can be caught in Belize City or Orange Walk, although they don't all go on into the village (check beforehand) but may drop you at the turn-off, from where it's a further 3½ mile walk. Jex Bus and Novelo's Bus (but *see* p.66) both operate direct services to Crooked Tree village from Belize City. Slightly inconveniently, travelling by bus will entail an overnight stay as the first return bus leaves at 7am.

Crooked Tree Wildlife Sanctuary

Crooked Tree Wildlife Sanctuary open 8–4.30; adm US$4

Founded in 1984 by the Belize Audubon Society (*see* p.96) to protect the large numbers of resident and migratory birds drawn to the area, the sanctuary covers over 16,000 acres of lagoons and wetlands, as well as stretches of logwood and broadleaf forest. The star attraction here is the rare **jabiru stork**, the largest flying bird in the western hemisphere, with a wingspan of up to 8ft/2.4m (it's pretty hard to miss), several pairs of which nest here every year from around November onwards. Black-bellied whistling ducks, herons, kingfishers, ospreys, snail kites and peregrine falcons have also been spotted here, as have a variety of non-avian wildlife, including crocodiles, iguanas, otters, turtles and monkeys.

There are **trails** (pick up a map at the visitor centre) and 6 miles of **elevated walkways**, dotted with observation towers, and you can also hire a boat at the visitor centre to tour the **waterways** (the best way to explore the sanctuary during the wet season). For the best spotting opportunities, aim to arrive as early as possible (there are accommodation options if you want to stay overnight, *see* below) when the birds will be at their most active.

The sanctuary also contains a Mayan site, **Chau Hiix** (pronounced 'chow heech' and meaning 'jaguarundi' in Maya), which is currently being excavated. Though there is much work still to be done, it's estimated that the settlement was occupied from around 1200 BC and encompassed an area of at least 10m sq/26km sq. So far, a large hydrological system, residential buildings and tombs have been discovered, but there is still much that lies buried beneath the ground. There is a viewing platform overlooking the site from where you can get an idea of the current state of progress.

Where to Stay in Crooked Tree

Although it has become an increasingly popular haunt with visitors, much of the accommodation in Crooked Tree remains at a very basic level – mainly simple, locally run places. Many allow camping for around US$5–10.

Bird's Eye View Lodge, south end of village, t 203 3040, f 222 4869, *www.birdseyeviewbelize.com* ($$$; US$60). Aimed primarily at bird-watchers, with whom it is very popular, this lodge offers 18 rooms, all of which overlook the adjacent lagoon (and, of course, the resident wildlife) and come with private bathrooms, although they do vary in size somewhat. Group savings can be made by staying in one of the quad rooms (US$80) or triple rooms (US$70). Home-cooked, traditional meals can be provided, as can canoes (US$5 per hour) and horse-riding (US$10 per hour).

Paradise Inn, north end of village, **t** 225 7044, **f** 223 2579 ($$$; US$50). The Paradise Inn comprises seven rustic, simple cabanas with private bath-

rooms and lagoon outlooks. The restaurant here gets very good reviews.

Sam Tillett's Hotel and Tours, **t/f** 221 2026, *samhotel@btl.net* ($$; US$30). Run by the eponymous Sam, a respected local bird expert, who runs daily tours out onto the waterways, the hotel offers value with comfortable rooms (all with private bathrooms) and decent food served in the restaurant.

The Northern Cayes

Belize's barrier reef, which stretches for 184 miles along the entire coastal length of the country, is the second largest in the world, after Australia's, and home to a stunning array of multicoloured marine wildlife. Just behind the reef lie the country's cayes (pronounced 'keys'), a slender string of islands that represent the topmost parts of a great limestone ridge. These, combined with the atoll cayes further east, constitute in excess of 450 Belizean islands. Though only a few of these islands are inhabited, two of the largest, Ambergris Caye and Caye Caulker at the northern end of the chain, have become extremely popular tourist destinations. Indeed, more people visit these two islands than anywhere else in the country.

09

Don't miss

⭐ **Encounters with rays and sharks**
Hol Chan Marine Reserve **p.125**

⭐ **Shops, golf carts and bars**
San Pedro **p.122**

⭐ **World-famous diving**
The Blue Hole **p.142**

⭐ **Snorkelling, beer and sunsets**
The Split, Caye Caulker **p.136**

⭐ **Hard-core, intense diving**
Turneffe Atoll **p.140**

See map overleaf

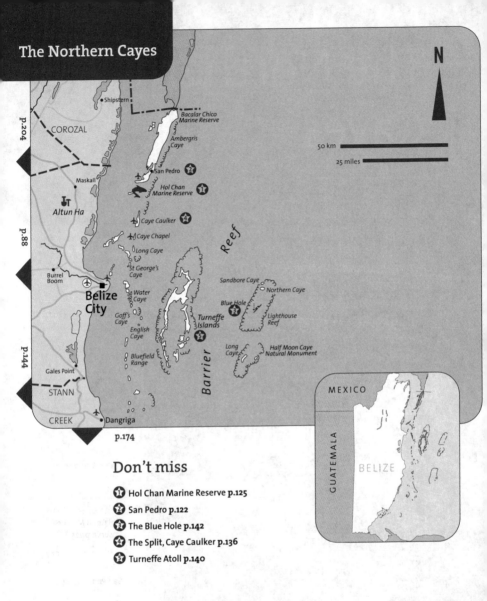

N

50 km
25 miles

p.204

p.88

p.144

p.174

Shipstern

COROZAL

Bacalar Chico
Marine Reserve

Ambergris
Caye

Maskall

San Pedro ⭐

Altun Ha

Hol Chan
Marine Reserve ⭐

Caye Caulker ⭐

Caye Chapel

Long Caye

Burrel
Boom

St George's
Caye

**Belize
City**

Water
Caye

Reef

Sandbore Caye

Northern Caye

Goff's
Caye

Blue Hole ⭐

English
Caye

Turneffe
Islands ⭐

Lighthouse
Reef

Bluefield
Range

Barrier

Long
Caye

Half Moon Caye
Natural Monument

Gales Point

STANN

CREEK

Dangriga

MEXICO

GUATEMALA

BELIZE

Don't miss

⭐ Hol Chan Marine Reserve **p.125**

⭐ San Pedro **p.122**

⭐ The Blue Hole **p.142**

⭐ The Split, Caye Caulker **p.136**

⭐ Turneffe Atoll **p.140**

Their appeal is simple to sum up: beautiful palm-tree-lined sandy beaches; warm tropical waters; a highly developed tourist infrastructure offering plenty of good-quality hotels, bars and restaurants; and, most importantly, ease of access to the great coral expanses of the reef itself, which lies less than a mile offshore. From Ambergris, when the wind is up, you can clearly see the white foamy line representing the point where the waves break over the reef.

Ambergris, with its funky little town of San Pedro, is the more up-market destination, with scores of high-end resorts and a growing number of luxury condominiums, while Caye Caulker is generally regarded as the budget, backpacker alternative. These things are relative, however, and you'll find costs, particularly for food and drink, generally higher on both than on the mainland.

While the availability of funds will probably dictate which island you end up staying on, whichever you choose it's worth popping over to the other for a day trip and a change of atmosphere (there are regular water taxis). In terms of the quality of beaches and swimming, there is very little to separate the two, although Ambergris does offer the better off-beach snorkelling, and the shallows of both islands are thick with clogging sea grass making swimming difficult close to the shore. Ambergris is also the more developed, although again, this is a relative comparison. San Pedro, its town and fulcrum, may not be a particularly large or hectic place, but it's positively heaving with activity compared to little Caye Caulker. Both islands have a plethora of tour companies and guides offering trips out to the main dive sites of Bacalar Chico National Park, the Hol Chan Marine Reserve (both off Ambergris Caye) and further afield to the Turneffe Islands and Lighthouse Reef, the last of which is the site of the famous Blue Hole, a vast underwater sunken cavern.

Ambergris Caye

Ambergris Caye is the beautiful island, 'La Isla Bonita', immortalized in song by Madonna (something which the islanders will no doubt keep reminding you; you'll be lucky to go a few hours without hearing it somewhere). It's also the largest, most heavily populated, most visited and most northerly of Belize's islands, located just a canal's width south of Mexico's Yucatán peninsula. In terms of tourism, it's the most developed area in the whole of Belize, with decades of expertise behind it catering to beach-loving, reef-diving, cocktail-sipping vacationers. And it hasn't stopped growing yet.

Its main community and point of arrival is the three-street town of San Pedro at the caye's southern end, where you'll find most of the island's shops, cafés and services (banks, post offices etc.), as well as its limited range of budget accommodation. It's a characterful little place, but very touristy, filled year-round with (largely American) visitors. Much of the rest of the island (particularly its northern end) is given over to high-end resorts and luxury condos, with more going up all the time. Despite this flurry of construction, tourism has yet to reach overwhelming levels, with plenty of peaceful, isolated stretches of coast remaining. Though popular, the caye's beaches are rarely chock-a-block with basking bodies, as most people spend their days exploring the reef, and the town is almost never crowded, except at festival time in early August.

Getting to Ambergris Caye

By Air

Flying is by far the quickest (but also the most expensive) way to get to Ambergris Caye, although the cost is hardly prohibitive. Both **Maya Island Air** (t 226 2435, *www.mayaislandair.com*) and **Tropic Air** (t 226 2012, *www.tropicair.com*) operate several flights a day to and from Goldson International Airport (15 mins, US$54), Belize Municipal Airport (15 mins, US$30), Corozal (30 mins, U$40) and Caye Caulker (10 mins, US$30) aboard small, propeller-driven aeroplanes. The island airstrip is located just a couple of minutes south of San Pedro.

By Boat

The cheapest way to arrive is by water taxi. The **Caye Caulker Water Taxi Association** (t 223 5752, *www.caye watertaxi.com*) runs boats from Belize City to San Pedro (stopping at Caye Caulker on route) at 8am, 9am, 10.30am, 12 noon, 1.30pm, 3pm, 4.30pm, with an additional service at 5pm. The journey takes around 1½ hours. Boats return at 7am, 8am, 9am, 11.30am, 1pm, 2.30pm, 3.30pm and 4.30pm. The 4.30 service only goes as far as Caye Caulker Mon–Thurs. Fares are US$15 to/from Belize City, US$25 return, and US$10 (US$15 return) if only travelling to/from Caye Caulker. Boats arrive and leave from the Tackle Box Pier, a few steps from the centre of San Pedro town. **Triple J** (t 207 7777) and **Thunderbolt** (t 226 2904) run similar services.

Getting around Ambergris Caye

By Golf Cart

San Pedro is very small, comprising just three main streets (only one of which is paved). However, unless you're staying in town (and planning never to leave its confines) you'll need to use another form of transport during your time on the island. The most northerly resorts lie over 5 miles (or a 2–3hr walk) from town, the most southerly around 2 miles (or a 20min walk) away. The most popular and fun form of transport are golf carts, which during the day seem to fill every square inch of San Pedro. There are a number of companies in town offering a rental service. They can also be hired from many of the island's more up-market hotels. Prices for a 4-seater cart start at around US$12 an hour for an electrically powered version, rising to US$14 per hour for a petrol (gas) powered one. Daily rates are around US$60–70, weekly ones around US$250–300.

The northern and southern halves of the island, which were once separated by a narrow channel of water, have recently been linked by a small bridge. Prior to its construction, the only way to cross this channel had been via a hand-cranked ferry, which golf carts had an alarming habit of falling off. Perhaps as a hangover from that era, some firms still won't allow their golf carts to be taken over to the northern half of the island. Check beforehand if you plan to venture north or are staying at one of the northern resorts. Cart drivers must pay a fee of US$2.50 to use the bridge. To rent (and drive) a golf cart, you must have a valid driver's licence.

Golf cart rental firms: Ambergris Golf Cart Rental, Angel Coral St, t 226 3455; Cholos Golf Cart Rental, east end of Caribeña St t 226 2406/2627; Polo's Golf Cart Rentals, Barrier Reef Drive (north end), t 226 3542/2467; Ultimate Golf Cart Rentals, corner of Pescador Drive and Tarpon St, t 226 3326.

By Bike

Bikes represent the cheaper alternative to golf carts, typically costing around US$6 a day/75c an hour to hire. Some resorts even provide complimentary use of bicycles for their guests. Bikes are allowed to cross the island's north–south bridge for free. **Bike rental firms**: Calvio Bike Rental, t 661 7143; Joe's Bike Rentals; and Mayan Bicycle Rentals are all located on Pescador Drive.

By Taxi

There are only a few cars on the entire island and most of these are taxis, which are available for trips between the town and the southern part of the island (including the airstrip) only. They cost a flat rate US$3/5, depending on how far you're going. Settle the price with the driver before you get in so as to avoid confusion.

By Water Taxi

The quickest way of getting around the island, and definitely worth looking into if you're staying in the very far north, is the **San Pedro Island Ferry** (t 226 3231) which leaves from Fido's Dock in the centre of town for all destinations north at 7am, 9am, 11am, 1pm and 3pm during the day, then hourly from 5pm till 10pm. On Wed, Fri and Sat there are additional services at midnight and 2am. This ferry will stop at whichever northern resort's pier you request and costs a flat rate US$5 to any stop up to Journey's End, US$10 to any stop beyond that. To attract diners from the town, some northern island restaurants offer discounts on the water taxi fare.

History

A few thousand years ago Ambergris Caye was simply an extension of the Yucatán peninsula. It was the Maya who first turned it into an island, digging a narrow canal (now known as the Bacalar Chico Channel and part of a Marine National Park) through which they could paddle their canoes and thus open up trade routes with (and speed up access to) the mainland. In the late 1800s, Mexico had the gap widened for pretty much the same reasons (they just had larger boats). The main **Maya** occupation of Ambergris lasted until around AD 1000, when most of the communities here, along with the majority of Mayan cities on the mainland, abruptly collapsed (*see* pp.23–4), although there is evidence to suggest that a few small settlements continued functioning for a couple more centuries, trading with the remaining mainland Maya communities, such as Lamanai (*see* p.210). There are a few small ruins on the island dating from this time, including Chac Balam in the north and Marco Gonzalez in the south, although they're not really worth seeking out, being rather difficult to access and not particularly well preserved.

The next group of people to utilize the island were **British pirates**, who in the 17th century briefly employed it as a base from which to launch attacks on Spanish treasure ships, and as a hideout to stow away their plunder. They also used the Bacalar Chico Channel as an escape route, fleeing in their small manoeuvrable craft away from the larger, lumbering Spanish ships. The British are also credited by some (though there is a good deal of dispute) with having been responsible for naming the island. It is believed that one of the pirates' other moneymaking schemes – aside from looting and pillaging – involved the collection of ambergris, an oily substance secreted by whales, which apparently used to wash up regularly on the island's beaches, and which, being one of the main constituent ingredients of perfume, could be sold on for a tidy profit to the fragrance industry.

A few buccaneers aside, the island remained largely uninhabited until the mid-19th century when hordes of mestizos and Maya fleeing the Yucatán Caste Wars just to the north arrived (*see* p.27), founding the community of San Pedro soon after. However, if they thought their problems were behind them, they were greatly mistaken. In the 1870s a wealthy British landowner, James Blake (by this time Ambergris Caye, along with the rest of Belize, had become part of the British Empire), bought the island, converting it into a vast **coconut plantation**. The islanders were presented with a stark Hobsonian choice – work on the plantation or face eviction. The coconut industry thrived until the 1950s, when a combination of hurricane damage and the growth of the local lobster-fishing industry (which allowed many workers to leave their plantation work) sent it spiralling into an economic decline. In the 1960s, the Blake family's holdings on the island were bought out by the Belizean government. Their legacy remains, however, in the look of Ambergris Caye, which is still dominated by great sweeping swathes of coconut palms.

Lobster fishing proved to be a short-lived economic panacea. Over-harvesting meant that the species was all but fished out by the 1980s, prompting the government to impose a strict fishing season. Happily, at around this time, **tourism** was just taking off, allowing many of the islanders to retrain as guides, hotel workers and restaurateurs. Lobsters, meanwhile, have come to be replaced on the island's menus (out of season at least) by conch, abundant numbers of which live in the coastal waters, for the time being anyway. You'll see conch shells adorning hotels and cafés throughout the island and conch meat crowbarred into all manner of recipes (even pizza).

San Pedro

 San Pedro

The first thing people tend to notice upon arriving in San Pedro is the large number of golf carts filling the streets, which represent the principal means of transport around here. The second is just how narrow the town is, with just three sandy roads separating the sea to the east and the lagoon a few hundred yards to the west. These roads now have the official and rather grand names of **Barrier Reef Drive** (the road nearest to the beach), **Angel Coral Street** (the road nearest to the lagoon) and **Pescador Drive** (the road between the other two, and the only one that's paved), but they're more commonly referred to by their simple, original and more explanatory titles – Front Street, Middle Street and Back Street. On these three streets you'll find the vast majority of the town's services, facilities and eating and drinking options (banks, ATMs, supermarkets, bars, Internet cafés, restaurants, golf car rental shops etc.). A thin sandy **beach** runs along the eastern edge of town, from where numerous piers, lined with dive shops and tour operators, jut out into the sea.

From town, Coconut Drive runs south down past the airstrip to the resorts and condos beyond, while Pescador Drive, which turns into Laguna Street, runs north up to the Boca del Rio, a narrow channel separating San Pedro from the northern part of Ambergris Caye. Until February 2006, the only way to cross this channel was via a rather slow hand-cranked ferry (which could only transport one vehicle at a time). Today, however, the island is the proud owner of brand-new **toll bridge**. The toll is payable by golf cart drivers and motorcyclists (US$2.50), but not cyclists or pedestrians. All monies collected go towards paying off the loan that made the bridge's construction possible. Cars aren't allowed to cross the bridge, as

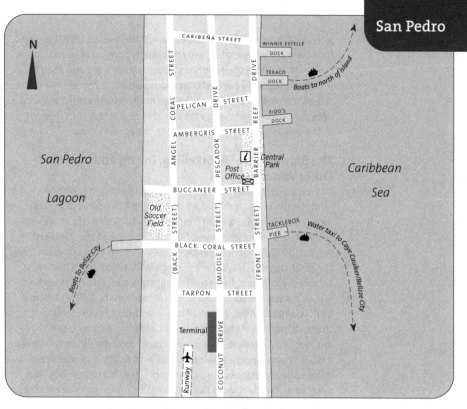

there isn't a suitable road on the other side. North of the bridge, the only artery running north up the island is a thin (and in places rather overgrown) track. You can also reach the northern end of the caye by walking along the beach, although this will take you a good 3hrs.

Almost all of the construction on the island has taken place on its eastern, reef-facing side.

Ambergris Caye Attractions

Sea and Sand

The quality of the beaches varies greatly along the island's length. Those stretches fronting upscale hotels and resorts tend to be clean and pristine (if not particularly wide), their golden sands carefully maintained by resort staff and often protected from erosion by sea walls. In between the resorts, however, it tends to be a different story with much of the sand littered with all manner of rubbish – plastic bottles, styrofoam cups, even oil drums. Swimming can be difficult from the shore as most of the shallows are thick with sea grass, a consequence of the barrier reef protecting the coast from the worst of the currents. This needn't be a problem, however, as the coastline is lined with piers/docks extending out beyond the limit of the sea grass which swimmers can use to launch themselves into the water. Safe swimming areas are clearly marked by buoys and you should be sure to stay within their confines as these waters are also used by plenty of propeller-powered boats. Mosquitoes and sandflies ('no-see-ems') can be a problem, although many resorts spray their area of beach. In any case, mosquitoes tend to be a severe nuisance only at the very height of summer, or when the breeze drops.

The Barrier Reef – Snorkelling, Diving and Other Watersports

In nature-watching terms, a coral reef is the very opposite of a rainforest. Where a trek through the jungle will, unless you're very lucky, usually involve a lot of fruitless searching, perhaps snatching a few furtive fleeting glimpses of creatures here and there (indeed, you can often go for hours without seeing much at all), down among the coral, there's always something to look at – shoals of multi-coloured fluorescent fish, scuttling lobsters, spiny scary sea urchins and, of course, the coral itself. **Coral** comes in many different forms, all of it very beautiful, and all of it wonderfully easy to identify, thanks to naturalists having taken a handy 'say what you see' approach to naming it. So, a piece of brain coral does indeed look like a brain (a large spherical lump riddled with ridges and channels), moose horn coral looks like moose horns, deer horn coral looks like deer horns, fan coral looks like (the most beautiful translucent blue) fans, and so on and so forth. All can be seen at Belize's **barrier reef**, which at Ambergris Caye lies less than a mile from the shore.

While an official tour to one of the reef's main dive spots will offer the best wildlife-spotting opportunities (particularly if you go to Shark Ray Alley where the animals are bribed with food to put in an appearance), it's quite easy to visit the reef independently, particularly from the northern resorts. Simply hire a kayak and snorkelling gear (many of the hotels let their guests use them for free), paddle out towards the reef and start exploring. The water here is very shallow, making it ideal for inexperienced snorkellers, although you must take care not to touch the coral, which is extremely delicate (and also extremely slow-growing, which means that any damage cannot easily be regenerated). If you don't feel that your snorkelling skills are quite up to negotiating a reef yet, you can put in some practice closer to shore. Many resorts feed the fish by their pier, thus giving you the chance to get close to the wildlife and hone your flipper technique.

There are a large number of tour operators on the island (most of whom are located in San Pedro) offering **snorkelling and diving tours** of the area. Though all operate different itineraries, most take in the nearby favourites of the Hol Chan Reserve, Tackle Box Canyon, Mexico Rocks and Tres Cocos. Routes tend to change according to the prevailing weather conditions or time of day, and an experienced guide should know which areas will provide the best viewing opportunities at any given time. However, if there is something in particular you want to spot – turtles, coral, or stingrays – don't be shy about letting them know. Many tour companies also offer night tours, as well as trips a little further afield to Turneffe Atoll and Lighthouse Reef (site of the famous Blue Hole), which are particularly popular with scuba enthusiasts. Three-day PADI certification courses are available for upwards of US$400.

Diving and snorkelling may be the most popular activities, but they're by no means the only water sports offered. You can also go **windsurfing**, **parasailing** and **deep-sea fishing**. Some tour operators also organize sightseeing tours over to the mainland, taking in such major attractions as Belize Zoo, Lamanai, Xunantunich and even Tikal, all the way over in neighbouring Guatemala.

Hol Chan Marine Reserve and Shark Ray Alley

⭐ Hol Chan
Marine Reserve
*www.holchanbelize.
org; adm US$10*

Located just 4 miles southeast of San Pedro, the **Hol Chan Reserve** is the most popular diving excursion with people staying on Ambergris Caye. The name is Maya for 'small channel' and refers to a 'cut', a natural surf-worn passage through a section of reef, which lies at the centre of the reserve. Just 76ft/23m wide and (up to) 33ft/10m deep, the cut is a great place for snorkellers and new divers to explore because of the huge amount of fish that congregate here, who are attracted by the high concentration of nutrients stirred up by the currents. It's particularly renowned for the amount of large fish that can be seen, including sharks, groupers and barracuda.

The area was established as a sanctuary in 1987, making it the oldest of Belize's now many marine reserves. Aside from the 'cut', Hol Chan covers an area of around 3 square miles (8 sq km), incorporating four separate habitats – the coral reef, mangroves, sea-grass beds and (not a true habitat) the popular Shark Ray Alley.

The evocatively named **Shark Ray Alley** is, unlike the reef itself, not a natural environment that now attracts sightseers, but rather an artificial one maintained for the benefit of sightseers. To be fair, its creation did come about informally and largely accidentally when local fishermen began cleaning their daily yield in an area south of the cut, in the process attracting great swarms of nurse sharks and southern stingrays, come to feed on the scraps. These days it's the dive masters that provide the daily nourishment, for which the sharks and rays are just as grateful, excitedly circling the groups of divers to earn their keep.

The Hol Chan and Shark Ray Alley trips provides a neat introduction to Belizean marine life, and can be undertaken as either a snorkelling or a diving tour (or, indeed, a combination of the two). A half-day excursion snorkelling at both sites will cost around

US$25–35, a dive trip with one tank from US$35–45, with two tanks US$55–65. Night dives are also available. Note, there is an entry fee to the reserve of US$10, which is not always included in the tour price. For more information and to see some photos of the animals you may encounter while diving, go to the visitor centre on Caribeña Street (*open 9am–5pm*).

Tourist Information on Ambergris Caye

Upon arriving in Ambergris Caye, it's worth getting hold of a copy of the *San Pedro Sun* (*www.sanpedrosun.com*). This is a free weekly paper with information, adverts and a map. The annually produced booklet, *Hot*, is also very handy, containing listings and money-off coupons. You should be able to pick these up from your hotel or from the tourist information booth located in Central Park. Try also checking out the Ambergris Caye website (*www.ambergriscaye.com*), which is packed full of information and has an active message board, as well as the official tourist board's site, *www.go ambergriscaye.com*.

Services on Ambergris Caye

All in San Pedro:

Banks: Alliance Bank, corner of Barrier Reef Drive and Ambergris Street, t 226 2136 (their ATM doesn't accept foreign cards); Atlantic Bank, corner of Barrier Reef Drive and Buccaneer St, t 226 2195; Belize Bank, northern end of Barrier Reef Drive, t 226 2482.

Books: Barefoot Books, south end of Pescador Drive, t 206 2577, *www. barefootbooks-belize.com*.

Hospitals: Lion's Health Clinic, t 226 4052, emergencies t 600 9071.

Internet: Carribbean Connection, Barrier Reef Drive, more or less in line with San Pedro Water Taxi Terminal, t 226 4664; Mousepad, Barrier Reef Drive, t 226 3690.

Pharmacy: Barrier Reef Pharmacy, Barrier Reef Drive.

Police: Pescador Drive, t 226 2022.

Post office: Barrier Reef Drive, opposite the Atlantic Bank.

Supermarkets: Mini Supermarket, Barrier Reef Drive (next to the Thomas Hotel); Island Supermarket, Coconut Drive (south of town), t 226 2972; The Greenhouse, Barrier Reef Drive, t 226 2084; Richie's Supermarket, north end of town, past police and fire stations.

Tour Operators and Dive Shops on Ambergris Caye

Note that park fees and equipment rental are not always included in the quoted tour price. Check first. All the following are in San Pedro:

Amigos del Mar Dive Shop, t 226 2706, *amigosdive@btl.net*, *www.amigosdive. com*. Offers: snorkelling tours to Hol Chan Marine Reserve/Shark Ray Alley (US$25); Mexico Rocks (US$30); Caye Caulker (US$50); the Blue Hole (US$125); sports fishing (half day US$160, full day US$220); local dives (1 tank US$35, 2 tanks US$60, 3 tanks US$85, 1 tank night dive US$40) as well as diving instruction.

Fido's Fun Sports, Fido's Dock, t 226 3513, *info@belizeparasailing.com*. Offers single (US$70), double (US$120) and triple (US$165) person parasailing (i.e. gliding through the air beneath a parachute, while attached to the back of a motorboat).

Grumpy and Happy, t 226 3420, *www. grumpyandhappy.com*. Water sports tours include: half-day group snorkelling trips for US$62.50 or full day from US$400 (up to 8 people); snorkelling/ diving at the Blue Hole for US$125/185; Caye Caulker snorkelling trip for US$40; manatee-watching for US$90; half-day sports-fishing tour for US$200 (2–4 people); night fishing for US$175 (2–4 people). It also offers a variety of sightseeing and activity day trips over to the mainland: Xunantunich and cave-tubing for US$180; Belize Zoo and cave-tubing for US$150; a jungle zip line and cave-tubing for US$210; the Lamanai Maya ruins for US$135; an overnight trip to Tikal for US$388.

Protech Dive Centre, Belize Yacht Club Dock, t 226 3008, *www.protechdive. com*. Offers: snorkelling/diving trips to Hol Chan and Shark Ray Alley, both during the day for US$25/45 and at night for US$35/50; snorkelling/diving trips to the Lighthouse Atoll, taking in the Blue Hole, Half Moon Caye Wall, Long Caye Wall and lunch, for US$125/ 185; an 'Island Circuit' taking in two snorkelling stops in the Bacalar Chico Marine Reserve and a beach barbecue for US$125; as well as reef fishing, glass-bottomed boat trips and diving instruction.

Sailsports, in front of the Holiday Hotel, t 226 4488, *www.sailsportsbelize. com*. Water-sports specialists offering: beginners windsurfing lessons (US$20/ 45/65 hr/day/week); intermediate/ advanced classes (US$25/55/75 hr/day/ week); kite surfing (from US$150) and sailing (from US$60).

SEAduced, Vilma Linda Plaza, t 226 2254, *seabelize@btl.net*. Offers a number of upscale watersports options, including: a catamaran day cruise with snorkelling at Hol Chan (US$65) and a champagne full moon cruise (US$65, only available three nights a month), as well as a number of mainland sightseeing trips: Altun Ha (US$76), Lamanai river trip (US$135). Cave-tubing and manatee-watching trips also available.

SEArious Adventures, t 226 4202, *searious@btl.net*. Water-sports options include: snorkelling trips to Hol Chan and Shark Ray Alley (US$25); Mexico Rocks and Tres Cocos (US$30); and Caye Caulker, combined with manatee-watching (US$90); as well as sports fishing (half day US$150, full day US$200). Sightseeing and activity trips to the mainland also available: Lamanai (US$135), Altun Ha (US$75); Belize Zoo and cave-tubing (US$150).

Tanisha Ecological Tours, t 226 2314, *www.tanishatours.com*. Offers a variety of combination sightseeing/activity tours: a Belize river trip and manatee-watching (US$90): Altun Ha and the Baboon Sanctuary (US$125); Belize Zoo

and cave-tubing (US$150); Lamanai Maya ruins (US$135).

Festivals on Ambergris Caye

Ambergris Caye's big yearly blowout is the **Costa Maya festival**, and it lasts a full seven days, usually taking place during the first or second week of Aug. It's officially a celebration of the Mundo Maya, the 'Maya World', welcoming visitors and contributors from Honduras, Mexico, Guatemala and El Salvador as well as mainland Belize, but it's really just an excuse for a big party with live bands, lots of loud music, even louder costumes, plenty of dancing and beauty competitions. It's such a major event that it's now televised throughout Latin America.

Shopping on Ambergris Caye

With so many tourists arriving here every year, it's hardly surprising that San Pedro has the highest concentration of gift shops in the whole country. You'll certainly find no shortage of knick-knacks and holiday keepsakes to choose from – T-shirts, key rings, hammocks – with just about every hotel operating its own shop, and numerous stores lining the main streets in town. You'll also encounter a good number of street salesmen (both on the streets and the beach) as you wander around, who will no doubt call you over to 'come take a look' at their wares (usually carved wooden statues of local animals – lobsters, sharks, manatees). While most of what's on offer falls firmly under the heading of basic holiday gear – bikinis, sunglasses, flip-flops, etc. – try Surf Guru at the Vilma Linda Plaza for branded beach and surf wear; you will also find, in among all the postcard browsers, a few more high-end places selling decent-quality (if rather pricey) handcrafted jewellery and colourful local art. Some of the most popular shopping haunts surround Fido's Courtyard on Barrier Reef Drive, and seem to have been strategically placed so as to allow bored partners to prop up the bar while their other halves browse. These include the **Belizean Arts Gallery** (t 226 3019, *www.belizeanarts.com*), which stocks canvases by local artists, as well as a range of Belizean (and other Central American) jewellery, wood-carvings, ceramics and other crafts; and **Ambar** (t 226 3101), which has a selection of handmade jewellery. There's more jewellery at the **Emerald Mine** (t 226 3225), on Barrier Reef Drive opposite the Town Hall, which specializes in rather kitschy mounted Spanish treasure coins and tropical fish pendants.

And if you need to get a look together in a hurry, head to **Carib Creations** (t 226 3803) on Barrier Drive, which promises to be able to run you up a skirt, a shirt or even a wedding dress within 24 hours. All you need to do is choose the fabric.

There are a number of grocery stores in town where you can pick up supplies if you're self-catering, including the **Greenhouse** on Barrier Street Drive, and **Richie's Supermarket** on the square half a mile north of town.

Where to Stay on Ambergris Caye

As a general rule, the more expensive luxury resorts and villas – the sort of places that have their own private beaches, swimming pools and dive shops – are located to the north and south of town (the further from town they are, the more expensive they're likely to be), while most of the cheaper options are located in San Pedro itself. Do note, however, there are only a handful of genuinely low-priced places on the entire island. When working out your accommodation budget, remember to factor in transport costs, as shuttling backwards and forwards between San Pedro and the island's remoter areas (be it on golf carts or water taxis) can be expensive, although some of the very high-end places do operate their own private water-taxi services for guests. Some hotels do also provide self-catering facilities, although again any savings are often offset by the cost of having to travel into town to pick up supplies. Discounts can be rooted out if you're prepared to book far enough in

advance, out of season or online (for the best prices, all three), but in general you should expect the accommodation here to be a good deal more expensive than on the mainland. The very top places charge the highest prices in the entire country.

San Pedro

While the hotels in town may not have the same 'private island' feel to them as those occupying their own private beaches to the north and south, many are a good deal cheaper (if still not exactly cheap) and provide easy access to the island's services and nightlife, even if those in the very centre can be a touch noisy.

Luxury ($$$$$)
Blue Tang Inn, t US 1-866 881 1020, **t** 226 2326, **f** 226 2358, *www.bluetang inn.com* (US$135). Named after a common local tropical fish, the Blue Tang Inn at the northern end of town offers a range of differently sized, differently priced, differently equipped suites. All are tastefully decorated and have fully equipped kitchens, wireless Internet access and small living areas. The best also have balconies and Jacuzzis. There's also a swimming pool and restaurant. Complimentary coffee and fruit are available daily.

Mayan Princess, t US 1-800 850 4101, **t** 226 2778, **f** 226 2784, *www.mayan princesshotel.com* (US$125). The Mayan Princess is a large, pink, three-storey concrete condo-hotel with a range of well-equipped sea-facing suites, all with balconies, kitchenettes, a/c and cable TV. Guests can use the complex's swimming pool free of charge, but (rather meanly) have to pay to use the tennis court and gym.

Ramon's Village, t 226 2071, **f** 226 2214, *www.ramons.com* (US$180). Just south of the town proper, this well-maintained, if rather anodyne resort has 61 spacious, air-conditioned thatched cabanas scattered around neatly manicured tropical gardens, just back from the shore (the most expensive are, as is traditional, right on the beachfront). It's all very professional, offering all the facilities one would expect from a major resort, including a large swimming pool, a decent restaurant, a dive shop, and a range of tour options. It also holds regular beach barbecues, which are open to the public.

Sunbreeze Beach Hotel, t US 1-800 688 0191, **t** 226 2191, **f** 226 2346, *www. sunbreezehotel.com* (US$147). Large, rather blocky-looking hotel on the beachfront at the southern end of town, a minute or so's walk from the airstrip. The rooms are spacious and tidily decorated in a generic, international hotel sort of a way and come with private bathrooms, a/c, double beds, TVs and telephones. The better equipped also have Jacuzzis (US$178). Additional amenities include a swimming pool, a good restaurant ('The Blue Water Grill') and a dive shop. Bike and golf cart rental also available.

Tides Beach Resort, t 226 2283, **f** 226 3797, *patojos@btl.net* (US$125). At the northern end of San Pedro, this small, quiet, friendly place has just eight large rooms, all with refrigerators and a/c, some with balconies and sea views. Additional amenities include a swimming pool, a bar, a restaurant and dive shop offering various diving packages.

Expensive ($$$$)–Moderate ($$$)

Changes in Latitude B&B, Coconut Drive, **t** 226 2986, *latitudesbelize@ yahoo.com* (US$105). This very friendly (if a touch overpriced) B&B has six cosy rooms, all with private baths. There's also a pleasant communal area with a refrigerator and kitchen facilities where guests can prepare their evening meals. Rates include a cooked breakfast with fruit and creole breads. Guests have access to the swimming pool next door at the Belize Yacht Club.

Coral Beach Hotel, Barrier Reef Drive, **t** 226 2013, **f** 226 2864, *www.coralbeach hotel.com* (US$70). Coral Beach's rooms are hardly outstanding, but they are perfectly serviceable coming with private bathrooms, a/c and balconies. The main draws here are the good-value diving packages and range of excursions offered, and the decent restaurant, the Jambel Jerk Pit (*see* p.132), a popular local meeting spot.

San Pedro Holiday Hotel, t 226 2014, **f** 226 2295, *www.sanpedroholiday.com* (US$103). It's a little overpriced (but then so is everywhere in San Pedro), but it does enjoy a great location right

on the beach in the town centre providing easy access to (and, more importantly a simple route home from) the surrounding bars and restaurants. Rooms are well equipped with private bathrooms, a/c and small terraces with sea views. Windsurfing, diving and snorkelling packages are available.

Spindrift Hotel, t 226 2174/226 2018, **f** 226 2251, *spinhotel@btl.net* (US$47.50/ 66 fan/a/c). Located right on the beach right in the centre of town, the Spindrift offers 22 slightly noisy rooms, as well as two self-catering apartments with kitchenettes (US$120). The best rooms (US$82.50) have sea views and a/c, while the more lowly ones have fans and face the street.

Inexpensive ($$)–Budget ($)

Martha's Hotel, t 226 2053, **f** 226 2589, *marthashotel@yahoo.com* (US$35). This sweet little wooden hotel has 12 comfortable rooms, all with private bathrooms, a supply of iced water and fans. It's right in the centre of town and reasonably priced.

Pedro's Backpackers Retreat, t 226 3825, *peterlawrancepl@gmail.com*. With prices starting as low as US$10 per person, Pedro's provides some of the cheapest accommodation on the whole of Ambergris Caye, and is thus something of a godsend for budget travellers. The communal rooms are pretty basic, but it has a nice, young, backpackery vibe to it, and barbecues are held every night. There's a sports bar with a pool table and TV. Internet access is available free of charge.

Ruby's Hotel, t 226 2063, **f** 226 2434, *rubys@btl.net*. Spread over two properties, one on the beachfront at the southern end of town, the other inland on the lagoon, this family-run operation offers a range of accommodation options and prices, from private rooms with sea views and a/c (US$35) to good-value lagoon-side rooms with shared bathrooms ($16). All rooms are pleasantly decorated.

San Pedrano Hotel, t 226 2054 (US$30). The San Pedrano is a small, popular budget choice located on the corner of Barrier Reef Drive and Caribeña Street. Rooms are clean with private bathrooms (some also have a/c) and guests can use the large wraparound veranda.

Camping

Camping is available near the airstrip at the **Boat Yard** (t 226 3245, *dolphin@ btl.net*), which has a private beach with shower facilities and secure storage. Prices are US$5 per night, plus US$7.50 if you need to hire a tent.

South of Town

The hotels and resorts south of town tend to be a good deal more upmarket (not to mention larger, quieter and more expensive) than those in and around town. Unlike the northern resorts, however, they do lie close enough to San Pedro to make a trip back into the centre (via taxi, golf cart or bike) a matter of a few minutes. The following are listed in the order you encounter them south from San Pedro.

Xanadu Island Resort, 1.15m south of San Pedro, t 226 2814, f 226 3409, *www. xanaduresort-belize.com* ($$$$$; US$150). A good self-catering option just south of the town, the Xanadu offers 18 comfortable, well-appointed thatched suites in a variety of sizes and prices (studio, 1-bed, 2-bed and 3-bed ranging from US$150 to US$360), all with full kitchens, sitting areas, wireless Internet and private outdoor decking areas facing either the pool, the sea or a palm-tree-lined garden. Complimentary bikes, kayaks and canoes available.

Mata Rocks, 1.45m south of San Pedro, t US 1-888 628 2757, t 226 2336, f 226 2349, *www.matarocks.com* ($$$$$; US$138). The Mata Rocks is one of the area's more low-key, less over-the-top resorts with just 11 rooms and 6 junior suites, spread out over two floors, all with fridges, TVs, coffee makers, a/c and sea views. The suites also have kitchenettes, making them a viable self-catering option. The resort doesn't have its own restaurant, but the beach bar serves light snacks, and there's a free buffet-style continental breakfast. Complimentary bikes available for rides into town, and there's a freshwater swimming pool. Tours offered.

Victoria House, 1.7m south of San Pedro, t US 1-800 247 5159, t 226 2067/ 344 3287, f 224 3287, *www.victoria-house.com* ($$$$$; US$194). Overlooking a spotless stretch of palm-tree-adorned, neatly raked sand (that looks like it's been vacuumed), this terribly fancy place offers pretty much what you'd expect (although that doesn't make it any less grand) – manicured grounds, rich guests lounging by the pool, a very good restaurant (with an award-winning chef), super-deferential staff and well-equipped accommodation. You can choose between hotel rooms in a central block (lots of polished hardwood), thatched *casitas* in the garden (flouncy mosquito nets around the beds, terraces and hammocks) and three private villas (a 2-bed, 3-bed and 4-bed), which have their own separate 'villas only' pool.

Royal Caribbean Resort, 1.8m south of San Pedro, t 226 4220, f 226 4221, *www. rcr-belize.com* ($$$$$; US$150). Situated next door to Victoria House, the Royal Caribbean is one of Ambergris' more recent additions to the lodging scene. Set amid 12 acres of land just steps from the beach, the 40 spacious thatched-roof wooden cabanas have kitchenettes, ceiling fans, cable TV and separate living areas. There's also a swimming pool, a restaurant and a bar. Good low-season deals available.

North of Town

This is where the island's most exclusive hotels can be found, the ones that conform best to the glossy, Caribbean getaway pictures in brochures. The very best places attract an equally up-market clientele (including the odd celebrity) and command big prices. Expect excellent facilities and food, lots of smiley attentive service, plenty of peace and quiet and a scary-looking bill. The following are listed in the order you encounter them as you head north from San Pedro Town.

Capricorn Resort, 2.87m north of San Pedro, t 226 2809, f 220 5091, *www. capricornresort.net* ($$$$$; US$185). This well-run 'micro' resort has just three cabanas, all decorated with bright cheery fabrics and art, with their own private patios with hammocks. Its location, less than 3 miles north of San Pedro, means that it's got a secluded feel to it without feeling too cut off from it all. The restaurant is highly acclaimed; complimentary breakfast.

Captain Morgan's Retreat, 3m north of San Pedro, t US 1-888 653 9090, t 226 2567, *www.captainmorgans.com* ($$$$$;

★ **Capricorn Resort** >>

★ **Victoria House** >

US$199). Captain Morgan's thatched-roof *casitas* are beginning to look a bit tired and frayed around the edges these days (perhaps now that they're TV stars – they featured in the first series of *Temptation Island* – they feel they don't have to try quite so hard), although the surrounding facilities, which include a large swimming pool, a bar and a restaurant, are still good. The presence of a team of salesmen at the resort, however, employed to drum up interest in 'vacation membership' deals (i.e. timeshares) has led to a number of complaints.

Journey's End Resort, 4.5m north of San Pedro, **t** US 1-800 460 5665, **t** 780 1566, **f** 780 1726, *www.journeysendresort. com* ($$$$$; US$155). Occupying over 50 acres of beach-front land, the Journey's End offers several accommodation choices, ranging from large hotel rooms overlooking the lagoon (US$155) to pretty garden-set cabanas (US$205/235). All come equipped with fridges, coffee makers, hairdryers, ceiling fans and a/c. Catering mainly to all-inclusive package guests (many of whom never leave the resort's confines), the Journey's End offers a range of additional facilities, including a large gift shop, a beach bar and grill, a restaurant and a spa. Fishing equipment is available for hire.

★ Azul >
★ Salamander Hideaway >>

Azul, 5.1m north of San Pedro, **t** 226 4012/13, **f** 220 5058, *www.azulbelize. com* ($$$$$; US$695/795 double/triple or quadruple occupancy). The absolute pinnacle of snazziness. Opened in March 2005, the Azul has just two identical villas, designed by their owners as the manifestation of their own ideal holiday dwelling. Luckily for their guests, the couple have impeccable taste (and no little ambition). This place is absolutely stunning. The villas are huge (3,000 sq ft/900 sq m) with high-ceilinged open-plan living areas with Bose sound systems, flat-screen TVs, large kitchen areas with top-of-the-range accessories and beautiful sweeping staircases. All the cabinets, window frames, doors and furniture have been hand-made from locally sourced wood. Each villa has two large bedrooms, two bathrooms and (the *pièce de résistance*), a rooftop terrace with views out to sea, a

sunbathing area and a private hot tub. There's a great restaurant (the Rojo Lounge, *see* p.132) next door run by the same management and a communal swimming pool. Kayaks and snorkelling equipment are available and tours can be arranged.

Mata Chica Beach Resort, 5.21m north of San Pedro, **t** 220 5010, **f** 220 5012, *www.matachica.com* ($$$$$; US$230). Mata Chica has a nice 'luxury rustic' feel, its casitas (US$350), suites (US$295), bungalows (US$230) and villas (US$650, with 2 bedrooms) all decorated in deep reds, oranges and yellows with lots of weather-beaten wood and Guatemalan/Mexican arts and textiles. All the accommodation options are very well equipped, none more so than the new beach mansion which has three bedrooms, three bathrooms, a huge patio and veranda, living area and kitchen, and sleeps up to six people. On the downside, the resort restaurant isn't quite as good as it might be (*see* p.133; you'd be better off going to the Rojo Lounge next door), the pool is a bit small and the Jacuzzi is located, slightly oddly, right by the restaurant, but, more positively, the service is slick and ever-smiley, a range of tours is offered, there's a spa, and guests can make use of a free water-taxi service to and from town.

Salamander Hideaway, 10m north of San Pedro, **t** 209 5005, *www. salamanderbelize.com* ($$$$$; US$130). Hidden away around 10m north of town, the Salamander is a peaceful and romantic escape amid a sand, sea and palm tree setting. The eight thatched stilt-set lodgings are simply yet stylishly decorated with screens, hardwood floors, fans and beds, but little else (the shower isn't even screened and the toilet is only protected by a rather meagre half-wall – something which has caused consternation for some guests). Everything here is understated (apart from the sumptuous six-course set meals, US$17.50), conveying a natural eco-friendly feel that's conspicuously missing from some of the larger, brasher, better-equipped resorts. Tours can be arranged, and you can hitch rides into town with the staff when they go in to pick up supplies (though a certain amount of flexibility is required), but to do so too often would be to miss the point slightly. After all, this is meant to be a 'hideaway', somewhere where you can snorkel, sunbathe, lounge in hammocks and not rush around.

Eating Out on Ambergris Caye

There's no shortage of choice. San Pedro town is absolutely packed with places to eat. While many are pretty generic establishments catering mainly to 'international' (i.e. American) tastes, there are also some pretty decent places serving up some pretty decent gourmet fare. Indeed, Ambergris Caye boasts some of the finest restaurants in all Belize. In fact, it's good-value budget cuisine that's actually rather harder to come by. Your best bet is probably the streetside barbecues – often set up at weekends – which sell reasonably priced burgers, chicken wings, ribs and rice and beans. **BC's** next to Ramon's Village operates a full grill on Sunday afternoons (often accompanied by live jam sessions). Quite a few of the restaurants in San Pedro will deliver to hotels in the southern part of the island for a small extra charge, while some of the restaurants on the northern half of the island offer discounts on the island ferry to their diners.

San Pedro
DandE's Frozen Custard & Sorbet, Pescador Drive. Decent ice-cream parlour serving a range of sundaes, sorbets, milkshakes, banana boats and frozen custards. 'Ice cream to the extreme' proclaim the adverts, and they're not far wrong.

★ Elvi's Kitchen >

Elvi's Kitchen, Pescador Drive, t 226 2176, f 226 3056, www.elviskitchen.com. Ask a local where the best place to eat is in San Pedro and nine times out of ten they will say 'Elvi's' (and that's not just because the owner has a large family). In the day, this offers a simple menu of burgers, sandwiches and salads, and at night lots of tasty elaborate seafood creations – crab claws in spicy lemon garlic butter (US$37.50), lobster and shrimp chardonnay (US$22) or coconut shrimp (US$33.50).

★ Rojo Lounge >>

Fido's Restaurant, Barrier Reef Drive, t 226 2056, www.fidosbelize.com. This large thatched-roof restaurant, bar and general all-round meeting place is (according to its staff T-shirts), pronounced 'Fee-doze' (feed and doze, get it?). The menu is a sort of American/Mexican smorgasbord aimed squarely at the crowds of American tourists who pass through here every day (many of whom are en route to the Island Water Taxi Terminal just outside), taking in quesadillas, burgers, burritos and nachos, all of which are reasonably priced (US$6–12). It's pretty lively all day and even more so at night when there's live music from 8pm.

Jambel Jerk Pit, Coral Beach Hotel, Barrier Reef Drive, t 226 3515. Occupying a large, slightly cavernous ground-floor dining room, this is a decent, reasonably priced hotel restaurant that serves up food with a spicy Jamaican flavour – jerk chicken (US$6), jerk tomato pasta (US$10), shrimp creole (US$14) – as well as a few blander choices (burgers, steak sandwiches) for less adventurous tastes.

The Reef Restaurant, Pescador Drive, t 226 2222. Another fishy favourite, The Reef cooks up seafood specials and Belizean fare in generous portions. It's located right next to Elvi's and, though not quite in the same league, cheaper.

Rice 'N' Roll, Fido's Food Court. This sushi and martini bar is the place to go if you fancy something a little different. Enjoy a wide range of freshly made sushi rolls and tempura dishes while looking out over the Caribbean.

North of Town
The following are listed in the order you encounter them as you head north from San Pedro town.

Capricorn, at the Capricorn resort 2.87m north, t 226 2809. A rather refined, rather expensive affair offering beautifully prepared European-influenced meals – escargots with button mushrooms, sautéed shrimp, crêpes, plus a wide array of seafood. Mains US$15–25.

Rojo Lounge, at Azul, 5.5m north of San Pedro, t 226 4012. One of the island's very top choices, the Rojo Lounge sits under a large palapa on the beachfront. It's certainly very 'rojo' (red roof, red walls, red furniture) but the whole thing is very stylishly put together with comfy, bespoke bamboo chairs and sofas. It welcomes boatloads of visitors throughout the night. The menu, which features lots of share platters, is dominated by seafood, particularly conch which finds its way onto a whole host of different dishes (including, slightly bizarrely, pizza at US$24). Other choices include cashew-crusted crab, scallop-stuffed grouper (US$33), crab and shrimp wontons (US$22) and some extremely potent cocktails – try the frozen *mojito* (US$8). The management have plans to open another branch in town soon.

Mambo Restaurant, at Mata Chica Resort, 5.21m north of San Pedro, t 220 5010. The Mambo Restaurant occupies a pleasant 'luxury rustic' dining space at the front of the Mata Chica Hotel with an adjoining bar and outside seating next to the pool. The menu offers tropical twists on international staples (mango-glazed pork chops, etc.) as well as a range of decent seafood dishes. However, considering the effort it takes to get here and the not inconsiderable prices (mains US$16–30), it's not quite as good as it should be. Surprisingly, for a place that is partly Italian-owned, it's the pasta dishes that particularly disappoint.

South of Town

The following are listed in the order you encounter them as you head south from San Pedro Town.

Tastes of Thailand, Sea Grape Drive, t 226 2601, *www.tastesofthailand.net*. The chef here cooks up some good authentic Thai dishes, with a comprehensive menu filled with curries, noodle dishes, rice dishes and several tofu choices for vegetarians. Open dinner only. You can request how spicy you want your curry.

Casa Picasso, off Coconut Drive, south end of airstrip, t 226 4507, *casapicassobelize@yahoo.com*. This trendy little place offers a high quality Mediterranean-inspired menu of fresh tapas and pasta dishes. Start slowly with olives, gazpacho and whole bulbs of roasted garlic (one of the more daring tapas choices, perhaps not recommended for a first date), before moving on to stuffed lobster tail (in

season), *sangria pollo* (chicken marinated in Spanish sangria) and a spicy *penne putanesca*. Best to book in advance.

The Palmilla, Victoria House Hotel, t 344 2340. Amy Knox, the executive chef at the Palmilla, has won a couple of awards for her internationally inspired menu, which includes lobster salad (when in season), pepper-crusted filet medallions, cashew-crusted grouper and the belly-bursting deep-fried banana *chimichangas* with coconut ice cream. It's pretty pricey: soups and salads US$6–8; mains US$20–25. Advance booking essential.

Entertainment and Nightlife on Ambergris Caye

There are lots and lots of bars in San Pedro. As a general rule of thumb, quieter places tend to be located back from the front while the noisier ones are right on the beach. Many put on live music. The most popular places include the cavernous **Fido's** (music every night from 8pm), the **Tackle Box** (music Tues, Wed, Sat and Sun from 9pm) and **BC's Beach Bar** (t 226 3289), which stages live music on Thurs and jam sessions on Sun afternoons, but there are plenty of others. Have a wander and see what takes your fancy. San Pedro also has a couple of clubs. Currently the most popular places for dancing the night away are the generically funky **Big Daddy's** and the kitschy **Jaguar Temple** (you enter through the mouth of a fibreglass jaguar head).

The **Palace Casino** (t 226 3571) can be found on the corner of Pescador Drive and Caribeña Street and is open six days a week (Thurs–Tues) 7pm–midnight. Even though the palace is closed on Wed, you'll still be able to get your gaming fix at the weekly 'Chicken Drop', the town's biggest event, which starts at 7pm at the Pier Lounge of the Spindrift Hotel. Here, a grid of numbered squares is marked on the floor, on which a chicken is then released and allowed wander around. Patrons bet on which square the chicken will eventually relieve itself. High stakes stuff.

Caye Caulker

Caye Caulker, Ambergris Caye's smaller (a mere 4 miles/6km long), cheaper, more chilled-out alternative lies just 11 miles south of the larger island. It's been a stop on the hippy trail, attracting small groups of travellers, since the 1960s. Backpacking, tie-dye-wearing explorers are still drawn to the island's colourfully painted guest-houses and relaxed atmosphere, but have been joined in recent years by a wider range of visitors, which has in turn spurred the expansion of the island's tourist infrastructure. The island's core of budget accommodation/eating options has now been augmented by a few pricier, more luxurious choices. Although the island is becoming more developed, this is by no means at the pace or level of Ambergris. Indeed, the resident community seems pretty determined to keep the island's way of life as low-key as possible.

History

Caye Caulker hasn't been inhabited for all that long. Though there is evidence to suggest that groups of Maya and bands of British buccaneers may have occasionally passed through (and perhaps even set up the odd temporary camp here), the island didn't see its first permanent community until the mid-19th century when it welcomed a significant influx of Maya and mestizos fleeing the Yucatán Caste Wars. In the late 19th century, one of these newcomers, Luciano Reyes, rather cleverly obtained a colonial grant giving him ownership of the entire island, which he then sublet to its other inhabitants. Reyes' descendants still inhabit the island (they run the Paradise Hotel).

The island is particularly susceptible to hurricane damage – which may go some way to explaining why it remained uninhabited for so long – being essentially just a sand bar set on top of a clump of limestone which, at its very highest point, is just 8ft/2.4m above sea level. Three devastating hurricanes have hit the island since the first communities were founded, the most severe of which, Hurricane Hattie in 1961, destroyed over 90 per cent of the island's buildings, including its school, which was torn from its foundations and deposited in the sea. Hattie was also the hurricane that wreaked such inordinate damage on Belize City that the authorities decided to move the capital inland to Belmopan (still, both communities fared better than the village on Calabash Caye Island in the Turneffe Atoll, which was completely obliterated). The community on Caulker recovered remarkably quickly, however, rebuilding its homes and restarting its businesses. Until recently, those businesses mainly involved shipbuilding (the name 'Caulker' derives from the practice of caulking – filling in the joins in a ship to make it watertight) and lobster fishing. The fishing industry expanded dramatically after the

Getting to Caye Caulker

By Air

Caye Caulker is just a short 10min hop by plane from the mainland. Both **Maya Island Air** (t 226 2435, *www.mayaislandair.com*) and **Tropic Air** (t 226 2012, *www.tropicair.com*) operate several flights to/from Belize City Goldson International (US$54 one way), Belize City Municipal (US$30 one way) and San Pedro (US$30 one way). The island's airstrip is to the south of village, from where you can walk or pick up a golf-cart taxi into town.

By Boat

The **Caye Caulker Water Taxi** runs from Belize City at 8am, 9am, 10.30am, 12noon, 1.30pm, 3pm, 4.30pm and 5.30pm and returns at 6.30am, 7.30am, 8.30am, 10am, 12 noon, 1.30pm, 3pm, 4pm and 5pm (the last one runs only on Fri, Sat and Sun). All boats leave from the main dock near the centre of town. Fares cost US$10 one way or US$15 return. Boats also run to and from San Pedro daily at 7am, 8.45am, 10am, 11.30am, 1pm, 2.30pm, 3.30pm, 5.30pm and return 7am, 8am, 9.30am, 11.30am, 1pm, 2.30pm, 3.30pm and 4.30pm (the last on Fri, Sat and Sun). Fares from Caye Caulker to San Pedro cost US$10 or US$15 return. **Triple J** (t 207 7777) and **Thunderbolt** (t 226 2904) also run similar services.

Getting around Caye Caulker

It's pretty easy. Caye Caulker is a small, 4-mile-long island made up of two chunks of land separated by a narrow channel of water known as the 'Split'. And, as almost all of the island's development has taken place in its southern half in an area less than one mile square, most people get around on foot or on bicycles (many hotels offer a bike rental service, some provide them for free to guests). Aside from a couple of delivery vans, there are no cars on the island. Golf carts are the main form of motorized transport, making up the island's (rather slow-moving) taxi fleet. Drivers will charge US$2.50 per person. You can also hire your own cart – Caye Caulker Golf Cart Rentals, t 226 0237, can provide them for around US$60–65 a day – although the island is so tiny, this hardly seems necessary.

1960s following the islanders' decision (in the face of much government opposition) to form a cooperative in order to acquire new technologies (better boats, freezer plants etc.) and to set fairer prices. The decline of lobster stocks in recent years, however, has led to the implementation of a three-month fishing season, which in turn has obliged many villagers to seek work elsewhere, mainly in the tourism industry. The island has welcomed a good deal of development in recent years with a number of new hotels opening and several foreigners building holiday homes here. This hasn't, as yet, reached overwhelming levels, and the island still has under a thousand permanent residents.

Beaches and Swimming

Caye Caulker's beaches may not be the most picturesque in the Caribbean but that doesn't stop people oiling up and stretching out

Orientation

There are just three main streets on Caye Caulker, all simple sandy affairs, named **Front**, **Middle** and **Back**. Most of the businesses reside on Front Street, the closest to the sea. Around half a mile north of the village is the **'Split'**, a channel dividing the island in two, created in 1961 by Hurricane Hattie. This northern section of the island is still largely uninhabited, although a small amount of development is currently taking place, which may lead to it becoming more touristified in the future. For now, most island life is concentrated in the southern region.

⚙ The Split

on them. The island's most popular spot is the artificial beach up by The Split, where the waters are clear and the lack of sea grass (a severe problem along the rest of the coast) makes swimming and snorkelling relatively easy, although you should take care as currents can be quite strong and the area sees quite a lot of boat traffic. There's also a decent bar here, the Lazy Lizard. As with every else in the cayes, the sandflies and mosquitoes can get quite aggressive when the breeze drops, so bring adequate supplies of bug spray.

Caye Caulker Lobster Fest

Caye Caulker's economy was once based almost entirely on the fishing of spiny lobsters, and although this has been supplanted in recent years by tourism, the practice still plays an important role in the local culture. The island's main festival is the Lobster Fest, which is held in July to celebrate the beginning of the lobster season. Festivities consist of lots of (lobster-heavy) food, plenty of music and a beauty pageant culminating in the official crowning of that year's Miss Lobster Fest (surely every little girl's dream).

Activities and Tours

With the barrier reef located just a mile offshore, most of the activities available on Caulker are sea-based. You can go snorkelling independently, from one of the piers up near the spit, or take an official tour to one of the main local snorkel/dive sites, including the **Caye Caulker Marine Reserve**, the island's own patch of preserved reef, a 5–10min boat ride away, which has an artificial feed site, the **Shark Ray Village**, that provides a similar experience to Ambergris Caye's Shark Ray Alley (*see* pp.125–6). Tours further afield to Hol Chan Marine Reserve and Shark Ray Alley (*see* p.125), Turneffe Atoll (*see* p.140), Lighthouse Reef (*see* pp.141–2) and the famous Blue Hole (*see* p.142) are also available, as are fishing, windsurfing and sailing tours.

It's also possible to take trips out to see (but not swim with) **manatees**, a sort of giant aquatic mammalian herbivore, who live in large numbers around **Swallow Caye**, a small island just 4 miles east of Belize City (*see* Chocolate Tours, opposite). And, if you don't fancy getting wet, the island, despite its small size, is a renowned **bird-watching** destination. Over 100 species have been recorded here. Guided bird-watching tours are given around the mini-reserve near the airstrip for around US$25, or visitors can follow a self-guided trail for free. The mangrove-covered north section of the island is also a good place for sighting wildlife, with over 100 acres of land protected as the **Caye Caulker Forest Reserve**. You can arrange boat trips to here from the village.

Tourist Information on Caye Caulker

There is no official tourist information office on the island, although the tourist board does operate a Caye Caulker dedicated website, *www.go cayecaulker.com*, which is worth taking a look at when planning your trip. Try also *www.cayecaulkerbelize.net*.

Services on Caye Caulker

Banks: Atlantic Bank, Middle St, t 226 2195. Unfortunately, the island does not have an ATM.
Internet: The Caye Caulker Cyber Café, Middle St.
Police: Front St, t 226 2022.
Post office: Back St, t 226 2325.
Supermarkets: Chan's Mini Mart, Middle St.

Tour Operators on Caye Caulker

Chocolate Tours, t 226 0151, *chocolate@ btl.net*. Lionel 'Chocolate' Heredia is the island's foremost expert on (and champion of) manatees. His campaigning on behalf of the gentle giants led directly to Swallow Caye, the manatees' favourite feeding ground in these parts, being designated an official sanctuary in 2002. The environmental protection group he formed, the Friends of Swallow Caye, now manage the area in conjunction with the Belize Ministry of Natural Resources. Lionel's enthusiasm remains undimmed, however, and he still leads daily tours out to see his beloved creatures. In order to safeguard the manatees' wellbeing, strict regulations are in place at the caye – no swimming and no speeding.

Dolphin Bay Travel and Tours, t 226 2351, *dolphinbay@btl.net*, *www.caye caulker.org/dolphinbay*. Tours include: local reef snorkelling (US$25); snorkelling at Hol Chan/Shark Ray Alley (US$30); manatee-watching and reef snorkelling (US$45). Mainland activities, including jungle tours and cave-tubing, also available.

Hicaco Tours Snorkel and Dive, t 226 0174, *www.hicacotour.com*. Tours include: snorkelling at Hol Chan, Shark Ray Alley and Coral Gardens (US$45); snorkelling at Shark Ray Village and two local reef stops (US$25); manatee-watching, snorkelling at Shark Ray Village and camping on Geoff's Caye (US$95, including food and drink); manatee-watching (US$50). Diving courses, fishing and boat charters also available.

Michael's Windsurf and Water Sports, t 226 0457, *www.windsurfbelize.com*. Offers windsurfing (lessons start at US$35; boards from US$10 an hour, US$45 per half-day, US$65 full day), and kiteboarding for both novices (day rental of trainer kite and ½ hour instruction US$80, one day introduction US$135) and the experienced – boards rented for US$15 per hour, US$10 each additional hour, or US$35 per half day, US$45 full day.

Raggamuffin Tours, *www.raggamuffin tours.com*. Tours include: day cruise stopping at Hol Chan, Shark Ray Alley and Coral Gardens (US$35, including park fees, lunch and snorkel gear); sunset cruise (US$20); moonlight cruise (US$30); three-day sailing trip to Placencia, with two nights camping on the cayes (US$250); three-day sailing trip to Lighthouse Reef, Halfmoon Caye and Blue Hole, with two nights camping on the cayes (US$250). Fishing trips and boat charters also available.

Tsunami Adventures, t 226 0462, f 226 0432, *www.tsunamiadventures.com*. Activities include: snorkelling at Hol Chan Reserve/Shark Ray Alley and lunch (US$45); three-hour local reef trip (U$25); glass-bottom boat tour (US$25); three-tank dive to the Blue Hole (US$115 including park fee and lunch); four-hour sports-fishing trips (US$175). Tsunami also offer a variety of sightseeing trips over to destinations on the mainland, including: Altun Ha, Lamanai and a river cruise (US$97.50) and Tikal (US$305).

Where to Stay on Caye Caulker

There is a wide variety of lodgings on the island, although you should be aware that many of the places at the budget end of the spectrum are very basic. You'll find none of the huge, super-equipped resorts of Ambergris Caye here. Indeed, the accommodation system works on a rather ad hoc basis, with most visitors to the island arriving without having made a prior reservation. However, unless you are very picky about where you stay, you shouldn't have too many problems getting a room. All the accommodation in Caye Caulker lies within 10 mins of the village centre, so nowhere feels cut off. Several nonresidents rent out their vacation homes when not on the island. Contact **Caye Caulker rentals** (t 226 0029, *www.cayecaulkerrentals. com*). Prices start from around US$75 a night. Incidentally, the slightly brackish smell arising from many of the bathrooms is an unfortunate consequence of desalinated sea water used here.

Luxury ($$$$)–Expensive ($$$$)
Auxillou Beach Suites, t 222 4600, *www.auxilloubeachsuites.com* (US$129). The Auxillou comprises several large, attractively decorated beach-front units with kitchenettes, living areas and private decking. The staff are very helpful and the views from the rooftop are probably the best on the island.
Caye Caulker Condos, t 226 0072/600 8485, *www.cayecaulkercondos.com* (US$100/120 1st/2nd floor). These eight air-conditioned studio-condos all come with wireless Internet, large showers (built for two), private sea-facing decks, and fully equipped kitchens (although if you don't fancy preparing your own meals, you can arrange for a cook to come in and do it for you).

⭐ Iguana Reef Inn >

Iguana Reef Inn, t 226 0213, f 226 0087, *www.iguanareefinn.com* (US$114). Located on the lagoon side, this place gets consistently good reviews for its spacious, well-equipped rooms and chirpy, eager-to-please staff. The rooms are comfortable with tiled floors, fridges and a/c. Outside there is a nice bar and plenty of places to relax in the sun with a good book.
Seaside Cabanas, t 226 0498, f 226 0125, *www.seasidecabanas.com* (US$95). The Seaside is a well-equipped resort offering a range of pleasant cabanas, all with bright décor (some with roof terraces), the only swimming pool on

the island (reserved exclusively for the use of guests) and a two-storey bar.

Moderate ($$$)
Barefoot Beach Belize, t 226 0205, *www.barefootbeachbelize.com* (US$59). This quiet, colourful guesthouse is located a 5min walk from the village centre. It comprises four bright sea-facing rooms with private bathrooms, coffee makers, fridges and ceilings fans/a/c; plus a separate cottage with a kitchenette and a futon, that sleeps up to four (US$79 for double occupancy, US$15 per additional person).
Costa Maya Beach Cabanas, t 226 0462, *www.tsunamiadventures.com* (US$45/55 fan/a/c). Costa Maya has six private cabanas, all equipped with fridges, coffee makers and wireless Internet access (two of the larger units also have kitchenettes) as well as a slightly grander beach house (US$75) with air conditioning and a futon that can accommodate up to four people. Complimentary bikes and kayaks are available.
De Real Macaw, t 226 0459, f 226 0497, *www.derealmacaw.biz* (US$50/60 fan/a/c). The De Real Macaw is a decent value choice with large private rooms, all with fridge, TV and fan (some with a/c), and a two-bedroom condominium that comes complete with kitchen (including microwave and washing machine) and can accommodate up to 6 people (US$130 per night for a minimum stay of two nights). At the other end of the scale, the hotel's cheapest double is just US$25.
Tree Tops Guest House, t 226 0240, f 226 0115, *www.treetopsbelize.com* (US$46/52 fan/a/c). Well-run and good value, the Tree Tops' six rooms are all clean, airy and spacious with light fresh décor, and come with fridges, TVs and ceiling fans. Four have private bathrooms, the other two share. There is also a large superior suite with its own private balcony.

Inexpensive ($$)–Budget ($)
Rainbow Hotel, t 226 0123, f 226 0172, *www.rainbowhotel-cayecaulker.com* (US$30/52 fan/a/c). This large two-storey blue hotel right on the beach offers clean, secure low-cost lodging. Rooms are quite simply furnished and decorated, with fans (or, for a bit more,

a/c) and TVs. There's also a two-bedroom *casita* with a full kitchen (including microwave) and living area (with TV) that sleeps up to six (US$107).

Tina's Backpackers Hostel, t 226 0351, **f** 226 0078, *tinasbackpackershostal@ yahoo.com.* The island's cheapest option offering bunks in a dormitory for US$7 per person. Additional facilities include a communal kitchen, a shared bathroom and hammocks strung up on the veranda.

Eating Out on Caye Caulker

Though prices on Caye Caulker are generally a bit higher than those on the mainland, they are still a lot cheaper than those on Ambergris Caye. The island's reputation as a haven for 'alternative' lifestyles has placed the emphasis on healthy, hearty dishes with lots of choice for vegetarians. For snacks or light breakfasts, head for the Bakery on Middle Street, which is renowned for its cinnamon buns in the morning and cheese pastries at lunch.

Cindy's Café, Front St, **t** 226 0095. Organic treats for the health-conscious, Cindy's is open only for breakfast, serving decent fresh coffee (with optional soy milk), breads and vegetarian snacks.

Don Corleone Caribbean Trattoria, Front St, **t** 226 0025. Despite the slightly cheesy name, this beach-front Italian is one of the island's top choices. Think fine wines, seafood and a pasta you can't refuse. Main meals, such as the excellent *pesce Catalaina* (fresh snapper with olive oil, tomatoes and olives), are priced at around US$14–16.

Glenda's, Back St. A popular local choice. Fill up on fresh orange juice, coffee, bacon, eggs and cinnamon buns (for around US$3) for breakfast, and burritos, rice and beans, and *garnaches* for lunch.

Habaneros, t 226 0487. This is one of the island's more expensive options, with a nice upstairs outdoor decking area and an international menu featuring plenty of fresh fish and vegetarian options.

Marin's Restaurants, t 226 0104. In season, seafood lovers flock here for the lobster, which is served for breakfast, lunch and dinner. In fact, if you don't like lobster, this is probably one best avoided. Mains are US$4–US$15, so there's something to suit everyone's wallet (if not everyone's palate).

Rasta Pasta Rainforest Café, Front St, **t** 226 0356/0358. The family-run Rasta Pasta offers a diverse menu of chicken, seafood and vegetarian dishes, much of it with a spicy Caribbean kick. Check out the super-size burritos (US$8) and the great value breakfast.

Sand Box, t 226 0200. This is one of the most popular eateries on the island with locals and tourists, who come to fill up on jerk chicken, seafood, pasta and several vegetarian options. There is a nice garden area for alfresco dining. Most mains come in at under US$10.

Syd's, t 206 0284. This is a great little place for a cheap (but tasty) meal. Burgers, burritos, tostadas and rice and beans dishes are available for under US$5. Saturday night is barbecue night.

Wish Willy. This creaky ramshackle building may not look too promising, but it offers a surprisingly up-market culinary experience. The seafood is delicious and the atmosphere friendly and lively.

Entertainment and Nightlife on Caye Caulker

Locals and guests alike tend to take life slowly here, chilling the day away. And while it can hardly be claimed that Caulker transforms into a party town come nightfall, it does liven up a bit.

Those who've spent the day hanging at the 'Split' can move to the popular local bar, the **Lazy Lizard,** which usually stays busy until closing (11pm) with plenty of reggae and snacks available.

Another popular choice for relaxing with a drink is the **I & I Reggae Bar,** spread over three floors with a cobweb-like assortment of swings and hammocks.

(★) Don Corleone Caribbean Trattoria >

Other Cayes

Caye Chapel Island Resort

Caye Chapel
Island Resort
t US 1-800 901 8938,
t 226 8250, f 226 8201,
golf@cayechapel.com,
www.belizegolf.cc;
US$300

The 265-acre Caye Chapel is a private island given over to a luxurious super-resort, which comes complete with its own 18-hole championship-standard golf course (US$50 a day for unlimited rounds). Though there are *casitas* available for US$300 per night, the most popular choices here are the luxurious villas (US$1,000 for four-person occupancy), which offer fine furnishings, marble floors, kitchens, living areas, two bathrooms, private decks and hydro spas. There's also a very good restaurant, sandy beaches and a swimming pool.

Non-guests can purchase a day membership for a not inconsiderable US$200, which entitles them to unlimited access to the resort's facilities, including the golf course, from 9am till 4pm. This is a request stop for water taxis travelling to/from San Pedro and Caye Caulker. There is also an airstrip here.

Turneffe Atoll

⭐ Turneffe Atoll

Belize has three atolls (ring-shaped coral reefs encircling lagoons), of which Turneffe Atoll, located 15 miles east of Belize City, is the largest, measuring some 10 by 30 miles (16 by 48km) and comprising over 200 islets. Many of the islands here are little more than uninhabited masses of mangrove that provide shelter for a whole smorgasbord of aquatic life, including manatees, wading birds, crocodiles, turtles and dolphins. It's a popular dive attraction, with several sites located towards the atoll's southern end, the most famous of which is **The Elbow**, right at the southern tip. This is generally recognized as a world-class site (best suited to advanced divers) with deep waters and strong currents that attract large schools of horse-eye jacks and snapper, as well as the odd shark. Turneffe also has some more easily accessible sites suitable for novices, including: **Triple Anchors**, whose 40–60ft (12–18m) depths house the coral- and sponge-encrusted remains of an 18th-century ship; **Hollywood** (20–50ft/6–15m), where you can see brain, tan lettuce leaf, flower and boulder coral; and **Sayonara**, which contains the wreck of a cargo boat that sank in 1985, as well as some impressive sponge formations. It's also a good place to spot parrotfish, who are indirectly responsible for creating many of the region's beaches. The fish eat the coral skeleton, crunching it up with their specially adapted, super-strong beaks, and excreting what they can't digest in the form of sand, which eventually ends up on the shore.

Where to Stay on Turneffe Atoll

Though Turneffe Atoll does have a number of options, it doesn't attract nearly the number of visitors that the larger islands to the north do, catering mainly to hard-core divers and snorkellers, plus the odd fishing fanatic.

Blackbird Caye Resort, t 463 0833, **f** 463 4081, *www.blackbirdresort.com* ($$$$$; from US$850/1,650 3/7-night snorkel package). This 166-acre resort offers snorkelling (two trips per day), diving (three tanks per day) and fishing packages (bring your own gear). Standard cabanas are large with wooden floors, a/c, ceiling fans, private bathrooms and porches, while the de luxe versions have separate bedrooms and living areas. Family-sized units also available.

The Oceanic Society, t US 800 326 7491, **t** 220 4256, *www.oceanic-society.org/index5.html* ($$$$$; from US$1,190/1,550 5/8-day snorkelling package). An alternative to staying at the Blackbird Caye Resort is to get a place on one of the snorkelling expeditions run by the Oceanic Society, who operate a few basic beach cabanas (with private bathrooms) at their Blackbird Caye Field Station. The snorkelling trips, led by a trained naturalist, include a visit to the Blue Hole (*see* p.142). It may not be as luxurious as some other caye accommodation, but at least it's more eco-friendly, with guests contributing to the preservation of the coral reef.

Turneffe Flats, t US 1-888 512 8812, **t** 298 2783, *www.tflats.com* ($$$$$; from US$1,749/ 3,289/3,439 diving/fishing/combination week-long package). This is a specialist fishing resort overlooking several miles of wadeable flats (ideal for catching bonefish, apparently) and offering a range of trips in specialist fishing skiffs. Bedrooms have private bathrooms, a/c and verandas.

Turneffe Island Lodge, t US 1-800 874 0118, **t** 817 0309, *www.turneffelodge.com* ($$$$$; from US$1,140/1,818 3/7 nights beachcombing). This private 14-acre island, at the southern end of the atoll, is surrounded by top-quality dive sites, and occupied by a top-notch luxury resort, offering a range of beachcombing, fishing and diving packages. The options run the gamut from pretty fancy (room with a/c and private bathrooms) to incredibly fancy (large ocean-front mahogany cabanas with huge windows and outdoor showers). Three meals a day are served at the beach-front dining room.

Lighthouse Reef Atoll

This, the furthest reef from mainland Belize, comprises six separate cayes and some renowned diving attractions, including Belize's most famous site, the Blue Hole, which is situated in the middle of the atoll's 30-mile-long lagoon. Of the cayes, the only islands of any real interest are **Northern Caye**, **Long Caye** and the protected **Half Moon Caye** (*see* below), although some dive boats include a stop at Sandbore Caye to the north, even if there is not much to see there other than a lighthouse. Northern Caye is a private island with just one resort, The Lighthouse Reef Resort (*www. scubabelize*), which has its own airstrip to fly guests in (at the time of writing, however, the resort was closed for refurbishment). Long Caye, in the southwest sector of the atoll, is the largest of the Lighthouse islands at around 620 acres. It's currently undergoing development, which will see the construction of an ecovillage and a couple of resorts with several acres set aside as nature reserve. At the time of going to print, however, only one resort was open for business – the **Calypso Beach Retreat**, which has just four beach-front rooms, all with four-poster

Calypso Beach Retreat
US **t** 303 523 8165,
www.calypsobeach retreat.com

beds, private bathrooms and access to a shared kitchen. Rates started at US$465 for three days including meals and transfers.

Half Moon Caye Natural Monument

Half Moon Caye
Natural Monument
adm US$10

When a small section of this caye was set aside as a reserve in 1928, it represented the first protected marine area in the whole of Central America. Since then, the reserve has expanded to include the entire island, as well as its surrounding reef and lagoon, which together have been declared a National Monument. Visitors to the caye, which is now managed by the Belize Audubon Society (*see* p.96), can enjoy nature trails, walk the beaches and climb an observation tower to see the colonies of red-footed boobies and frigate birds that nest here. Many tour companies (and hotels) offer snorkelling and diving trips to the caye, usually combined with a stop at The Blue Hole. From Ambergris Caye or Caye Caulker, this can be done as a day trip or with an overnight camp on Half Moon Caye.

The Blue Hole

✦ The Blue Hole
adm US$40 – not
always included in tour
price. Check first

The chances are that even those people who haven't heard of Belize will have seen a picture of the Blue Hole. The image of the huge, almost perfectly spherical circle of deep blue water set against the lighter blue of the encompassing ocean has become the defining icon of the country. The pictures are usually composed with a yacht positioned at the hole's edge so as to emphasize its vast size. The hole is actually a giant limestone cavern that began its life on land before being flooded and submerged beneath meltwater following the end of the last Ice Age. The weight of the water on the top of the cave eventually caused its ceiling to collapse, forming a large pit of around 1,000ft/300m in diameter and over 400ft/120m deep, the water of which appears darker than the surrounding sea. It was the great underwater explorer Jacques Cousteau who first brought the site to international attention, when he filmed inside in the early seventies, revealing to the outside world its strange half-land, half-marine landscape of stalactites and sharks, stalagmites and stingrays. Today, local dive shops offer tours here several times a week. To be honest, despite its fame, it's not the best dive the area has to offer. The extreme depth – up to 150ft/45m – means that it's only really suitable for experienced divers, and even they must begin their ascent back to the surface after just 11 minutes. For this reason, a trip to the Blue Hole is nearly always done in conjunction with a dive at some of the other sites at Lighthouse Atoll. These include **Tres Cocos**, near Long Caye, which has a wall with overhangs; the **Silver Caves**, with its dark coral caves; and the best and most popular site (second only to the Blue Hole itself), the **Half Moon Caye Wall**, a seemingly never-ending face of coral riddled with tunnels and canyons and home to a superabundance of marine life.

Cayo District and the West

Bordering Guatemala, Cayo is Belize's most westerly district. It's also the country's largest administrative area, encompassing over 2,000 square miles (3,200km) of territory, taking in everything from mountains, cave systems and waterfalls to broadleaf jungle, savannah and pine forest. Many (certainly many that live there) believe it to be the country's most picturesque region, although its lack of a coastline (or, more specifically, its lack of any beaches) means that it attracts significantly fewer tourists than the cayes or the southern resorts, and has a less developed tourist infrastructure.

10

Don't miss

⭐ **Subterranean landscapes**
Barton Creek Cave **p.152**

⭐ **Scenic drive**
Hummingbird Highway **p.149**

⭐ **Hi-octane adventure**
Ian Anderson's Jungle Lodge **p.150**

⭐ **Bustling charm**
San Ignacio **p.153**

⭐ **Caves, waterfalls, Mayan ruins**
Mountain Pine Ridge Forest Reserve **p.166**

See map overleaf

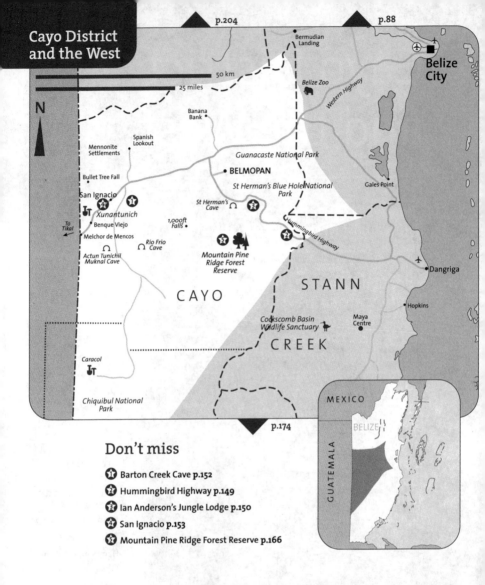

Belize City

50 km

25 miles

N

Bermudian Landing

Belize Zoo

Western Highway

Banana Bank

Mennonite Settlements

Spanish Lookout

Guanacaste National Park

Bullet Tree Fall

• BELMOPAN

Gales Point

San Ignacio

Xunantunich

St Herman's Blue Hole National Park

St Herman's Cave

To Tikal

Benque Viejo

1,000ft Falls

Melchor de Mencos

Rio Frio Cave

Hummingbird Highway

Actun Tunichil Muknal Cave

Mountain Pine Ridge Forest Reserve

Dangriga

CAYO

STANN

Hopkins

Cockscomb Basin Wildlife Sanctuary

Maya Centre

CREEK

Caracol

Chiquibul National Park

Don't miss

⭐ Barton Creek Cave **p.152**

⭐ Hummingbird Highway **p.149**

⭐ Ian Anderson's Jungle Lodge **p.150**

⭐ San Ignacio **p.153**

⭐ Mountain Pine Ridge Forest Reserve **p.166**

MEXICO

BELIZE

GUATEMALA

p.174

Nonetheless, there's plenty to do, with a wealth of high-adrenaline adventure activities on offer – including cave-tubing, canoeing and rappelling – as well as a number of more sedate pursuits, such as nature-watching in the region's national parks and reserves (which make up no less than 60 per cent of the district's area) and touring the various Mayan cities, which include Xunantunich and Caracol, the country's largest pre-Columbian site (in fact, climbing to the top of Caracol's great pyramid probably does count as an adventure sport). Visits to Tikal, just across the border in Guatemala, can also be arranged.

The district's more modern urban centres will perhaps hold slightly less appeal for visitors. The country's capital, Belmopan (which took over from Belize City in 1970) in the northeast is, in truth, a rather lacklustre metropolis, of more interest for its transport links than its own purpose-built charms.

Bustling little San Ignacio in the west, with its busy market and supply of good-value hotels and eateries, is a lot more fun. It's also home to several tour operators and hotels, making it a good base for exploring the nearby Mountain Pine Ridge Reserve, with its cascading waterfalls and spooky cave systems.

Although you won't find the range of accommodation options here that you will on the cayes, there's still plenty of choice, with everything from small low-cost rustic cabanas with few facilities to some of the best equipped and most exclusive (not to say expensive) lodges in the country on offer.

Belmopan

Belmopan, the country's capital, has for nearly four decades now sat squarely in the shadow of its larger, more populous, more glamorous rival, Belize City, the city it was supposedly built to replace (which, other than in a purely administrative sense, it has singularly failed to do). With just 8,000 inhabitants, Belmopan is one of the smallest capitals in the world. Its conception began in 1961

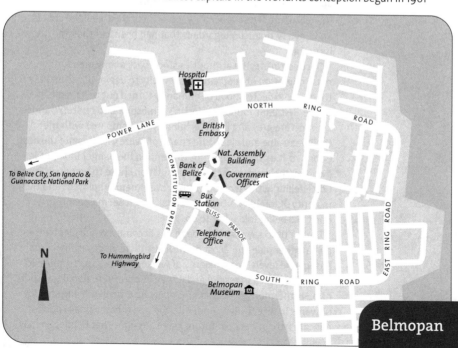

Belmopan

Getting to and around Belmopan

As one of the region's major transport hubs, Belmopan is both easy to get to and away from. Most **buses** running along the Western Highway and Hummingbird Highway stop here. Novelo's, the country's main bus company (but *see* p.66), operates a half-hourly service from Belize City. The last bus leaves at 7pm. Passengers are dropped at Market Square, from where return services to Belize City (every half-hour till 7pm) also depart.

If **driving**, Belmopan lies around a mile east of the Hummingbird Highway. The turn-off is just south of the T-junction where the Hummingbird Highway meets the Western Highway. The main road into town is Constitution Drive, which passes along the western side of the city, before joining the ring road that encircles much of the centre. Just east of Constitution Drive is the Market Square, Novelo's bus terminal and Independence Plaza, which marks the official centre of the city.

when Hurricane Hattie ripped through Belize City, the then capital, destroying many of its buildings and much of its infrastructure. It was the second major hurricane to hit the capital that century. The first, in 1931, killed an estimated 10 per cent of the population. The government, fearful that a third assault by the weather might not just destroy the capital, but effectively decapitate the body politic from the rest of the country, decided that it would be a good idea to relocate the capital – and in particular the parliament and government offices – inland away from the worst ravages of the coastal storms. However, rather than adopt an existing urban centre, and risk offending any particular community, it was decided to create a brand-new city more or less in the geographic centre of the country. By 1970, the new capital was ready. It was given the name 'Belmopan', a portmanteau amalgamation of the first syllable of 'Belize' and the district's river 'Mopan', although it also acquired the nickname, 'The Garden City', because of the tree-lined streets and flowery, manicured gardens that had been incorporated into its design.

Once complete, the authorities stood back and waited for the mass migration of people to the new city to begin. Unfortunately, for them, the expected flood of humanity turned out to be more of a trickle. Belizeans found Belmopan's atmosphere to be sterile and its architecture grey and boxy, certainly when compared with the Caribbean vibe and clapboard charm of Belize City. Despite the best efforts of the government, not to mention the danger inherent in living on the coast, most of the population chose to remain in Belize City – tellingly, this included most government employees and the majority of foreign embassies. Sometimes, it seems, people just don't like being told what to do.

That's not to say that Belmopan has become a white elephant – just a rather pale one. Most of the institutions of government are based here (even if the majority of workers choose to commute to the city rather than reside) and it is an important regional transport hub. Furthermore, population numbers have been moving steadily upwards in recent years. And, with the US Embassy finally due to relocate here in the near future, there are signs that Belmopan may finally be ready, if not to emerge entirely from its rival's shadow, then at least to dip a toe or two into the light.

The Town

Pretty much everything of interest in Belmopan can be seen within a relatively short period of time. If you are just in the area waiting for your next bus, a quick wander around the market (Tuesday and Friday mornings) and a look at the rather unusual (not to say rather kitschy) **National Assembly**, which is built around a central plaza in the style of a Mayan temple, is possible in about half an hour. If you've got a bit longer, the **Belmopan Museum** has an interesting collection of archaeological finds, but is currently closed for refurbishment and not due to re-open until January 2007. Information on the museum, along with leaflets and brochures on the various Mayan sites currently being excavated in the region, can be obtained from the **Department of Archaeology** (within the National Assembly buildings, **t** 822 2106). The **Belize National Archives** are also located here, although their (admittedly extensive) collection of images and documents will be primarily of interest to scholars and researchers.

Belize National Archives
*26/28 Unity Blvd, **t** 822 2247, www. belize archives.org; open Mon–Thurs 8am–9.30pm, Fri 8–5*

ⓘ **Belmopan Ministry of Tourism >**
*14 Constitution Drive, **t** 822 2303*

Services in Belmopan

Banks: Belize Bank, 60 Market Square, **t** 822 2303; Scotia Bank, Ring Rd, **t** 822 1414.

Books: The Angelus Press, Constitution Drive, **t** 822 3861.

Hospitals: Belmopan Hospital, Constitution Drive, **t** 822 2264.

Internet: Techno Hub, Market Square (by Novelo's Bus Terminal), **t** 822 0061.

Post office: Independence Square, by the police station.

Souvenirs: Art Box, next to the roundabout on the way into town, **t** 822 2233. Stocks a good range of gifts, slate carvings, T-shirts and books.

Supermarkets: The Everyday Supermarket, Ring Road (East).

Telephones: The main BTL office is on Bliss Parade, **t** 822 2193.

Tour Operators in Belmopan

Roaring River Adventure Tours, t 820 2025, *www.rratoursbelize.com*. Offers tubing and rainforest treks in the area.

Most of the hotels in and around Belmopan should also be able to help you arrange tours.

Where to Stay in Belmopan

Not many people opt to stay in the capital itself, not even most of those people who work here, so the quality (and quantity) of lodgings is not high. Thankfully a more diverse selection of accommodation is available in the surrounding area.

Bullfrog Inn, 25 Half Moon Ave, **t** 822 3425, **f** 822 3155, *www.bullfroginn.com* ($$$; US$75). The Bullfrog has the reputation for being the best hotel in the capital (to be fair, the competition isn't exactly fierce), with spacious rooms, large beds and balconies, as well as a reasonable restaurant and a popular bar. It's a bit motel-like and impersonal, but perfectly acceptable for a day or two.

El-Rey Inn, 23 Moho St, **t** 882 3438, **f** 882 2682, *hibiscus@btl.net* ($–$$; US$20–30). 12 simple tiled rooms, all with fans and private bathrooms, located in a quiet part of town. Although the units are nothing special, they are clean, the hotel serves decent (and cheap) meals, and offers a range of tours. It's around a 10min walk to the city centre.

Eating Out in Belmopan

If your visit is brief and your budget tight, you needn't stray too far from the bus terminal. Inexpensive meals and speedy snacks can be bought from the stalls in Market Square, or from one of the restaurants surrounding the bus station. If you've got a bit more time (but are still looking to save the pennies), the **Surprise Café** on the east side of town by Brodies dishes up basic Belizean/American snacks and sweet treats, while **Piccini's** on Constitution Drive offers a nice range of cheap(ish) Italian meals. For Chinese cuisine, **Guang Dong** on Constitution Drive, opposite the Belize Bank, has a large and inexpensive menu.

Bull Frog Inn, 25 Half Moon Ave, t 822 3425. This is a popular, dependable eatery and a particular favourite with government employees. Its varied menu features a range of Belizean and regional specialities, including conch soup and *escabeche* (a cold concoction of marinated fish).

Caladium, Market Square, t 822 2754. With most dishes coming in at under US$10, this is frequented as much by locals as tourists. The menu is made up mainly of Belizean and Central American staples. They also serve very good breakfasts, burgers and fresh juices. Look out for the value specials.

Pepper's Pizza, 86 Ring Rd, t 822 0666. Good, reliable pizza place with an outdoor seating area on the east part of the ring road. Takeaway service too.

Arts, Entertainment and Nightlife in Belmopan

As most of the city's workers commute to their offices, leaving Belmopan at the end of the day to return to their homes in Belize City and other regional towns, there's not much of a nightlife scene here. Still, there are a few places you can go once evening falls. The bar of the **Bull Frog Inn** (*see* above) stays open till midnight every night, and has karaoke on Thurs and live music on Fri. Concerts and film screenings are also regularly put on at the **George Price Centre for Peace and Development**, Price Centre Road (t 822 1054, *www.gpcbelize.com*; *open Mon, Wed, Thurs, Fri 8–6, Tues 8–8*).

Around Belmopan

Guanacaste National Park

Guanacaste National Park open 8–4.30; adm US$5

Guanacaste National Park is pretty easy to find. The entrance lies on the Western Highway, a few miles north of Belmopan, at the T-junction where the Western Highway connects with the Humming- bird Highway. Despite covering over 50 acres of tropical forest filled with all manner of flora and fauna, the park, which is managed by the Belize Audubon Society (*www.belizeaudubon.org*), is named after a single inhabitant – a huge, and very grand-looking guanacaste tree, which stands over 130ft (39m) high, has a diameter of over six feet (1.8m), and is crowned with a decades-old collection of epiphytes, bromeliads and vines dangling regally from its mighty branches. It's a relatively compact reserve with just 2 miles of well-maintained self-guided trails to explore – alongside which labels have been erected allowing you to identify some of the resident plants – as well as a swimming hole (don't forget your swimsuit) and picnic areas. If you're lucky you might catch sight of some of the wildlife that lives among the park's cohune and broadleaf forest,

Where to Stay at Guanacaste

★ Belize Jungle Dome >

Belize Jungle Dome, Mile 47, Western Highway, **t** 822 2124, **f** 822 2155, *www.belizejungledome.com* ($$$$; US$105). Neighbouring the Banana Bank Lodge, this is a small, stylish, peaceful lodge set against a stunning rainforest backdrop. Family-run (by British ex-professional footballer Andy Hunt and his Dutch wife), it has just three rooms – one standard and two spacious suites – that can accommodate up to five guests. All the rooms have pool-side terraces, a/c, TVs, fans and wireless Internet access. Meals, which feature fruit and vegetables grown organically in the Dome's garden, are served on the pool terrace and at the Tree Top Café, which looks over the pool and surrounding jungle. Various tours and activities are offered, including yoga, Pilates and, for the more adventurous, cave-tubing and bike-riding.

Banana Bank Lodge and Equestrian Centre, Mile 47 Western Highway, **t** 820 2020, **f** 820 2026, *bbl@starband.net*, *www.bananabank.com* ($$$/$$$$$; US$77/130 shared/private bathrooms). Occupying some 4,000 acres of land (no less than half of which is primary growth rainforest) on the banks of the Belize River, this ranch and lodge is owned and managed by John Carr and his wife, the local artist Carolyn Carr, whose work is shown in an on-site gallery (as well as at galleries countrywide). Accommodation is cheerful and comfortable with brightly coloured cabanas with private bathrooms, as well as 'budget' rooms with shared bathrooms. Facilities include Internet access, a swimming pool and a good restaurant. There's even a small Mayan ruin on site. The lodge also has its own equestrian centre catering for riders of all levels, as well as a small zoo, in which live a range of exotic birds, two spider monkeys and a rescued pet jaguar called Tika. Interestingly, Tika is probably the most photographed cat in Belize, starring in many Belizean websites and tourist brochures, not to mention untold numbers of tourist snaps (but then, he is a lot easier to photograph than a wild one).

which includes howler monkeys and over 120 species of birds (the red-lored parrot and the blue-crowned motmot among them). Opposite the park entrance is the **National Agricultural Show Ground**, where events are often staged and market stalls set up.

South from Belmopan along the Hummingbird Highway

② The Hummingbird Highway

As seems entirely appropriate for such a prettily named road, the Hummingbird Highway offers some of the most picturesque driving in the country. Past Belmopan, the vegetation becomes increasingly greener, thicker, lusher and generally more tropical looking as the jungle begins to crowd in on either side of the highway. The road rises over and around a series of hills and passes over a number of rickety bridges as its meanders its way south, with all the while the Maya Mountains coming into clearer focus in the distance.

St Herman's Blue Hole National Park

St Herman's Blue Hole National Park
open 8–4.30; adm US$4 (park), US$10 (cave)

The country's other slightly less famous 'blue hole' is located around 12 miles (19km) from Belmopan at this 575-acre national park managed by the Belize Audubon Society. The '**Blue Hole**' is actually a water-filled karst sinkhole feeding into the Sibun River, its deep shadowy colour the result of the water's depth – around 25 feet (7.6m). Despite its depth, and the coldness of the water, it's become a popular swimming spot in recent years. Access is via a set of steps and there are changing rooms on site.

The park's other principal attraction is **St Herman's Cave**, a 1½-mile (2.4km) hike from the Hole. Though you are allowed to enter the chamber alone (bring a flashlight or rent one from the visitor centre), you must have a guide with you if you wish to explore any further than 300 yards (275m) in. Within the cave, several pieces of pottery and other Maya remains dating back to the Classic period have been found (and subsequently removed). It's believed that pots were placed to catch the clean water dripping from the roof. Above ground level, there are also plenty of marked nature trails through the park's stretches of forest, an observation tower for spotting the local wildlife, and dedicated picnic areas.

Five Blues Lake National Park

This 4,200-acre national park is run and maintained by the local community of Margaret's Village. Although the turn-off to the park is located on mile 32 of the Hummingbird Highway (by the village), and thus accessible by bus from Belmopan, the actual park entrance lies another 3.5 miles along the road, beyond the limit of public transport. Hiring a bike in the village might be a worthwhile investment (or you could try asking for a lift from a friendly local), if you are without your own vehicle; otherwise, you'll have to walk. Within the park, there are around 3 miles of trails (you can pick up a map or hire a guide at the village), taking you through areas of forest and past the Five Blues Lake itself, so named because its waters are supposed to reflect five different shades. Swimming and canoeing are allowed on the lake (there are changing facilities) and there's a picnic area. Tents can be pitched near the entrance for US$2.50 (per person). You can also contact the community directly (*fiveblues@hotmail.com, www.5blueslake.org*) if you're interested in arranging a homestay in the village.

Ian Anderson's Caves Branch Adventure Company and Jungle Lodge

Canadian-born Ian Anderson has been running adventure expeditions in Belize for around 12 years from his home at Caves Branch. Indeed, he largely pioneered caving tours in this country, now one of Belize's most popular activities. All his guides are highly trained, which is just as well as some of the tours on offer here are a touch on the dangerous side. Activities range from the merely challenging – cave-tubing at nearby river caves (US$95) – to the much more daunting 'Black Hole Drop', which consists of a rappel

Where to Stay at Caves Branch

If you really feel like getting active, you could book a few days at the company's on site lodge, which is located smack bang in the middle of the jungle.

Here, you can opt to rough it in budget cabanas (US$98), bunkrooms (US$15) or tents (US$5), but you'll have to make do with shared facilities, which include outdoor, screened warm water showers (although the setting is so stunning beneath the jungle canopy that this hardly feels like much of a hardship) or, if you feel your weary bones need a bit of pampering after a hard day's rappelling, you can upgrade to a bungalow with private bathroom, ceiling fan and window screen (US$138) or suite (all of the above, but larger, US$158).

A range of honeymoon (for active newlyweds, obviously), family and adventure packages is available.

★ Ian Anderson's Jungle Lodge >

down into a 300ft (90m) pitch-dark sinkhole (US$105). And if that doesn't sound intense enough for you, four-day jungle treks and survival training courses are also available. There are a few slightly more leisurely activities to choose from (with the emphasis on the 'slightly'), including kayaking, bird-watching, mountain-biking and zip-lining (US$75), but this is a place primarily aimed at the sort of people who feel that a day spent without an intense adrenaline rush is a day wasted. Lazy scaredy-cats need not apply.

The Western Highway to San Ignacio

The well-maintained Western Highway follows the Belize River southwest from Roaring Creek (near the Western Hwy/Hummingbird Hwy junction) for just over 22 miles to San Ignacio, western Belize's major town. On the way, the road passes through a number of towns, which will involve slowing for numerous speed humps (be careful: many are not properly signposted). Various areas of interest lie off this stretch of highway. The first is the pretty (and prettily named) Creole village of Teakettle, from where a rough road leads south to the **Tapir Mountain Nature Reserve** (which, unfortunately, is currently not open to the general public), **Pook's Hill Lodge** (see p.153) and **Actun Tunichil Muknal Cave**. Further along the highway sits the village of Georgeville, from where the Chiquibul Road heads south towards **Barton Creek Cave**, the **Green Hills Butterfly Ranch**, **Mountain Pine Ridge** (see p.166), and **Caracol** (see p.171). Just east of Georgeville, a right turn heads north from the Western Highway up towards the Mennonite village of **Spanish Lookout**.

Actun Tunichil Muknal Cave (The Cave of the Crystal Sepulchre)

Unfortunately a trip to these caves is an option open only to fit and adventurous people, who can swim and are happy getting completely soaked. What happens is this – after an initial 45-minute

Xibalba – Caves and the Mayan Underworld

The Maya were fascinated by caves. Almost every cave that's been discovered in Belize – and the country's landscape is absolutely riddled with them – has revealed some evidence of a prior Mayan presence, usually in the form of pottery or burials. The Maya believed these caves were entrances to the underworld and the realm of gods, a place they called Xibalba (pronounced she-bahl-*bah*), which roughly translates as 'Place of Fear'. It's an appropriate name. To the Maya, caves were obviously scary, sacred places where the divine had to be appeased with blood-letting and sacrificial rituals – the remains of which (human skeletons, altars, weapons) often litter the cavern floor. When visiting the country's caves, take special care to avoid disturbing any of these ancient relics. Resist the temptation to touch any of the cave formations or artefacts, and watch your footing to make sure you are not stepping on something you shouldn't.

trek, some of which will be through ankle-deep creeks, you reach the cave opening, where you don helmets with headlamps. Now comes the difficult part, a swim across the cave river (around 20ft deep) followed by a climb up a steep passage until you finally reach your goal, a series of truly spectacular cathedral-like caverns, the sight of which will hopefully make you forget your former discomfort. The cave's floors are littered with Mayan remains – pottery, blades etc. – that have lain undisturbed since placed here centuries before. There are also a number of rather more sinister-looking human skeletal remains, the most amazing of which being a shimmering female skeleton encrusted with calcite. Due to the importance and fragility of the cave's contents, access is only granted to those in the company of a registered guide from one of just two tour companies. Tours cost around US$80, including food and transport, and can be arranged (only) through **Mayawalk Tours** (t 824 3070, *www.maya walk.com*) or **Pacz Tours** (t 804 2267, *www.pacztours.net*), both of which are based in San Ignacio. Remember to take a change of clothes and a waterproof bag for your camera.

Barton Creek Cave

⭐ Barton
Creek Cave
*off Mile 4
Chiquibul Road*

Much easier to access than Actun Tunichil, and thus a lot more popular, Barton Creek Cave is certainly a favourite with tour companies, and was evidently well used by the Maya as well. Many ceramic pots and human bones have been found here (some of which remain *in situ*), indicating that the cave may have been used for some sort of ceremonial purpose. You explore the cave via its waterway, drifting along in either a canoe or an inner tube for about a mile (before turning back). Along the way, you'll pass some stunning illuminated stalagmite and stalactite formations (which make the caverns appear quite magical) and past banks dotted with skeletal remains (which make them seem a bit scary). The whole thing is a bit like a sort of antique aquatic ghost train. Entry is around US$10. Most people visit as part of an organized tour, although it is possible to rent canoes (or inner tubes), torches and a (compulsory) guide at the entrance. The bumpy drive from

Where to Stay on the way to San Ignacio

Pook's Hill Lodge, 5m from Teakettle village, t/f 820 2017, www.pookshill lodge.com ($$$$$; US$162). Arranged around a Maya plaza in the depths of the lush jungle, this peaceful lodge has attractive thatched cabanas with private bathrooms and fans. Trails lead through the surrounding 300 acres of forest, which can be explored either on your own or (for a fee) in the company of Pook's own resident naturalist guide, who can help you to identify some of the abundant wildlife, which include numerous species of bird (it's a particularly popular destination with bird-watchers, and has a library of bird books). The nearby Roaring River is great for swimming or tubing.

Caesar's Place Guest House, Mile 60 Western Highway (Georgeville), t 824 3296, f 824 3449, www.blackrocklodge. com/caesars/guesthouse.htm ($$$; US$50). Owned by the same family as the Black Rock River Lodge (see p.162), Caesar's has simple rooms, all with private bathrooms and fans. Meals served in the guesthouse restaurant are pretty decent, but cost extra (US$7 breakfast/ lunch, US$14 dinner). The complex also contains the Caesar's Place Gift Shop, one of the area's best source of souvenirs, with a good range of carvings and books. Internet access also available.

Georgeville to the cave entrance along the Chiquibul Road will take about half an hour. There's no public transport.

Green Hills Butterfly Ranch and Botanical Collections

Green Hills Butterfly Ranch
Mile 8 Chiquibul Road, merman@btl.net; open 8–4.30; adm US$4 (min. 2 people)

Run by Jan Meerman and Tineke Boomsma, who are known throughout the country for their environmental and ecological work, the Green Hills Butterfly Ranch gives visitors the chance to view all stages of the butterfly life cycle, and to get up close to flocks of the fluttering colourful creatures in the flight room. The entry fee includes an hour-long tour with a knowledgeable guide, who will regale you with a whole range of butterfly facts, and access to the surrounding tropical gardens.

San Ignacio

⭐ San Ignacio

Scruffy, potholed, bustling, cheery San Ignacio, on the banks of the Macal River, is (with apologies to poor old neglected Belmopan) western Belize's main tourist hub. With its twin town, Santa Elena, just across the river, it boasts the second-largest urban population (just under 20,000) in Belize, after Belize City. It's an intense, friendly little place with a heavy Spanish influence (as you'd expect from somewhere just a few miles from Guatemala) and a diverse mix of cultures, where there always seems to be something going on – a market, a concert, a football match, a religious meeting. There are few formal attractions within the town, but plenty of tour operators (who can be utilized for exploring the numerous attractions of the surrounding area,) plus a good collection of hotels and restaurants. Burns Avenue, Hudson Street and Waight's Avenue are the main streets for lodgings and food.

Getting to San Ignacio

By bus: Novelo's buses (but *see* p.66) run around every half-hour from Belize City along the Western Highway to Benque Viejo del Carmen, stopping en route in San Ignacio. Passengers are dropped off on Burns Avenue.

By car: Although finding Santa Elena, San Ignacio's twin town, is pretty easy – just follow the Western Highway till you reach it – finding your way from here to San Ignacio can be a little bit more tricky, with signs suddenly disappearing, roads being blocked off and one-way streets bringing you back to where you started. The easiest way in, when you arrive at Santa Elena, is to take the first (and only) sign right for 'low lying bridge'. Follow the road to the end and turn left. Now take the first right, which will take you down a hill to the river and the wooden bridge. Once across the bridge, follow the road as it bears right. You'll see a sports stadium directly ahead of you. Turn left here for the centre of the town. If you want to pass through the town, turn right. Go straight past Macal River Park. Follow the road as it bears left. Continue past the cemetery, after which the road will bear left becoming Survey Street, more commonly known in the area as Double Street (you'll see why). This finishes up at the corner of Old Benque Road (which back leads into town and to Hawkesworth Suspension Bridge back to Santa Elena) and Buena Vista Road, which heads out to the hotels on the town's outskirts.

Locally, the town is known simply as Cayo, meaning 'island' in Spanish (from which the words 'cayes' is also derived), a reference to the area's somewhat isolated position, flanked to the west by the Mopan River and to the east by the Macal River. Entrance to the town is from Santa Elena (which lies on the Western Highway) via a bridge across the Macal River, where at weekends you'll often see families picnicking on the banks, and swimming, canoeing and even washing their clothes in the water. There are in fact two bridges linking Santa Elena and San Ignacio. The first, a simple wooden affair, serves traffic travelling in both directions, while further south, the more sturdy, metal Hawkesworth Suspension Bridge only serves traffic travelling from San Ignacio to Santa Elena.

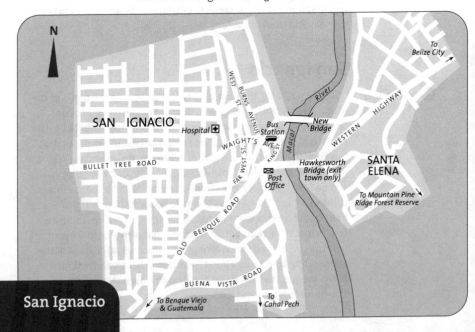

San Ignacio

San Ignacio may today form the centre of western Belize's tourist industry, but for centuries it was one of the country's lonelier outposts: where, in the 16th and 17th centuries, the Maya held out against Spanish incursions; where, in the 18th century, British Baymen came searching for mahogany; and where, in the late 19th century, Belizeans came to tap sapodilla trees for chicle to export to Britain (where it would be turned into chewing gum). It was a region where men came to undertake lonely, independent pursuits far removed from mainstream society. That all changed in the 1930s when the Western Highway was built, at a stroke reducing the time it took to travel from San Ignacio to the then capital, Belize City, from several gruelling days (sailing down the river) to several hours.

Cahal Pech

Cahal Pech
t 824 4236; open 6–6;
adm US$5

Perched high above San Ignacio sits Cahal Pech, a small, compact, medium-interest Mayan site. The name translates as the rather unappealing 'place of ticks', and was coined in the 1950s when cattle (riddled with ticks) grazed in the area. Today, the cows and their attendant parasites are long gone, although the dusty 15-minute uphill hike to the site from town may have you wishing you had a host of your own to cling to. Thankfully, the site itself is quite easy to get around, with all the buildings lying close together. And none of the structures is of an overwhelming size, so you won't be required to put in one of the thigh-burning ascents that characterize visits to some of the region's other Mayan sites. In fact, you could regard your visit to Cahal Pech as a sort of primer for those more challenging ruins. In total seven plazas, and 34 structures (including two ball courts and a couple of modestly sized pyramids) have been discovered, dating from around 900 BC–AD 800, when Cahal Pech would have been a significant, if not dominant, regional centre. The lack of any truly grand structures, plus the density of the surrounding woodland, which blocks the views out over the area, means that the site lacks the 'wow factor' of other places, particularly Xunantunich and Caracol. Still, it's a pretty, serene place and a good deal of work has gone into the restoration of the ruins. There's a **visitor centre** and **museum** by the entrance (where you buy your ticket), where you can see a scale model of the site, read histories of its construction and see a collection of artefacts found both here and at other regional ruins. To get to the site on foot, follow the Buena Vista or Old Benque Road south and take the dirt track on the left, located just before the Texaco petrol station. If travelling by car, this stretch of road may require a 4WD in poor weather.

Green Iguana Project and Medicinal Jungle Trail

Green Iguana
Project
San Ignacio Resort
Hotel, 18 Buena Vista St,
t 824 2034/2125,
www.sanignaciobelize.
com/iguana.html;
adm US$5.45

This conservation project was set up a few years ago by the San Ignacio Resort Hotel to try and arrest the decline of the country's green iguanas, numbers of which have plummeted in recent times. The hotel programme breeds, hatches and raises baby lizards in a protected environment, before releasing them into the wild when they reach a year old. You can tour the breeding centre – and see the scaly beasts close up – as part of an hour-long tour, that also includes a trek along the hotel's medicinal trail which is laid out through 14 acres of jungle.

Tourist Information in San Ignacio

There's no official tourist information office, but **Eva's Restaurant** (22 Burns Ave) has for some time, under the patronage of its friendly and knowledgeable owner Bob Jones, been the town's main unofficial source of information, for locals and visitors alike, its walls adorned with advertisements and posters. Unfortunately, at the time of writing, Eva's was up for sale, but not yet sold, so it remains to be seen whether the legacy will be continued. Still, it may be worth a minute of your time to take a quick look. Otherwise, look out for flyers and ads in the town's hotels and restaurants (Café Cayo has a decent collection of leaflets and notices).

Services in San Ignacio

Banks: Atlantic Bank, t 824 2596/2347; Belize Bank, t 824 2031; Scotia Bank, t 824 2347. All are located at the southern end of Burns Ave and open Mon–Thurs 8–1, Fri 8–4.30.
Bike rental: Max's Place, Burns Ave, t 804 0829.
Books: The Green Dragon on Hudson St has a small collection of books (open Mon–Sat 8–8); The Angelus Press, JNC Mall 3rd Floor, t 824 4474.
Hospitals: San Ignacio Hospital, off Waight's Ave, t 824 2066; La Loma Luz Hospital, in Santa Elena, t 824 2087 (a private hospital with 24hr emergency services).
Internet: Green Dragon, Hudson St; Tradewinds, Hudson St (access for around US$1.5 per hour).
Laundry: Martha's Guest House Laundry, 10 West St, t 824 3647 (service washes for US$3 per load, drying US$3 per load).

Pharmacies: There's a pharmacy on Hudson St, opposite Tradewinds Internet.
Post office: Hudson St, t 824 2049.
Supermarkets: Celina's Superstore, 43 Burns Ave, t 824 2972; Hudson Supermarket, Hudson St.
Telephones: BTL, Eve St, t 824 2049.

Tour Operators in San Ignacio

San Ignacio is home to a number of tour operators offering a variety of activities – river trips, cave-tubing, horse-riding, mountain-biking, rappelling, etc. – as well as tours to all the major local attractions, the Mountain Pine Ridge Reserve, Xunantunich, Caracol, Cahal Pech, and day trips across the border to the Guatemalan Mayan site of Tikal.
Cayo Adventure, t 824 3246, *www.cayoadventure.com*.
David's Adventure Tours, Savannah St, t 804 3674, *www.davidsadventure tours.com*.
Mayawalk Tours, 19 Burns Ave, t 824 3070, *www.mayawalk.com*.
Pacz Tours, 4 Far West St, t 804 2267, *www.pacztours.net*.

Shopping in San Ignacio

Every Saturday morning a **market** is held in the square by the bus terminal to the north of the town, where you can browse fresh locally farmed produce, as well as a small selection of crafts/gifts. There are also a few second-hand stalls. The café-cum-health store, **Green Dragon**, on Hudson Street has a nice range of Belizean-made gifts, books and beauty products, as does **Caesar's Place Gift Shop** (*see* p.153) on the Western Highway.

Events in San Ignacio

La Ruta Maya Belize River Challenge: Once upon a time, a boat trip of several days represented the only means of getting from San Ignacio to Belize City. Today, with the two cities linked by the Western Highway, it's an option rarely taken up by locals, except as a 'bit of fun' during the first week of March (to coincide with the Baron Bliss celebrations), when a multi-day canoe race is held. Everyone is welcome to enter the event, with participants divided into a variety of different categories, according to age, sex and experience. However, before you rush to sign up, remember that, fun or no, this is still a pretty gruelling experience, involving no less than 170 miles of solid paddling up to Belize City. Still, it's all in a good cause, with the proceeds from the race donated to organizations working to preserve the region's environment.

Where to Stay in San Ignacio

In and around San Ignacio, there's a pretty strict demarcation between budget accommodation – reasonably priced hotels and guesthouses – which can usually be found right in the centre of town, and the larger, more expensive resort-style places, which tend to be located on the outskirts. Some of the more up-market places are very well-equipped, particularly those on the Chial Road (see p.162), and thus ideal for tourists planning long stays or families, although some of the places in the immediate vicinity of the town are a bit disappointing and a touch overpriced.

Luxury ($$$$$)–Expensive ($$$$)
San Ignacio Resort Hotel, Buena Vista Rd (½ mile from town), t US 1-800 822 3274, t 824 2034/2125, f 824 2134, www.sanignaciobelize.com (US$110). The most up-market and best-value choice in the immediate environs of the town, this has 24 spacious, comfortable rooms with balconies (and good views), as well as a gift shop, a restaurant, a swimming pool, a basketball court and a new tennis court. The hotel occupies 14 acres of forested grounds, on which a Medicinal Jungle Trail has been laid out, and operates a green iguana captive breeding programme (see pp.155–6).

Windy Hill Resort, Mile 69 Western Highway, t 824 2017, f 824 3080, www.windyhillresort.com (US$185). If its rooms were around US$100 cheaper, then the Windy Hill Resort, just outside San Ignacio, would be a decent, convenient, mid-range choice. As it is, it's just convenient. Its wooden cottages – which come with rather shabby bathrooms, twin beds, a/c, balconies and hammocks – are rather spartan. To get the best out of the hotel, you'll have to make full and repeated use of the facilities, which include a swimming pool, a bar (with pool table and table tennis), a rather scrubby medicinal trail, a small fitness centre, a restaurant (set meals by prior arrangement only), an equestrian centre (the horses graze on the adjacent field) and a tour desk, which can arrange trips to local attractions.

Moderate ($$$)–Inexpensive ($$)
Cahal Pech Village Resort, t 824 3740, f 824 222, www.cahalpech.com (US$79). The Western Highway seems to be lined almost along its entire length by billboards advertising this hotel, which make it out to be some sort of modern Shangri La. The truth is rather different – it's a mid-range, mid-quality hotel perched on a hill next to the mid-interest ruins of the same name (see p.155). There are two types of accommodation on offer here – thatched cabanas and motel-style rooms in a main block. Neither is particularly outstanding, although all have the requisite private bathrooms and a/c. The rooms have balconies, and those on the top floor good views out over the town and hotel garden (where fruit is laid out to attract the local birdlife), but are badly soundproofed, which is a bit of a problem with tour groups marching in and out throughout the day. Additional facilities include a swimming pool and a large refectory-style, open-sided restaurant.

The Log Cab Inn, Mile 68 Western Highway, t 824 3367, f 824 2289, www.logcabinns-belize.com (US$65). Situated a mile out of town in 45 acres of hillside flora, this relaxed resort has 12 spacious 'rustic' mahogany cabins, all with two beds, private bathrooms, coffee makers and fans. Additional facilities include a swimming pool, gift shop and restaurant, which serves reasonable (and reasonably priced) meals.

Martha's Guest House, 10 West St, t 824 3647, f 824 2917, *www.marthas belize.com* (US$40–45/55 fan/a/c). Martha's, right in the centre of town, offers a range of inviting, homely rooms to suit different budgets. The most expensive is the First Lady Suite (double US$75, quadruple US$95), which has a kitchenette and a veranda with views of the mountains. There is also a Laundromat on site and a popular restaurant downstairs (particularly with ex-pats who congregate here throughout the day, *see* p.159).

Midas Tropical Resort, Branch Mouth Rd, t 824 3172/3203, f 824 4845, *www. midasbelize.com* (US$39). A 5min walk north from town brings you to this small, basic and pretty good value river-side lodge. There are 13 rooms to choose from, made up of a mixture of cabanas and cottages, all with private bathrooms, hot water and fans. Facilities are minimal, although there is a *palapa* restaurant serving up decent (and decently priced) local dishes, and the adjacent Macal River makes up for lack of swimming pool. Camping on the grounds is allowed for about US$5.

Casa Blanca Guest House, 10 Burns Ave, t 824 080, *bettyguerroo1@yahoo. com, www.casablancaguesthouse.com* (US$37.50). This friendly little guesthouse in a central (but relatively quiet) location, offers clean, pleasant rooms with private bathrooms, cable TV and fans (some have a/c, but you'll need to book in advance). The communal areas include a kitchen where guests can prepare their meals (and take advantage of the complimentary tea and coffee) and a roof terrace overlooking the town.

Budget ($)
Hi-Et Guest House, 12 West St, t 824 2828, *thehiet@yahoo.com* (US$10–20).

The Hi-Et occupies a large wooden family home and offers small, basic, clean rooms (some with private bathrooms, most with shared). The various communal areas are a great place to meet fellow budget travellers. It's popular, so book ahead.

Pacz Guest House, 4 Far West St, t/f 824 4538, *www.paczguesthouse. com* (US$12.50/20 shared/private bathroom). Nice little guesthouse with five simple rooms – three with en-suite bathrooms, two with shared, all with fans. There's a handy book exchange on site, as well as a pleasant sitting area to chill out, watch TV and make friends.

Rosa's Hotel, 65 Hudson St, t 804 226, *rosashotel@yahoo.com* (US$20). The rooms at Rosa's all come with private bathrooms, fans (or a/c) and a complimentary continental breakfast, but do vary in size rather. If this bothers you, ask to see what you're getting before committing. Discounts available for long stays.

Tropicool Hotel, 30 Burns Ave, t 824 302 (US$20). The Tropicool has simple, basic rooms with shared bathrooms for budget guests, plus three pleasant cabins with private facilities and cable TV aimed at a more selective, mid-range clientele. Inside the main building there is a helpful bulletin board and a small gift shop, while outside there's a leafy garden. Bikes are available to hire.

Camping
Inglewood Camping Grounds, Mile 68.25 Western Highway, t/f 824 3555/ 4589, *www.inglewoodcamping grounds.com*. Large camping ground just off the highway that is suitable for RVs (water and electricity hook-ups are available) and tents (US$7 per person per night). *Palapas* are available to provide respite from the midday sun.

Eating Out in San Ignacio

Central San Ignacio has a good selection of low-priced cafés and restaurants with a number of different cuisines represented including, of course, Belizean, as well as American,

Indian and Chinese (in fact, there are a number of Chinese restaurants).

If self-catering, you should investigate the **market** on Saturday mornings (behind the bus terminal), a good source of snacks, fruit, vegetables and other fresh local produce.

Café Cayo, Burns Ave, t 823 2709. Café Cayo is a stylish little bistro offering reasonably priced Italian cuisine, a fully-stocked bar and Internet access.

Café Sol, West St. Good coffee and healthy eats (pastas, salads, soy burgers) with an emphasis on vegetarian dishes at this decent backstreet café.

Chingo's Bar and Grill, Burns Ave, t 608 6932. A laid-back little place, Chingo's menu is made up of the usual Belizean/American fare – steak sandwiches (US$4), burgers (US$4), burritos (US$6) served up in a pleasant, leafy little courtyard. It's one of the few places in town to open on Sunday afternoons.

Green Dragon, 8 Hudson St. Pleasant little café occupying a distinctive orange building in the town centre, serving a range of good imported coffees, cakes, smoothies and local ice cream. Internet access is also provided.

Erva's, 4 Far West St. Located next to Pacz, Erva's is open all day, dishing up full breakfasts (US$5), pancakes (US$2.50) and waffles in the morning, and a whole variety of dishes – including rice and beans (US$4), steaks, chops, burgers, fish dishes, burritos (US$3), pizzas and salads – for lunch and dinner.

Hannah's Restaurant, 5 Burns Ave, t 822 3014. Hannah's menu of organic Belizean, Southeast Asian and Indian cuisine, with plenty of vegetarian options, make it one of the town centre's more gourmet choices, although with most dishes coming in at US$10, it's not too expensive. Also open for breakfast.

Martha's Restaurant, 10 West St, t 824 3647. Popular local meeting spot (particularly with ex-pats), the café of Martha's Guest House serves a wide menu of Belizean, Mayan, creole and international cuisine, featuring regular specials and vegetarian options – pizzas, *garnaches*, burritos, seafood, burgers and more. If possible try to get a table in the shaded courtyard rather than the stark interior.

Maxim's, 23 Far West St. A very popular Chinese restaurant located on the corner of Waight's Ave and West St, with a good reputation for value and cuisine. Locals flock to this one for takeaways on Sundays.

Pop's Restaurant, West St. Popular with locals, this rather basic-looking café serves large, filling (and above all cheap) breakfasts all day (US$4–5), as well as a range of quite decent ice creams.

The Royal Indian, corner of Waight's Ave and Far West St. Local favourite, this little air-conditioned restaurant serves spicy hot curries and rice dishes for lunch and dinner.

Serendib, Burns Ave. Alongside the usual steaks, burgers and rice and beans, which have been added to the menu to assuage local tastes, are a range of spicy Sri Lankan curries. *Open from 4pm Sun.*

Entertainment and Nightlife in San Ignacio

The scene here isn't really at all bad, and certainly the best the Cayo District has to offer. Though it's hardly a case of wall-to-wall clubs and bars, there is a fair bit of choice for those who want something a bit livelier than a chat over a cool beer in a restaurant.

Live music events are normally posted on boards around town (cafés, hotels and lampposts usually), but for weekend DJs check out the **Roomba Room Nightclub** located behind the ice-cream parlour on the corner of Buena Vista Rd and the Old Benque Rd or see what's going on at the **Pitpan Tavern** (formerly known as Coconutz). **Hodes** and **Champions Sports Bar** can also get quite lively.

If you're feeling lucky, the **Princess Gaming Salon** is situated next to the San Ignacio Resort Hotel (you'll have to show your passport).

Around San Ignacio

El Pilar

El Pilar
adm US$5

Around 5 miles northeast of San Ignacio is the small village of Bullet Tree Falls, a few miles beyond which lies El Pilar, one of Belize's largest Mayan sites. By way of comparison, it's over twice the size of Xunantunich, itself a pretty big site, encompassing over 100 acres, some of it in Guatemalan territory. Unfortunately, as archaeological work on the site only began in the early 1990s, under the direction of the University of California Santa Barbara, there's not a great deal to see as yet. There are plans to excavate the site more fully and turn it, and the surrounding jungle, into a sort of combined Maya/nature reserve, but these are still at the preliminary stages. Despite this, and the difficulty of getting here (there's no public transport), El Pilar is still worth a visit. Welcoming far fewer tourists than many other ruins in the district, it's a peaceful place with marked environmental trails through lush surrounding vegetation (the tranquillity means that you stand a good chance of seeing some of the area's resident wildlife), picnic sites and good elevated views of the area. Furthermore the deep jungle, which covers much of the site, gives it a romantic, Indiana Jones-esque allure.

Archaeologists believe that El Pilar was occupied from around 500 BC–AD 1000, during which time it managed to amass over 20 plazas and 70 major structures, some of which stand over 70ft (21m) tall. You can find out up-to-date information on the project and see a scale model of the site (and buy some locally produced gifts and crafts) at the **Be Pukte Cultural Center**, run by 'Amigos de El Pilar' (Friends of the El Pilar Society, *www.interconnection.org/elpilar*) in Bullet Tree Falls, on Bullet Tree Road (*open Fri, Sat, Sun and Mon 9–3*).

Where to Stay and Eat in Bullet Tree Falls

Quiet little Bullet Tree Falls, the nearest village to El Pilar, has a surprisingly large range of accommodation to choose from, much of it a good deal cheaper than what you'll find around San Ignacio. And there's the added bonus that many of the places lie just a couple of steps from the river (and the prospect of cooling dips).

Cohune Palms, t 609 2738/600 7508, *www.cohunepalms.com* ($$$; US$45/55 shared/private bathroom). The Cohune Palms offers nicely decorated cabanas with ceiling fans (a choice of private or shared bathrooms), as well as a large loft cabana that sleeps up to five people (something of a bargain at US$60). There's also a good thatched-roof restaurant, and an art shop selling a wide range of jewellery, carvings, books, music and other local products.

Parrot Nest Lodge, t 820 4058, *parrot@btl.net*, *www.parrot-nest.com* ($$$: US$40–50). One of the area's best and longest-established choices, the Parrot Nest offers tree houses and thatched cabins (with shared bathrooms) and decent home cooking in a peaceful leafy environment. A wealth of birdlife (including the eponymous parrots) inhabit the surrounding trees. There are good views from the dining-room veranda. Guided horse tours to El Pilar can be arranged.

Iguana Junction, t 820 4021, *www.iguanajunction.com* ($$; US$30/40 shared/private bathrooms). Clean, wooden cabins and guest rooms located close to the river. Freshly cooked meals are served three times a day, inside or out.

Maya Rooms & Restaurant, t 608 2208, f 605 3569, *www.mayarooms.com* ($; US$15–20). The 'Mayan' theming of this friendly little budget place is pretty all-encompassing, taking in everything from the rooms (traditional thatched cabanas) and décor (authentic Maya fabrics) to the restaurant menu, which features tamales and corn juice. Camping is also available.

Along the Western Highway towards Guatemala

The Chial Road

Around 5 miles (8km) southwest of San Ignacio (just past mile 70) is the turning for the Chial Road (be careful not to miss the sign, which is on the right-hand side of the road). This bumpy track leads to several places of interest, including the Belize Botanical Gardens, as well as some of the region's most up-market and best-equipped lodges.

Belize Botanical Gardens

Belize Botanical Gardens
Chial Road (adjacent to DuPlooys Lodge), t 824 3101, www.belizebotanic.org; open 7–5; adm US$2.50

DuPlooys are justly proud of their botanical gardens, which provide a fascinating overview of the country's rich and abundant (not to mention supremely colourful) flora. Two miles of trails traverse the 45-acre site, taking you on a tour past all manner of tropical fruit trees, towering palms and various exotic flowers. There's also a Native Orchid House (containing over 100 species), a couple of ponds that provide a home for a wide range of wildfowl and a 25ft/7.5m 'fire tower' providing bird's-eye views of the gardens. Self-guided tours are US$3.75, guided tours are US$7.50, while horseback tours, if you really want to explore the area in style, will set you back a not unreasonable US$35.

The Chaa Creek Natural History Centre and Blue Morpho Butterfly Farm

Chaa Creek Natural History Centre
adm US$5

The small Natural History Centre at Chaa Creek Lodge holds an eclectic, curiosity-shop-like collection of exhibits – Mayan items discovered in the vicinity, mounted insects as well as books, slides and scientific studies on the area. The real draw here, however, is the attached butterfly farm, where giant blue morpho butterflies are bred for commercial sale. You can watch all the stages of their intricate life cycle.

Where to Stay on the Chial Road

The Lodge at Chaa Creek >

The Lodge at Chaa Creek & Spa, Chial Rd (on banks of Macal River), t US 1-877 709 8708, t 824 2037, f 824 2501, *www.chaacreek.com* ($$$$$; US$210). Set in lush, neatly tended gardens (which give the place the look of a sort of eco golf course), on the banks of the Macal River, this is one of the region's top choices. The whitewashed thatched cabins are beautifully decorated with mahogany beds, pieces of original artwork and Mexican tiled floors. The larger suites have Jacuzzis and balconies overlooking the river (and cost a cool US$320), and there's a spa (*www.belizespa.com*), offering facials, massages and body wraps, and a pretty decent restaurant serving three-course Belizean-special dinners each night for US$26. A number of free activities are included in the room price – including tours of the Natural History Centre and Butterfly Farm, access to the Ix-Chel Rainforest Medicinal Trail, which adjoins the lodge, guided morning bird-watching, and use of canoes which can be used to paddle up and down the river – making it a good option for families with children to tire out (sorry, entertain). The lodge also operates its own stables.

DuPlooys Jungle Lodge >

DuPlooys Jungle Lodge, Chial Rd, t 824 3101, f 824 3301, *www.duplooys.com*. Another of the area's very grand lodges, DuPlooys is spread out over the side of a hill and offers a variety of accommodation options: spacious rooms with two queen-sized beds, private bathrooms and private screened porches (US$145); large bungalows that can sleep up to four, with king-sized beds, futons and private porches (US$185); and a very large two-storey house, La Casita, sleeping up to eight people with two wraparound verandas and a Jacuzzi (US$275). All of these are quiet, attractively decorated and provide easy access to the river with its sandy beach. A range of tours is offered to nearby attractions, including the lodge's own botanical gardens (*see* p.161).

Black Rock River Lodge, off Chial Rd, t 824 2341, f 824 3449, *blackrocklodge.com* ($$$/$$$$; US$50/95 shared/private bathrooms). Set on a 250-acre estate overlooking the Macal River, the Black Rock River Lodge is a rather pleasant, rather remote ecolodge offering decent, functional (but not particularly luxurious) cabanas. A good open-air dining room serves up dishes made from ingredients grown organically on site, and there are plenty of activities to choose from, including horse-riding, canoeing, tubing, bird-watching and caving, as well as sightseeing tours in the region.

Macal River Jungle Camp, *www.belizecamp.com* ($$$; US$55 per person). The budget wing of Chaa Creek lies separated from the more up-market cabins by a stretch of forest – it's around a 10min walkway. In contrast to the luxury and pampering available at the lodge, this is a more low-key, rough-and-ready affair, comprising a river-side 'camp' of 10 stilt-set *casitas* (small bungalows), each with two beds, private porches and shared bathrooms. Though it's a lot more rustic (and a good deal less private) than the lodge, this is still a pretty fancy form of camping, especially as guests have the use of many of the facilities of the main lodge, including the canoes and trails. The price includes breakfast and dinner in the camp's own thatched *palapa*.

On The Western Highway

Tropical Wings Nature Centre
Mile 71, Western Highway; open 9–5; adm US$2.50

Past the Chial Road turn-off, the Western Highway heads southeast down to the small village of San Jose Succotz. The main attraction here is the Mayan site of Xunantunich, one of the region's largest, although if you are in the area the Tropical Wings Nature Centre also provides a pleasant way of whiling away an hour or two. Occupying 22 acres of forest, the centre has landscaped gardens, on which feeders have been set up to attract hummingbirds, a medicinal garden, nature trails, a butterfly house and an interpretive centre with exhibits on birds, insects and ecology. There is also a snack bar and gift shop selling books and crafts.

Xunantunich

Xunantunich
open 8–5; adm US$5

This Mayan site's mouthful of a name (it's pronounced *shoo-**nahn**-too-netch*) means 'the Stone Lady', and was coined at the end of the 19th century when the ghostly apparition of a woman was apparently seen floating around the site, before mysteriously disappearing into the stone. She hasn't been seen since, but the name has stuck. The site is one of the most spectacular in the country, with several large structures rising imperiously over the grassy compound. The most prominent building is the mighty **'El Castillo' pyramid**, which at around 132ft (40m) tall, is still the second tallest man-made structure in the country (after Caracol). A series of steps leads up and around the building to the summit, from where there are great views of the region and over to Guatemala. Take care, if you're at all nervous about heights, as there are no guardrails at the top. The flanks of the pyramid bear intricate carved friezes (to be accurate, they actually bear intricate plaster copies of friezes, set protectively over the originals), representing the Sun God (Kinich Ahau), the Moon and Venus.

Finds from the site, as well as a scale model of the complex, are displayed in the rather good **visitor centre**, which also provides a neat overview of the history of Mayan occupation in this area. Xunantunich may have been inhabited from as far back as 400 BC, although most of the site's construction took place between AD 600 and 900, the late Classic Period, during which time the area thrived as a great ceremonial centre, maintaining close links with the even greater ceremonial centre of Caracol to the south. An earthquake in AD 900 is thought to have been the main cause of the site's ultimate abandonment, a process no doubt exacerbated by the widespread

Where to Stay near Xunantunich

Clarissa Falls, Mile 70 Western Highway, **t** 824 3916, *www.clarissafalls. com*. This family ranch's range of accommodation options include, in order of price: camping facilities (US$7.50); 10-bunk dormitories (US$15); cottages with private bathrooms (US$75); and large family-sized suites with two bedrooms, kitchenettes and private bathrooms that sleep up to four (US$175). There's also a thatched restaurant serving up good basic food, including a number of vegan and vegetarian options. Breakfasts are US$5, dinners around US$9.

The Trek Stop, Mile 71 Western Highway, **t** 823 2265, *www.thetrekstop. com* ($/$$; US$20/35 shared/private bathroom). Simple ecofriendly accommodation and camp ground (US$5 p/p) situated next to the Tropical Wings Nature Centre, offering single, double or group cabins with a choice of shared or private bathrooms. Internet access, a simple restaurant, a fully equipped kitchen and a lounge area are available to guests, and inner tubes, kayaks and bikes can be rented.

Getting to Xunantunich

Xunantunich may be one of the most accessible major Maya sites in the country, but it still lies beyond the reach of the public transport system. Getting to the site, by either car or ferry, will entail crossing the Mopan River at San Jose Succotz via an old-fashioned hand-cranked **ferry**. There is no official charge, although you may want to leave a tip on the way back (it's quite heavy work). It takes around a minute to cross the 20m span of water, from where it's a further mile hike up to the site entrance, or a quick drive if you have a car – the ferry can accommodate vehicles, one car at a time. The village of San Jose Succotz itself lies on the Western Highway 7m (11km) southeast of San Ignacio, from where there are frequent buses.

decline of lowland Mayan communities at this time, for reasons that are still as yet not fully understood. Hopefully, ongoing archaeological work by the Universities of California and Pennyslvania may provide a few more answers in the future. Snacks, drinks, picnic tables and toilet facilities are all available on site.

Benque Viejo del Carmen

This is the last Belizean town on the Western Highway before the border at Guatemala, 2km away. It's a relatively sleepy place with an understandably strong Spanish influence. Though good, regular public transport links make visiting easy enough, there isn't much reason to make a special trip unless you are planning to enter Guatemala. If making a connection here and at a loose end, there a **House of Culture** that holds regular exhibitions and lectures.

Tickets and information can also be picked up here for the **Poustinia Land Art Park**, which lies 2½ miles south of Benque Viejo del Carmen on the Hydro Road. This is a sort of outdoor art gallery (it describes itself as 'environmental art') comprising a series of installations made from organic materials placed along a network of trails and then left to return to nature. Visits are by appointment only and cost US$10, plus an extra US$25 for a guided tour.

A few miles past the park on the Hydro Road, at mile 8, is **Chechem Hah Cave** (it is signposted), the walls of which are adorned with paintings thought to be over 2,000 years old. A hike of around 45 minutes is required to get to the cave. The owner of the land, Mr Morales, only discovered the cave in 1999 and has since set up a little restaurant and a couple of cabanas for visitors. Members of the family will show you around if you are not part of a tour. There are also some lovely waterfalls with swimming holes in the area.

House of Culture
64 St Joseph Street,
t 823 2697

Poustinia Land Art Park
www.poustinia
online.org

Where to Stay in Benque Viejo

⭐ Mopan River Resort >

Mopan River Resort, Riverside North, Benque Viejo del Carmen, **t** 823 2047, **f** 823 3272, *www.mopanriverresort.com* ($$$$$; US$260). This resort has 12 luxurious wooden thatched cabanas, all equipped with a/c, cable TV, safes, mini-bars and kitchens. Additional amenities include a swimming pool, a Swedish massage service and bird-watching trails. The owner, Pam Picon, is an ordained minister so you can even tie the knot or renew your vows here, should you so desire.

Crossing the Border to Guatemala

To get to the border from Benque Viejo del Carmen, you'll need to pick up a shared taxi (known as a *colectivo*), which run between 6am and 7pm. At the crossing your passport will be stamped and vehicle papers checked (if applicable). There is a departure tax of US$18.75 (BZ$37.50) for all non-Belizean citizens, which can be paid in US$ or BZ$, but no charge for entering Guatemala. British and North American citizens do not require a visa to enter Guatemala. Buses to Flores and Tikal, a popular day-trip destination, can be caught at the border after all the formalities have been dealt with.

Tikal

Tikal
*t 502 2361 1399; open
daily 6–6; adm US$7*

One of the most popular day trips available in Belize actually involves leaving the country for a few hours to visit the ruins of Tikal, generally regarded as the most spectacular of all the region's Mayan cities. In fact, if you can afford it, it's worth staying overnight and spending a whole day exploring the vast site. Located right in the heart of the jungle, Tikal is at its most magical in the early morning, when the thick fringing trees reverberate to the excited shrieks of parrots and the low threatening whoops of howler monkeys. At this time, the **five great granite pyramids** that dominate the centre of the site (the largest of which is over 200ft/60m tall) can seem as ominous and awe-inspiring as they must have appeared to the Maya. There are, as you'd expect, great views from the top.

Despite involving crossing an international border, a trip to Tikal from Belize should be a relatively smooth, stress-free process. The tourist infrastructure is well-oiled, with bus and plane timetables arranged for maximum ease of access, and there are a number of accommodation options lying right on the site's doorstep. There are also a good number of tour operators in Belize who can organize the whole thing for you (*see* p.64).

Tikal was settled from around 900 BC onwards, but didn't reach the peak of its powers until the 4th century AD when, under the leadership of King Great Jaguar Paw, it became the dominant Maya kingdom in the lowland area. Throughout the next couple of centuries, it would keep up an intense rivalry with that other great Mayan city of the time, Caracol, in southwest Belize. The inevitable war between the two in the 6th century saw Caracol emerge victorious, after which it briefly succeeded Tikal as the region's dominant force. Tikal fought back in the 8th century, restoring a measure of its former primacy, and it was during this second late flowering of the city that most of the large structures (including the pyramids) you see today were built.

Tikal, as with the majority of lowland Mayan kingdoms, abruptly collapsed and was abandoned some time around the beginning of

Where to Stay at Tikal

Accommodation at the site – just outside the entrance – includes a camp site (US$5 per person) and three rather overpriced hotels. You'll need to book in advance for the hotels as they often fill with tour groups.

Jungle Lodge, t 2477 0754, *www.jungle lodge.guate.com* ($$$$; US$86).

Tikal Inn, t 7926 1917, *hoteltikalinn@ itelgua.com* ($$$; US$75).

Jaguar Inn (t 7926 0002, *www.jaguar tikal.com* ($$$; US$50). Also has camping space available.

the 10th century, for reasons still not fully understood. The city was rediscovered in the 19th century, but serious excavation work didn't begin here until the 1950s. It's still ongoing. Indeed, so enormous is the site (covering over 200 square miles in its entirety) that many structures remain covered in dense foliage. Entire temples still await uncovering.

Despite the limited scope of the site's excavation, with only those structures at the very centre having been fully revealed, this still makes up a pretty large area. If you're hoping to cover it all, you'll have to do a lot of walking, so bring stout, comfortable shoes and plenty of water.

Tikal Museum
open 9–4.30;
adm US$1.50

Your journey begins at the **visitor centre** by the entrance, where there's a small **museum** containing finds from the site and a ticket booth. If you arrive after 3pm, your ticket will also be valid for the next day. You can also engage the services of a guide here for around US$45.

South of San Ignacio

Mountain Pine Ridge Forest Reserve

Mountain Pine Ridge Forest Reserve

A great 300-square-mile (777-sq-km) swathe of pine forest is probably not the first thing you'd expect to see in an area set at the heart of the sweltering tropics, but then this region has always been a bit different. A geological pioneer, it was the first part of Central America to poke its head above sea level, existing for millions of years as an island while the rest of the isthmus remained submerged beneath the waves. The thinness and sandy nature of the soil here means that the area is unable to support the great broadleaf forests that blanket much of the rest of the country, but instead sustains a slightly incongruous, rather European-looking ridge of pines, bracken and grass. It's also made the area pretty much uninhabitable, as agriculture is virtually impossible here, something which has aided its preservation since people first arrived in the region several thousand years ago. Even the Maya were unable to sustain communities here.

Unfortunately, since the area's designation as a national reserve in 1944 (making it the country's oldest protected area), nature seems to have taken over where humans have failed, with forest fires and,

Getting to and around Mountain Pine Ridge Forest Reserve

If not coming as part of a tour (see p.156 for San Ignacio-based tour operators), you'll need your own transport – which essentially means a sturdy **4WD**, as all the roads within Pine Ridge are unpaved and very bumpy. Some become impassable in wet weather. To access the reserve, you'll need to take the Chiquibul Road from Georgeville, 6 miles (10km) east of San Ignacio. Alternatively, you could take the Cristo Rey Road from Santa Elena which passes through several villages, including San Antonio, before connecting with the Chiquibul Road around 1½ miles from the reserve gate. It's largely un-made, with only those sections that pass through the villages having been paved. Remember to fill up with petrol before you set off, as there are no petrol stations within the park. There is one in Santa Elena, opposite the Cristo Rey Road turn-off.

The **entrance** to the reserve is marked by a gate and a small ranger hut, where you'll have to stop while a ranger emerges to ask you your business and take down your car registration and name. If you think you need directions to anywhere, this is the time to ask.

more devastatingly, a plague of mountain pine beetles destroying much of the vegetation in recent decades. Everywhere you go, you'll see dead trunks shorn of their branches protruding sadly from the ground. Happily the forest floor is also littered with bright-green pine saplings, suggesting that the area is over the worst of the blight, although it will take a good many years for the forest to return to its former glory. At the plague's peak, over 90 per cent of the park's pines were believed to have been affected.

Notwithstanding the rather forlorn-looking stretches of straggly vegetation marking the beetle's lethal path, much of the park is still strikingly beautiful, the whole area riddled with stunning valleys, hills, rivers, waterfalls and caves. There is plenty to do here, making it a popular destination with tour groups who generally try and combine visits to a couple of the park's natural attractions – such as a cave or a waterfall – with a trip to Caracol in the southwest region (in the adjoining Chiquibul National Park). Despite the number of visitors the Mountain Pine Ridge Reserve attracts, the sheer size of the place, and the poor condition of the roads, means that it rarely feels crowded, and in the early morning or late afternoon, in particular, you may find that you have some of the pools and caves to yourself.

It's a very large area and, in order to explore it fully, a stay of a few nights in one of the park's lodges is recommended, many of which hire out bikes and horses. However, if you do, remember to pack a sweater. As stifling and hot as it can be during the day, the park's high elevations mean that it can also get pretty nippy at night.

Pacbitun

This, one of the area's least celebrated (and least visited) Mayan sites, lies outside the confines of the reserve proper. To find it, take the last turning on the left on Cristo Rey Road before it intersects with the Chiquibul Road (about 1½ miles from the reserve gate), from where a thin track leads down to the site. The track isn't signposted and is quite overgrown, making it rather difficult to spot.

Look out for the rather ominous-looking cow's skull that has been nailed to the gatepost. The land on which this little site sits is private and owned by a Mr Tzul, from whom you'll have to gain permission before visiting the site. His home lies down this track. A small fee will probably be requested.

Pacbitun (pronounced locally as *Pack-by-ton*) is believed to have been continuously occupied from around 1000 BC to around AD 900, during which time it became a major ceremonial centre. Over 24 temples have been discovered here along with stelae (inscribed tablets), ball courts, élite residencies and raised causeways, although many have only been partly excavated and today, in truth, there's not a great deal to see and there are no visitor facilities. The name of the site, which means 'Stones Set in Earth', was coined by the villagers of nearby San Antonio, to whom the site was known well before its official registration (in 1971) and subsequent (partial) excavation, carried out in 1980 and 1986 by Trent University, Ontario.

Five Sisters Falls

This group of tumbling cascades can be found on the property of the Five Sisters Lodge (*see* 'Where to Stay', p.170; a small fee is charged for visitors not staying at the lodge). The base of the falls are ideal for swimming, and there are thatched *palapas* providing much-needed shade for when you're not in the water. The easiest way to access the falls is via a hydro-powered rainforest tram that shuttles guests to and fro.

Thousand Foot Falls

Thousand Foot Falls
open 8–5; adm US$1

It's a catchy name, albeit not a particularly accurate one. This great cascade actually plunges down over 1,600ft (480m), making it the highest waterfall in Central America. It's a very impressive sight (whatever some other guidebooks may say), a thin ribbon of water plummeting down into a heavily forested gorge. The falls can take some getting to – which probably explains their other name, the 'Hidden Valley Falls'. You'll need to follow the challenging Cooma Cairn Road east until you reach the signposted turn-off (around 5 miles after the Hidden Valley Inn). Be warned, Cooma Cairn is an extremely badly maintained red mud track rutted with deep troughs, some stretching across the entire width of the road. This is strictly 4WD territory, and then only in dry weather. Note that the British Army regularly train in this area (even they consider the terrain challenging) so you may come across trucks.

Once at the site, you'll find a ticket booth (and the guard, who lives on site, probably just emerging from his cottage to collect your money) and a small picnic area (with an alarming-looking seismic crack through the middle), from where paths lead 10m or so down to a small concrete viewing area facing the falls. Once you've had your fill of tumbling water, you can explore trails leading through the surrounding forested valley.

Río On Pools

A collection of smooth granite pools formed by the gurgling action of the small Río On, and linked by a series of gentle cascades, this is a popular spot with both locals and tourists for swimming, sunbathing, picnicking and clambering about on the rocks. There are no formal facilities here, apart from a small parking area. The pools are clearly signposted and located just off of the sandy Chiquibul Road before the village of Douglas da Silva.

Río Frio Cave

Swathed in vines and creepers, a great Hollywood-esque, dragon's-lair-style 65ft (20m) stone archway marks the entrance to one of the most visited caves in the country. Its popularity is principally due to the fact that, unlike many of the region's other caves, which require the use of headlamps and boats to explore (at some you're even obliged to swim across stretches of river), this is a relatively easy place to access, being just a quarter of a mile long. The light of the exit becomes visible soon after you enter. Nonetheless, it's still an extremely intriguing place, the great cavern walls awash with beautiful stalagmites and stalactites. There's even a small sandy beach that's been formed by the erosive action of the river as it flows through the cavern. A walkway has been cut into the rock on the right-hand side of the cave allowing you to explore the interior. Although the size of the entrance and the proximity of the exit means that the cavern is reasonably well lit (by cavern standards), it's still a good idea to bring a torch as it can still get a bit gloomy and the ground is very uneven. The entrance is located close to Douglas da Silva (it's well signposted). The cavern actually forms part of a larger 45-minute nature trail taking you into the surrounding jungle, to a wildlife lookout and a smaller cave.

★ Blancaneaux
Lodge >>

Where to Stay at the Mountain Pine Ridge Forest Reserve

The Mountain Pine Ridge Reserve is home to some of the grandest, best-equipped, most exclusive, most expensive resorts in the country, the sort that could only be dreamed up by Hollywood directors. The only place where **camping** is permitted is at Douglas de Silva. You'll need to obtain permission from the ranger at the gate when entering the reserve.

Luxury ($$$$$)
Blancaneaux Lodge, t US 1-800 746 3745, t 824 3878, www.blancaneaux. com (US$250–650). It seems entirely fitting that the top hotel in such a dramatic-looking, photogenic region should be owned by a famous Hollywood director. This is actually one of two resorts in Belize owned by Francis Ford Coppola, the other being an equally luxurious beach resort in Placencia. Everything about the place is terribly grand, with wooden cabanas, beautifully decorated with antiques and native art, occupying neatly

tended tropical gardens overlooking a tumbling waterfall and swimming hole. If money is no object, then go for one of the two-bedroom villas (US$485), which have open-air living rooms with decks looking out onto the river, kitchenettes and stylish tiled semi-outdoor Japanese-style bathrooms. The restaurant is Italian influenced and very good (even if the balcony dining area is plagued rather by flies), with meals largely made from ingredients grown in the hotel's own organic garden, cooked up in an authentic Italian brick pizza oven. Additional facilities include complimentary bikes, a croquet lawn, a hot tub and a Thai massage service. A variety of tours is offered, including horse-riding (the hotel has its own stables) from US$60 for 2–3 hours, US$90 full day.

⭐ **Hidden Valley Inn** >

Hidden Valley Inn, Cooma Cairn Road, t US 1-866 443 3364, t 822 3320, f 822 3334, www.hiddenvalleyinn.com (US$170). This small luxury hotel has just 12 cottages, all with tasteful décor, fireplaces and mahogany furniture, but over 7,200 acres of forested land with over 90m (144km) of trails to walk or cycle (use of mountain bikes is free). Two-way radios are provided so you can stay in contact with the Inn. For a small fee they will even set up lunch and drinks for you at a point on your route. And if you really want to hike in luxury, US$100 will get you exclusive use of a waterfall for a day, complete with your own personal *palapa* (with bathroom) and lunch. The cottages are arranged around the main house, which contains several cosy lounge areas and an elegant restaurant where local and international dishes are served. There's also a swimming pool and hot tub.

Mountain Equestrian Trails, Mile 8 Chiquibul Road, t 820 4041, www.met belize.com (US$120). The main reason for staying at this lodge is to take advantage of the on site equestrian centre, which offers a variety of tours through the local countryside (by far the best way to explore its waterfalls, rivers and caves. It's certainly a lot more pleasant than being stuck in a car or tour bus). Rain gear, water bottles, camera bags and packed lunches are provided. Accommodation

takes the form of 10 simple but comfortable thatched-roof cabanas, all with private bathrooms and decorated with Mayan tapestries, and lit with kerosene lamps (there's no electricity in the rooms). Riding trips are also available to non-guests: half-day riding from US$55, full-day from US$75. A range of packages is also available.

Expensive ($$$$)–Moderate ($$$)
Five Sisters Lodge, t US 1-800 447 2931, t 820 4005, www.fivesisterslodge.com (US$105). Overlooking the set of waterfalls (see p.168) that gave it its name, this very swish lodge was opened in 1995 by Belizean-born Carlos Popper. There are 14 prettily decorated cabanas, all with thatched roofs, wooden floors, private bathrooms and verandas with hammocks, all providing easy access to the swimming pools at the base of the falls. The pick of the bunch is definitely the tranquil Riverside Villa (US$250), which has its own kitchen and a decking area overlooking the tumbling river, and is set away from the other cabanas on its own little trail.

Pine Ridge Lodge, Chiquibul Rd, t US 1-800 316 0706, t 606 4557, www.pine ridgelodge.com (US$89). One of the park's more modest offerings, the Pine Ridge Lodge has pretty grounds on which sit six cosy cottages, all with private bathrooms and decorated with Mayan and Caribbean art and Guatemalan fabrics. There's also a good restaurant serving meals largely made with produce grown organically in the lodge's garden (breakfast US$7.50, dinner US$21.50). A range of tours is offered.

Cristo Rey

Crystal Paradise Resort, Cristo Rey village, t/f 824 2772, www.crystal paradise.com ($$$; US$75). This lodge, which was hand-built by its Belizean owners, the Tut family, in the traditional way with palm-thatched roofs, offers a choice of three different lodgings: regular rooms (with private bathrooms); cabanas with private porches and views of the Macal River valley; and very large family loft cabanas that sleep up to eight people. Tasty home-cooked fare made with fresh vegetables is served in the restaurant, followed by coffee grown in the grounds.

Getting to Caracol

Due to the remoteness of the site most visitors arrive with a **tour**, usually combining the trip with a stop at the Río On Pools and one of the other tourist destinations in the Mountain Pine Ridge area. If you want to go it alone, be prepared for a long drive and make sure you have a full tank and spare tyre. To get there, follow the Chiquibul Road south through the Mountain Pine Ridge Reserve past Douglas de Silva and the Río Frio Caves, through San Luis and into the Chiquibul National Park. From San Ignacio (50m/81km north) it will take around 3hrs, although note that access may not be possible in the rainy season, even with a tour. There is no public transport.

Caracol

Caracol
open 8–4;
adm US$7.50

Over 50 miles (80km) south of San Ignacio, nestling in the Chiquibul Forest, an area rich in wildlife, lies the largest Mayan site in Belize, Caracol, the main building of which is still famously the tallest man-made structure in Belize. Despite the difficulty of getting here – travelling independently will involve a three-hour drive along some very poor roads – this remains one of the country's must-see sights. Occupation of the settlement is believed to have taken place from at least 600 BC to around AD 1100. At its peak, during the late Classic Period, Caracol may have supported a population of up to 150,000, a staggering number, especially when you consider that today Belize's largest urban centre, Belize City, supports less than half that. The entire site is vast, spread out over 30 square miles (77 square km), the epicentre of which is made up of five plazas and over 30 structures. In total there may be over 50,000 structures here, linked by over 30 miles of roads. Unsurprisingly, archaeologists have, since excavation work began here in the 1950s, uncovered a myriad of artefacts, including pots, jade beads, obsidian jewellery and animal bones. Many **glyphs** (Maya inscriptions) have also been revealed, the recent translations of which have provided tantalizing glimpses into the history of this great ceremonial site. For instance, one of the glyphs on Altar 21 seems to recount military victories inflicted by Caracol on its regional rivals Tikal and Naranjo in the 6th century AD. If true this would go some way to explaining Caracol's expansion and growth from AD 600–900, a time when it may have exerted greater dominance over the area than even Tikal.

After the city's eventual collapse, the site was swallowed up by the jungle and not rediscovered until 1937 when it was stumbled upon by a logger hunting for mahogany. It was given the name Caracol, which means 'shell' in Spanish, although for reasons that are not entirely clear today. It may simply have been because there are a lot of snails living in the area, or it may be a reference to the road that winds its way up to the site. Despite the importance of the discovery, the first serious excavation of the site didn't take place until the 1950s, under the stewardship of A. Hamilton Anderson of the University of Pennsylvania. Subsequent excavations took place in the 1970s and '80s, although a lack of funds meant that these were

10 Cayo District and the West | South of San Ignacio

necessarily short lived and limited in scope. Indeed, it's only been in recent years, thanks to an injection of cash by the tourist board, who are hoping to turn this into a major, easily accessible tourist attraction (once again re-igniting its rivalry with Tikal), that full-time year-round excavations of the site have been possible. New discoveries are being made every year, although there is still much of Caracol that remains to be uncovered.

The Site

Your first stop is the very informative **visitor centre**, by the main entrance, in which you can see a scale model of the site as well as various artefacts uncovered here, and read the history both of the rise and fall of Caracol itself and of its subsequent excavation. From here, a member of staff (or your own tour guide if you have one; you cannot explore the site independently) will guide you around the core of the site. The first major site you come to is '**Caana**' (Maya for 'Sky Place') in Plaza B, Caracol's (and indeed Belize's) tallest structure. Measuring 143ft (43.5m) high, it's a terribly grand and imposing place, comprising several palace complexes, and is topped with three pyramids (known as B18, B19 and B20). The climb to the summit is well worth the shortness of breath you'll inevitably experience for the vistas it affords out over the surrounding thick jungle canopy. Be sure to bring some water. Apparently, this is a great vantage point for spotting birds, with several rare species, including keel-billed motmots and scarlet macaws, having been spotted in nearby trees. Once back on terra firma, you'll be guided around the various plazas, ball courts and altars that make up this section of the complex. On your way look out for the **The Temple of the Wooden Lintel** (structure A6), which is believed to be oldest building (built in AD 70) in Caracol, beneath which an intriguing discovery of a cache of liquid mercury and a jadeite mask hidden within a stone box was made.

The South

The south represents a Belize that is both rapidly changing and staunchly unchanged, ever more developed and singularly untamed. There are areas here that are transforming so fast, most notably the Placencia peninsula, where new tourist and housing developments are going up by the month, that any guidebook is necessarily out of date by the time it hits the shelves. But there are also sections of the far south and areas around the Maya Mountains that support few roads and almost no human habitation, where the thickly forested landscape has altered little in thousands of years.

11

Don't miss

⭐ **The world's only jaguar reserve**
Cockscomb Basin Wildlife Sanctuary **p.187**

⭐ **Jungle-fringed river trip**
Monkey River Town **p.196**

⭐ **Whale shark migration**
Gladden Spit **p.191**

⭐ **Garifuna culture**
Dangriga **p.175**

⭐ **Reef snorkelling**
Laughing Bird Caye **p.196**

See map overleaf

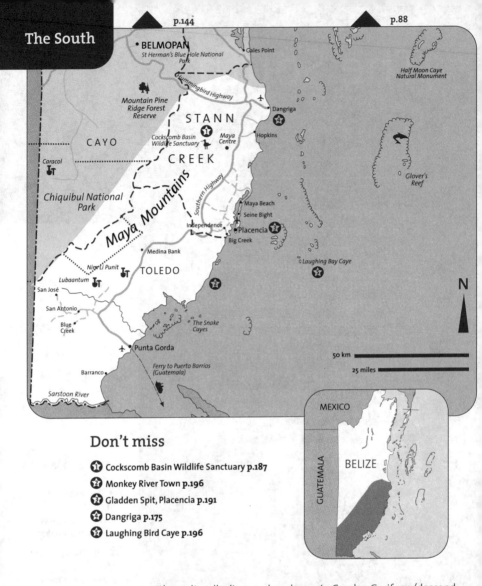

The South

p.144 p.88

BELMOPAN
St Herman's Blue Hole National Park

Gales Point

Half Moon Caye
Natural Monument

Mountain Pine
Ridge Forest
Reserve

STANN

Dangriga

CAYO

Cockscomb Basin
Wildlife Sanctuary

Maya
Centre

Hopkins

Caracol

CREEK

Glover's
Reef

Chiquibul National
Park

Maya Mountains

Southern Highway

Maya Beach
Seine Bight
Placencia
Big Creek

Independence

Medina Bank

Laughing Bay Caye

Nim Li Punit

TOLEDO

Lubaantun

San José

San Antonio

Blue
Creek

The Snake
Cayes

N

Punta Gorda

50 km

Barranco

Ferry to Puerto Barrios
(Guatemala)

25 miles

Sarstoon River

MEXICO

GUATEMALA

BELIZE

Don't miss

1 Cockscomb Basin Wildlife Sanctuary **p.187**
2 Monkey River Town **p.196**
3 Gladden Spit, Placencia **p.191**
4 Dangriga **p.175**
5 Laughing Bird Caye **p.196**

It's a culturally diverse place, home to Creoles, Garifuna (descendants of African slaves and Carib Indians), mestizos, Maya and, ever more so of late, ex-pat westerners investing in vacation properties. Most of the region's communities, and thus most of its tourist infrastructure, are located on the coast, where visitors have the opportunity to experience different ways of life, particularly in the Garifuna communities of Dangriga (the region's largest town) and Hopkins, and to take part in a wide range of sea-based pursuits. The barrier reef is the focus for most tourist activities, with operators offering snorkelling and diving tours out to two of the country's largest marine reserves, Glover's Reef and South Water Caye, as well as to a whole host of smaller cayes and sites, including Gladden Spit near Placencia, where at certain times of year it's possible to see migrating whale sharks.

The region comprises just two districts. The first, Stann Creek, to the north, is the smaller, but also the more populous, home to most of the south's major urban communities. The more southerly, Toledo, supports significantly fewer inhabitants (at least since the collapse of Mayan civilization here in the 10th century AD), most of whom reside at Punta Gorda, Belize's southernmost town. Indeed much of Toledo's western extent is swathed in thick lush virgin rainforest which rises up to swaddle the flanks of the Maya Mountains, the foothills of which hide a number of remote Mayan ruins. Much of this area is completely inaccessible to vehicles, and can be explored only on foot or horseback (and even then only with considerable difficulty). The most readily accessible section of jungle lies at its northern extent within the confines of the relatively well-developed Cockscomb Basin Wildlife Reserve, which was established in the 1980s to protect the area's community of jaguars, and which has numerous well-marked trails.

Dangriga

 Dangriga   Just over 100 miles (161km) south of Belize City and 55 miles (88km) east of Belmopan lies the coastal town of Dangriga, the largest town in the Stann Creek district and the centre of Belize's Garifuna community. Indeed, with around 80 per cent of its 11,000-strong population claming Garifuna descent, Dangriga is the largest

The History of the Garifuna

The Garifuna's route to Belize has been anything but straightforward. In 1635 two Spanish ships carrying slaves from Africa to the West Indies were wrecked off the coast of St Vincent, an island then inhabited by Carib Indians (or, more precisely, a mixture of Arawak Indians, the original inhabitants, and Kalipuna Indians, who had subsequently conquered the island and whose men, having killed all the Arawak warriors, then intermarried with the Arawak women). Survivors swam ashore and settled among these Carib Indians, intermixing, and over time forming a new group of people who called themselves the Garinuga (or Black Carib). Interestingly, the word Garifuna was actually coined to describe the people's language – a great stew of African, Caribbean, Spanish, French and English influences – and not the people themselves, but has over time become the term more generally utilized for both.

For several generations, this new culturally intense community lived peacefully enough, until, in 1763, St Vincent was invaded by the British, who wanted to turn the island into a sugar plantation. The Garifuna fought back and several decades of bloody battles ensued. Eventually, in 1795, the British quashed the Garifuna resistance and took control of the island. They were less than magnanimous in victory, taking over 4,000 Garifuna prisoners and transporting them to the nearby island of Baliceaux where over half died of disease (principally yellow fever). In 1798, the remainder were exiled to the island of Roatán, off the coast of Honduras. From here, the Garifuna eventually escaped to the mainland, forming new communities in Honduras, Guatemala and Nicaragua. Legend has it that on 19 November 1802 the very first Garifuna arrived in British Honduras (as Belize was then known), a date now celebrated in Belize as 'Settlement Day'.

Getting to Dangriga

By Air

Maya Island Air (t 522 2659, *www.mayaislandair.com*) and Tropic Air (t 422 3435, *www.tropicair.com*) both operate daily flights (7–9 a day) from Belize City to Dangriga (US$54 from Goldson International, US$35.50 from Belize Municipal). The flights take just 20 mins and touch down at Dangriga's tiny airstrip, just north of the town centre. There are also several flights a day to/from Punta Gorda (US$44) and to/from Placencia (US$26).

By Bus

Buses link Dangriga with all the main regional hubs, including Belize City, Belmopan, Placencia and Punta Gorda. The journey from Belize City takes around 3hrs, 5hrs if going via Belmopan along the Hummingbird Highway. Punta Gorda is around a 4hr journey away. Novelo's buses (but *see* p.66) pull in at the bus depot on Havana St, while James Buses stop at the north end of Commerce St. Southern Transport (t 502 2160) run several services a day to Belize City and Belmopan and two a day to Punta Gorda.

By Car

Dangriga can be accessed via three roads, the Hummingbird Highway from Belmopan, the Coastal Highway off the Western Highway near Belize City, or the Southern Highway from Punta Gorda.

Getting away from Dangriga

By Boat

For boats to Tobacco Caye and other nearby cayes, ask around the Riverside Café. The boats leave from the south bank of the North Stann Creek. You can also hire a kayak to explore the local area from Island Expeditions, Magoon St (single US$35, double US$55 per day).

It's also possible to catch a boat from Dangriga to Puerto Cortés in Honduras every Saturday (check-in 9am) and Thursday (check-in 8am) from North Riverside Street, two blocks west of the bridge. The journey takes around 3hrs and costs US$50. A return trip is made on Mon and Tues (*see* Travel, p.60). This service is run by Nesymein Neydey, t 522 0062.

Garifuna community in the world and thus something of a cultural hub. The town was founded as a simple fishing village in the early 19th century, although it's been known by its current name only since 1971 when a growing pride and awareness of its Garifuna heritage lead to the original English 'Stann Creek' being replaced by the Garifuna for 'sweet water close at hand'. Though the name may have changed, Dangriga's essence is much the same, and it remains for the most part an old-fashioned fishing town of weathered wooden clapboard houses, where the pace of life is slow and easy (the exception being the week around 19 November, Garifuna Settlement Day, when the town is a mass of partying – a must-see if you're in the area). Despite a degree of expansion and development in recent years, Dangriga makes little fuss about welcoming tourists. That's not to say it's not accommodating – the townspeople can be very friendly, eager to tell stories of their forefathers and show off a little of their drumming or craftwork – but its infrastructure remains low key and its hotels and restaurants geared primarily towards local not foreign tastes. But then, this is exactly what makes it so attractive to many tourists, particularly those averse to the more

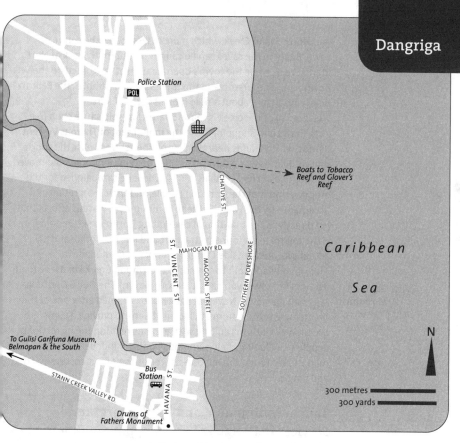

generic, first world-orientated, Esperanto charms of the Placencia peninsula. As long as you don't go expecting services on tap, Dangriga can make a very pleasant, simple base from which to explore the nearby cayes.

The Town

After several hours of driving along winding, jungle- and plantation-lined roads, you will eventually reach a sign bearing the legend, 'Mabuiga!', which means 'welcome!' in Garifuna and marks your official entrance to the town. Just past here is a roundabout, at the centre of which stands the bronze 'Drums Of Our Fathers Monument' depicting three traditional Garifuna *dügü* drums and a pair of *sísira* shakers, which together are supposed to symbolize the past, present and future of the Garifuna people. Turn left at the monument and you're on Dangriga's main street, which will take you right into the centre of town, changing name (but not direction) as it goes, from Havana Street to St Vincent Street to Commerce Street. As you head in you'll notice that the town spans two creeks, **Havana Creek** to the south, just past the bus depot and monument, and **North Stann Creek**, which more or less marks the centre of town. Boats to the cayes can be caught on the south bank of North Stann Creek, while the town's open-air market is situated on the north bank. The airstrip and the town's swankiest hotel, the Pelican Beach Resort, are about a mile (1.6km) north of here.

Just north of the creek is Marie Sharp's flagship sauce shop (see 'Arts, Crafts and Shopping') and the **monument of Thomas Vincent Ramos**, which stands near the pier, on the seafront past the sports-ground. Ramos was a Garifuna leader, born in Honduras, who moved to Dangriga at the age of 36 in 1923 where he campaigned for the empowerment of the Garifuna people, and their recognition and acceptance by the wider Belizean community. It was his efforts that led directly to the tradition of celebrating Garifuna Settlement Day.

The town's main tourist attraction, and its latest pride and joy, is actually located outside Dangriga proper, at Chuluhadiwa Monument Park, next to the hospital on Stann Creek Road (the road leading into town; you pass it on your way in). The **Gulisi Garifuna Museum** opened in November 2004 and is named after one of the first female settlers from St Vincent. It aims to provide a complete overview of Garifuna culture with exhibits relating the history of the peoples – including their numerous fights for independence and migrations around the region – as well as their food, costumes, art and dance.

Gulisi Garifuna Museum
Stann Creek Road,
t *502 0639,*
gulisi@btl.net; open
Mon–Fri 10–5, Sat 8–12;
adm US$5

Tourist Information and Services in Dangriga

There is no official tourist information office in Dangriga. The friendly Riverside Café, which has a comprehensive notice board, acts as a sort of unofficial information hub for travellers, and is the place to find a boatman or a tour guide to arrange any water-based trips.

Banks: Belize Bank, 24 St Vincent St, **t** 522 2903; First Caribbean, Commerce St; Scotia Bank, St Vincent St.

Hospitals: Dangriga Hospital, Stann Creek Valley Rd, **t** 522 2078.

Internet: Val's Laundry, Sharp St (opposite post office).

Laundry: Val's Laundry, Sharp St (opposite post office).

Library: Front St.

Post office: Mahogany Rd.

Supermarket: Supersaver Supermarket, Commerce St; Everyday Supermarket, St Vincent St.

Arts, Crafts and Shopping in Dangriga

Austin Rodriguez' Workshop, 32 Tubroose St. Music, and in particular drumming, has long been an important part of Garifuna culture. Drums are still made in the traditional fashion, stretching a piece of leather tight over a hardwood (often mahogany) frame. At the workshop of Austin Rodriguez, one of the town's most celebrated drum-makers, you can watch the entire process, see a demonstration of traditional drumming (perhaps even have a go yourself) and browse a range of Garifuna drums (from US$150), as well as a selection of smaller crafts and gifts, including handmade dolls.

Benjamin Nicholas's Studio, Howard St. Benjamin Nicholas is Belize's most celebrated artist, having displayed his canvasses in galleries worldwide, and even received an MBE for his colourful and lively depictions of Garifuna culture. He works in his studio every day and is usually happy to show off his work to anyone who calls in.

Pen's Art Gallery, 3 Aranda Crescent, *www.cayetano.de*. This is the gallery of Pen Cayetano, another of the town's (and country's) most famous artists. However, not content with winning awards for his paintings, Pen is also a skilled musician, credited with the creation of Punta Rock, a blend of traditional Garifuna music and modern rock. Although born in Dangriga, Pen now lives in Germany but every November returns to his home town to display his most recent art (and play his new music).

Marie Sharp's Fine Foods, 3 Pier Rd, **t** 522 2370, *www.mariesharps-bz.com*. Dangriga, and its surrounding region, is a creative environment that's produced numerous successful artists, musicians and bands. None, however, have managed to enjoy anything like the success of Marie Sharp. Her creation, a patented range of superhot sauces made with carrots, onions, garlic and *habanero* peppers (the world's hottest peppers, apparently), now adorn almost every restaurant (and home dining table) in the country. And they are very hot – the top of the range XXXXX 'Comatose Level' sauce bottles carry a warning against using the sauce to play tricks on 'the weak or the elderly' – but also very popular, having been for many years now the country's number one tourist souvenir. Marie's story is a classic tale of a local girl made good. From her start, selling a range of home-made sauces (made with leftover *habanero* peppers from the family farm) door to door, she now oversees a vast operation from her factory located 8 miles northwest of Dangriga, where thousands of bottles of hot sauce (plus an array of slightly-easier-on-the palate chutneys and jams) are produced daily for both the domestic market and export. You can take a tour of the factory to see sauce being made and bottled (**t** 522 370) and browse her full range of products at this store.

Festivals in Dangriga

Garifuna Settlement Day (19 November): Every year, for one whole week, the town of Dangriga (and other Garifuna communities across Belize) celebrates the arrival of the first Garifuna settlers in Belize, through re-enactments of that first landing, dancing, drinking, parades and a whole lot of drumming. For more information on the Garifuna culture and information on upcoming events, check out the National Garifuna Council of Belize, *www.ngcbelize.org*.

Where to Stay in Dangriga

There are just a handful of hotels scattered throughout the town (there's no hotel district, as such), some better value than others. For most of the year, you shouldn't have too much trouble getting a room, although if you plan to stay on or around Garifuna Settlement Day, you will have to book in advance.

Expensive ($$$$)–Moderate ($$$)
Pelican Beach Resort, Ecumenical Drive (north end of town, near airstrip), **t** 522 2044, **f** 522 2570, *www.pelicanbeach belize.com* (US$95). The Pelican is the town's most upscale resort. Its standard rooms come with private bathrooms, TVs, phones and fans; its superior ones (US$111) also have porches, while the very best rooms have all of the above (US$119), plus a/c. The Pelican also operates a resort on South Water Caye (*see* p.183). Frequent excursions to here are offered, as well as tours to a variety of other nearby destinations. It's quite a walk out of town to the hotel (15–20 mins), but at least that means it's quiet (so long as a plane isn't taking off at the nearby airstrip), and when you do get here you can relax on the hotel's own sandy beach (with *palapas* and hammocks).

Bonefish Hotel, 15 Mahogany Rd, **t** US 800 798 1558, **t** 522 2243, *www.blue marlinlodge.com/bonefish.html* (US$56–89). The two-storey Bonefish Hotel is operated by the Blue Marlin Lodge on South Water Caye (to which diving and fishing trips can be arranged, *see* p.183) and offers seven rooms with a/c, cable TV and minibars. There is a lounge area with views over the sea and a restaurant on the ground floor serving international cuisine.

Seaclift Bed and Breakfast, 1738 Southern Foreshore, **t** 522 3540, **f** 522 3538, *www.seaclift.com* (US$75). Two modern beach-facing buildings offering a total of six rooms (some with shared bathrooms) and various communal areas including a kitchen, a veranda and a volleyball court. This could be a good choice for groups or families who wish to rent an entire building. Breakfast is complimentary.

Inexpensive ($$)–Budget ($)
Bluefield Lodge, 6 Bluefield Rd, **t** 522 2742 (US$20). This is a popular, well-run, budget choice with nice simple rooms with fans (some have TVs and private bathrooms). Miss Louise, the owner, is a friendly host, happy to share information and tips about the town and surroundings. Book in advance.

Chaleanor Hotel, 35 Magoon St, **t** 522 2587/2481, **f** 522 2481, *chaleanor@btl.net* (US$10–16/30 shared/private). The tallest hotel in town, the Chaleanor has opened a roof terrace to show off its panoramic views. Beneath is a collection of reasonable rooms with private bathrooms, TVs and a/c. There are also a few more basic choices with shared bathrooms (US$10) in a neighbouring annexe as well as a small gift shop in the lobby. This place is often full with block bookings, so it's advisable to ring ahead.

Pal's Guest House, 868A Magoon St, **t** 522 2365, **f** 522 2095, *www.palsbelize.com* (US$19/23 shared/private bathroom). Pal's provides small, basic budget rooms (a choice of shared or private baths) at a beach-side location in the south side of town. All rooms come with cable TV and fans, and some have private beach-front balconies (US$33). The owner Mr Flores, a retired teacher, is a fount of knowledge about the Garifuna people and the local area.

Riverside Hotel, 135 Commerce St, **t** 522 2168 (US$10–12). Centrally located, next to the bridge, the Riverside has 11 rooms with fans and shared bathrooms. It's clean and cheap and there is a large sitting area to hang out and swap stories with other guests.

Ruthie's Cabanas, 31 Southern Foreshore, **t** 502 3184 (US$30). Ruthie and her husband Meeto rent out cheap-and-cheerful beach-side cabanas, and offer real home-cooked Garifuna food. Basic but comfortable (and very friendly).

Eating Out in Dangriga

For fresh cassava bread, snacks and barbecued foods, look out for vendors on the main drag or go to the open-air market on the north bank of North Stann Creek. The town also has several Chinese restaurants, most of which can be found along Commerce St and St Vincent St. The most popular is probably Starlight at 121 Commerce St. The Pelican Resort (near the airstrip, *see* above) is your best bet for fine cuisine.

Riverside Café, south bank of North Stann Creek. The Riverside is more than just a café. It's also the unofficial tourist centre for the town, as well as the place to book a boat trip out to the cayes. The notice board is a great source of information on tours or events. The food is actually pretty basic fare but reasonable value. They do particularly filling breakfasts.

King Burger, 135 Commerce St. Cheap and popular, this little fast-food joint features a range of burgers, milkshakes, breakfasts and simple meals, such as chicken with rice and beans.

Entertainment and Nightlife in Dangriga

It can be a bit rough and ready. The main street has numerous bars, but these cater mainly for locals and can be a bit intimidating. Much more fun are the demonstrations of **traditional Garifuna drumming** staged on the streets, often by groups of boys. **Griga 2000** near the Stann Creek Bridge is one of the town's longest-established clubs, holding regular karaoke evenings (which are extremely popular) and hosting DJs on weekends, when it's packed, sweaty and intense. A more refined, leisurely drink can be enjoyed at the bar of the **Pelican Resort**, a 15min walk north of town near the airstrip, which has a happy hour 6–8pm Fri.

Nearby Attractions

Mayflower Bocawina National Park

Mayflower
Bocawina
National Park
open 8–4; adm US$5

One of the more recent additions to Stann Creek district's attractions, this area was only declared a national park in 2001. It covers an area of around 7,000 acres, incorporating mountains, thick swathes of jungle, three Mayan sites (Mayflower, Maintzunun and T'au Witz), several rivers and three large waterfalls (Bocawina, Three Sisters and Antelope Falls), with a network of trails linking the various elements together.

Over 230 bird species have been recorded within the park perimeters, including toucans, parrots and motmots, and the jungle is also home to jaguars and howler monkeys, so be sure to pack your binoculars, plenty of water and a swimsuit.

Getting here with your own transport is relatively easy – just follow the signs off the Southern Highway down an unpaved road for about 4½ miles until you reach the visitor centre. Getting here under your own steam is less so as there's no public transport. You pay your entrance fee and pick up a map of the trails at the visitor centre.

Nearby Cayes

There are a number of small cayes within easy reach of Dangriga, offering a wide range of activity and accommodation options.

Coco Plum Caye

Coco Plum is a private island, 8 miles (13km) from the coast of Dangriga, occupied by just a single, exclusive resort. If it's seclusion you are after then this may well be the choice for you, as there are only five cabanas on the whole 16-acre island, which come with A/C, fans, bath tub/shower combos and large verandas. Prices start from US$735 for four days, including meals and free use of kayaks and

Where to Stay at the Mayflower Bocawina National Park

★ Mama Noots >

Mama Noots, t 606 4353, f 522 3687, www.mamanoots.com ($$$; US$75). Located inside the Mayflower Bocawina National Park, Mama Noots is a very ecofriendly, self-sufficient sort of place, organically growing its own fruit and vegetables and using solar, wind and micro-hydro for electricity. The accommodation is in the form of six comfortable thatched bungalows (all with private bathrooms) and a larger family-sized duplex. The restaurant dishes up three meals a day (breakfast US$10, lunch US$10, dinner US$18), made mainly from ingredients from the lodge's garden.

snorkelling equipment. Fishing, scuba and honeymoon packages are also available.

Tobacco Caye

Just 30 minutes from Dangriga by boat, this little 5-acre island situated right over the tip of the barrier reef provides a rough-and-ready yin to Coco Plum Caye's classy exclusive yang. Appealing mainly to tourists on a lower budget, the accommodation is pretty basic and facilities minimal, with the emphasis on diving, kayaking and snorkelling rather than pampering. Expect simple rooms on coral-white sands, views out over the clear blue sea, and decent, basic meals. If you just want to sunbathe, lounge in a hammock and take to the water then this is a fairly inexpensive way to go about it.

There is a dive shop at Reef's End where training and certification is available to all guests on the island. Kayaks, fishing equipment and trips to other parts of the reef can also be arranged through any of the hotels listed.

South Water Caye

South Water Caye, more commonly referred to by locals simply as Water Caye, is 5 miles (8km) south of Tobacco Caye and around 14 miles (22.5km) from Dangriga (about 45 minutes away by boat). Encompassing over 15 acres of land – including palm-tree-lined beaches and some rather incongruous-looking stretches of pine forest – it's quite a lot larger than Tobacco and, because of the superiority of the accommodation options available, a fair bit pricier, although there isn't a great deal of difference between the two islands in terms of what can be seen. The quality of the snorkelling is slightly higher at Water Caye.

Glover's Reef

Named after the British pirate, John Glover, who used to launch raids against Spanish treasure ships from here, Glover's is the smallest and most southerly of the country's three atolls (oval-shaped coral reefs encircling lagoons). There are some great places to dive here, with turtles, sharks, barracuda and manta rays all commonly spotted in the coastal waters. Because of the relative difficulty of getting here from Belize City or the northern cayes, the reef is pretty quiet, welcoming just a steady flow, rather than a deluge, of tourists. The atoll has several islands, all located on its southeastern section, on which you'll find several reasonably priced accommodation options. However, when factoring your budget, do take into consideration the entrance fee – the reef is an officially protected marine reserve. Check with your resort to see if their package covers the cost.

Where to Stay in the Cayes around Dangriga

Tobacco Caye

Although it's always advisable to book in advance, the island's lodges are rarely fully booked, so it's perfectly possible to get a boat over (ask outside the Riverside Café in Dangriga during the morning, around US$18) to check the options for yourself and see what deals can be had before deciding. As there are no other restaurants on the island, all prices quoted include meals. The cheapest lodges (US$25–35) are **Gaviota Reef Resort** (**t** 509 5032, office **t** 502 0341, *gaviotareefresort.com*), **Lana's on the Reef** (**t** 520 5036), both of which have shared bathrooms only, and the **Tobacco Caye Paradise** (**t** 520 5101), which has a few private bathrooms. All three are basic but offer friendly service and good meals. Slightly more expensive options include:

Tobacco Caye Lodge, t 520 5033, **f** 227 6247, *www.tclodgebelize.com* ($$$$$; US$146). There are six cabins here, all with private bathrooms, ceiling fans and balconies (with hammocks) facing the sea. The piña coladas at the *palapa* bar come highly recommended.

Reef's End Lodge, t US 1-866 225 3581, **t** 522 2419/520 5037, **f** 522 2828, *www.reefsendlodge.com* ($$$; US$65). Eight large rooms (US$65) with private bathrooms and verandas, spread over a two-storey wooden building. There are also two private cabanas available (US$75) and a honeymoon suite. The restaurant and very popular bar are situated on stilts over the sea.

South Water Caye

Prices include all meals.

Pelican's Pouch, t 522 2044, **f** 522 2570, *sales@pelicanbeachbelize.com*, *www.southwatercaye.com* ($$$$$; US$235). This, the sister property of the Pelican Beach Resort in Dangriga, occupies 3½ acres of the southern end of Water Caye. Cabins (US$265) are nicely decorated with private bathrooms, although the rooms (US$235) are a little simpler. For groups, there is a two-storey dormitory (referred to as

the 'university'), which comes with a shared bathroom, kitchen and recreational areas. Packages, including transfers and trips, offered.

Blue Marlin Lodge, t US 1-800 798 1558, **t** 522 2243, **f** 522 2296, *www.bluemarlinlodge.com* ($$$$$; packages start at US$1,300 per person per week). The sister resort of the Bonefish Hotel in Dangriga, the Blue Marlin offers several types of accommodation: air-conditioned wooden beach cabins; guest rooms with fans; and the rather unusual-looking 'domed' cabins. Additional facilities include a full dive shop, a bar, and plenty of tour options.

Lesley Cottages at International Zoological Expeditions, t US 1-800 548 5843, **t** 523 7076, *www.ize2belize.com* ($$$$$; US$140). Although the accommodation at IZE is primarily reserved for groups of visiting students and naturalists, they do also rent out their simple, but pleasantly furnished, cottages on an individual basis. Packages start at around US$1,000 per week (or US$140 per day). If you are hoping for a bit of peace and quiet, however, you may want to check if any groups are staying before booking.

Glover's Reef

Manta Resort, t US 1-800 326 1724, **t** 463 0833, **f** 463 4081, *info@caye resorts.com*, *www.mantaresortbelize.com* ($$$$$; packages start at US$1,600 per week). The island's grandest choice, the Manta offers very comfortable, beautifully decorated mahogany cabanas (the hexagonal de luxe versions are particularly sumptuous). Exceedingly good meals are dished up in the new cantina at the end of a 50ft pier and cocktails are served out on a deck over the ocean. Manta has a full dive shop and offers PADI training.

Isla Marisol Resort, t US 1-866 990 9904, **t** 522 0235/520 2056, *www.islamarisolresort.com* ($$$$$; packages start at US$625 for 3 days). Owned by a Belizean family, the Ushers, who offer nice cabanas and good cuisine. During the day there are lots of dive trips available to guests, as well as kayaking and fishing. Evenings are spent relaxing with a Belikin on the bar over the sea.

⭐ Glover's
Atoll Resort &
Island Lodge >

Glover's Atoll Resort & Island Lodge, t 520 5016, f 223 5424, *www.glovers.com.bz*. Great budget choice offering a range of penny-pinching options, from thatched cabins on stilts over the sea (US$40 per day or US$249 a week) and beach cabins (US$30 per day or US$199 a week) to dormitory bunks (US$15 per day, US$149 a week) and camping space (US$10 per day, US$99 a week).

All cabins have shared toilets and showers and you can make use of the kitchen facilities. You'll have to bring your own food (or get it brought in by the resort at cost plus 20%). Otherwise meals are US$212 a week (more if bought separately). And all savings made can be put towards the variety of snorkelling and diving tours offered, all of which cost extra.

Hopkins

Hopkins, a Garifuna fishing village approximately 20 miles (32km) south of Dangriga, does rather wear its culture on its sleeve, albeit in a very charming way. Dangriga may be Belize's largest, oldest and most prominent Garifuna community, but it's at this smaller, more recently founded village that this culture is more readily and openly expressed, and where the language is more commonly spoken, making it perhaps a better bet for visitors wishing to immerse themselves in the Garifuna lifestyle (and taste real Garifuna cooking). The people are famously friendly and eager to talk about their way of life. Indeed, it's been argued that it's the community's relative youth – it was founded in 1937 – which has led to it ostentatiously upholding traditions and customs as a way of establishing and confirming its identity.

Hopkins is still one of Belize's more minor tourist towns, but it's growing all the time as people begin to wake up to its charms, and there are a growing number of accommodation options, particularly on the outskirts. The town itself is not much to look at – a jumbly, slightly tumbledown stretch of wooden clapboard houses, running parallel to a long stretch of palm-tree-lined beach. Everything you need is either on or just off the main road. There aren't any road names but that shouldn't be a problem. There aren't that many wrong turns you can take. If you get into difficulties, just ask a local.

For a relaxing getaway, providing access to beautiful scenery, a fascinating insight into another way of life and a handy HQ for diving trips out to the barrier reef, the village could hardly be bettered, but don't go expecting too much in the way of excitement unless, of course, it's Settlement Day (19 November), which, unsurprisingly, is celebrated with no little fervour here. The sights consist of the sea, the beach, the people – and that's it. This is a small village but one with a big personality.

Getting to Hopkins

By bus: Buses run to Hopkins from Dangriga at 12.15pm and 5pm and return at around the same times. The journey take about 30 mins. There is also an early-morning bus service to/from Placencia. It's best to ask in the village (or where you are travelling from) for the latest information on bus timetables as they seem to change regularly.

By car: The turning for the village is at Mile 15 on the Southern Highway. The road continues for roughly 4 miles (6.5 km), only a few sections of which are paved, before hitting Hopkins.

Tourist Information in Hopkins

There's no official tourist office, but www.hopkinsbelize.com is a useful website that's been created by the good people of the village and certainly worth checking out when planning a visit.

Services in Hopkins

Internet: Windshief Internet Café, on the beach, south of the old school (30 mins US$2.50, 1hr US$4), wireless connection available; Harbour House Internet Café, north end.

Laundry: Hopkins Laundry on the Hopkins/Sittee Rd.

Police: The police station is located at the northern end of town opposite Hopkins Rd (the road connecting Hopkins with the Southern Highway).

Supermarket: Everyday Supermarket, northern end of town, opposite police station.

Tour Operators and Equipment Hire in Hopkins

Most of the town's hotels should be able to arrange snorkelling, diving and fishing tours. The **Tipple Tree Beya Hotel** rents out bicycles and kayaks; the **All Season's Guesthouse** rents out motor scooters (US$37.50); while **Windschief Windsurfing School and Rental** (t 523 7247, www.windsurfing-belize. com) offers windsurfing lessons (and board hire) and fishing as well as a variety of other water-based sports/activities. It also rents out cabanas and can provide Internet access. It's located at the southern end of town, on the beach past the old school.

Shopping in Hopkins

Handmade crafts, gifts and jewellery are available at **Kulcha Gift Shop**, just south of the centre. Also in the southern end of town is the punningly named **Sew Much Hemp**, which offers a range of organic hemp-based products.

Where to Stay in Hopkins

Hopkins Inn, on the beach opposite the basketball court, t 523 7283, www.hopkinsinn.com ($$$; US$50). Several breezy tiled beach cabanas, with private bathrooms, refrigerators, fans, coffee makers and verandas. A continental breakfast is included in the price.

All Seasons Guesthouse, south end, t 523 7209, www.allseasonsbelize.com ($$$; US$43). Three clean, airy rooms, all with private bathrooms, coffee makers, fridges and fans (or, for US$7 more, a/c).

Whistling Seas Inn, t 608 0016, f 609 1263 ($$$; US$40). Five clean, spacious (albeit not particularly attractive) concrete beach cabanas with fridges, private bathrooms and coffee makers. The cabanas still feel quite fresh and new and this is fast becoming a pretty popular place for travellers.

Tipple Tree Beya Hotel, south end on beach, t 520 7006, www.tippletree.com ($$; US$30/40 shared/private bathrooms). Three rooms (one with shared bathroom) in a two-storey wooden building with fridges, coffee makers, shared verandas and plenty of hammocks. There's also one separate cabin, which comes with a private bathroom and kitchenette for US$50. Camping is allowed for US$5.

Windschief Cabanas, past the old school and on the beach (at the windsurfing school/Internet café/bar), t 523 7247, *www.windsurfing-belize. com* ($; US$25). The Windschief has just two cabins, both stilt-set affairs on the beach. The smaller cabin has one double bed (US$25), while the large one has two (US$40 for two people, US$50 for four). Both have toilets, cold showers (there is a separate shared hot shower), coffee makers, refrigerators, and balconies facing the sea.

South of Hopkins

Hamanasi Adventure & Dive Resort, t US 1-877 552 3483, t 520 7073, f 520 7090, *www.hamanasi.com* ($$$$$; US$250). This luxury beach resort boasts 18 stylish units, including two large honeymoon suites (with draped 4-poster beds, US$310), several beach-front rooms (US$250 or US$280 for de luxe) and, the pick of the bunch, six fantastic tree houses (US$300). These last have shady porches with hammocks where you can recline watching the abundant local birds flitting from branch to branch right in front of you. Additional facilities include a bar, a swimming pool, a gift shop, kayaks, bikes and a full diving and snorkelling centre. A range of diving and sight-seeing tours is available.

★ Toucan Sittee >>

Jaguar Reef, t US 1-800 289 5756, t 520 7040, f 520 7091, *www.jaguarreef.com* ($$$$$; US$175). The Jaguar Reef offers roomy cabanas with tile floors and comfy beds, as well as several even larger two-bedroom suites with kitchenettes, TVs, DVD players and stereos. Guests also have use of Iguana Lodge, a river-side thatched shelter with bar and seating area from where you can go kayaking or fishing. The staff here are very friendly and helpful.

★ Beaches and Dreams >

Beaches and Dreams, t US 1-907 388 9073, t 523 7259, *www.beachesand dreams.com* ($$$$; US$95). The Beaches and Dreams lodge consists of just four rooms, all beautifully decorated with dark hardwood interiors and colourful paintings and bedspreads. There is a good bar and an extremely popular restaurant offering a huge menu (with something for even the fussiest of eaters; meal plans cost US$40 per person per day). Complimentary bikes and kayaks are available to all guests, and tours can be arranged.

Sittee River

Just to the south of Hopkins village, the Sittee River village is a peaceful picturesque area of lush greenery adjoining a gently flowing river. Although it's officially been designated a village there isn't much to the place beside a few guesthouses.

Bocatura Bank, t 606 4590, *possumpt@ btl.net*, *www.bocaturabank. com* ($$$; US$45). The Bocatura Bank offers rooms for different budgets, ranging from the Mini Cabana (US$45) to the Treehouse Cabana (US$65), all with private bathrooms and refrigerators. Meal plans are US$30 per person per day and feature hearty local dishes and filling breakfasts.

Toucan Sittee, t 523 7039, *birdcity@btl. net*, *www.toucansittee.info* ($–$$$; US$22/50 shared/private bathroom). Occupying a lovely location next to the river, close to the beach and surrounded by greenery, this little family-run river-side lodge offers superb value. There are only five stilt-set rooms, varying in size and price from a bunkhouse (US$11.50 per person) to a private apartment with a kitchen (US$77 for two people, US$99 for four). Food is fresh, wholesome and home-cooked by the owner, with plenty of choice for vegetarians.

Eating Out in Hopkins

Hopkins is the ideal place to taste some real Garifuna home cooking, literally so in some instances, as a few village households offer visitors the chance to join them for a traditional family meal. If this appeals, your hotel should be able to arrange it for you.

Restaurant menus tend to revolve around the staples of rice and beans and simple preparations of the day's freshly caught seafood, often augmented with a Garifuna or Creole 'special of the day'. If you want to sample a particular dish, you'll need to ring ahead and arrange it in advance. **Innie's** (t 523 7026) and **Iris's** (t 523 7019) are old favourites, and **King Cassava** (t 503 7305) and **The Watering Hole** (t 614 8686) are also very reliable.

For more internationally oriented (and more expensive) cuisine, head down towards the resorts of the Sittee River area, most of which operate decent restaurants (*see* 'Where to Stay').

Entertainment and Nightlife in Hopkins

There are several bars dotted around the village. Popular local haunts include **King Cassava** (at the intersection), which often puts on live music and **The Watering Hole**, which has a pool table.

Garifuna drumming, often accompanied by dancing, is the traditional form of entertainment here. Practitioners don't come much better than the LeBeha Boys at the **LeBeha Drumming Centre** (north end of beach, *www.lebeha.com*). This is where the village boys (aged around 10–14) come to learn how to drum, sing and dance according to Garifuna custom. They perform every night with great concentration, dedication and enthusiasm, making for an enjoyable evening's entertainment. The boys have even released an album to help fund their centre. Their CD can be bought online from a variety of places including UK and US online music retailers (check their website for details) and from the centre itself.

Cockscomb Basin Wildlife Sanctuary (Cockscomb Jaguar Reserve)

① Cockscomb Basin Wildlife Sanctuary
t 223 5004; open 4.30am–4.30pm; adm US$5

In the early 1980s, a young American naturalist, Dr Alan Rabinowitz, arrived in the Cockscomb Basin – so called because the nearby stretch of the Maya Mountains resembles a cockscomb (sort of) – to make a study of the region's jaguars, the first ever conducted in Belize. The doctor's intense, sometimes hazardous work, undertaken over a couple of years, led directly to a part of the region being designated an official jaguar sanctuary – the first in the world – in 1986. In 1990, the sanctuary's range was extended to cover the entire basin. However, this was not simply a case of marking the sanctuary's limits and leaving the jaguars to get on with it. The basin was at that time home to several hundred Mopan Maya, who were understandably reluctant to leave their homes. After much debate, they agreed to relocate to a purpose-built centre just outside the sanctuary, known as the Maya Centre, in return for being given jobs working in the sanctuary. Though Cockscomb is officially administered by the Belize Audubon Society (*see* p.51), much of its tourist infrastructure remains in the control of the local Maya who run its gift shops and visitor centre, and act as guides.

The sanctuary is a stunning place, set between three banks of mountains that protect over 128,000 acres of lush jungle, in which can be found (if, like the doctor, you're prepared to look long and hard enough) all five species of Belizean wild cats – **jaguars**, **pumas**, **jaguarundis**, **margays** and **ocelots**. Of course, this is no Belize Zoo and, given big cats' secretive, predatory (not to mention nocturnal) nature, it's pretty unlikely that they'll reveal themselves to visitors meandering along the sanctuary's trails (although you never know). Still, don't be too disheartened. The sanctuary is also home to a number of more commonly spotted creatures, including **howler monkeys** (for your best chance, come in the early morning when

Getting to Cockscomb Basin Wildlife Sanctuary

The **Maya Centre**, which sits on the border of the sanctuary, can be found at Mile 14 of the Southern Highway. If travelling by **bus** to/from Dangriga, Placencia or Punta Gorda, you may have to ask the driver to stop. Stock up on drinks and snacks in the village, if you haven't already done so, as there is nowhere to eat once in the reserve. It's another 6 miles from the Maya Centre to the visitor centre and the sanctuary entrance, along an unpaved road. If without your own transport, you can get a **taxi** (US$15) from the village, and also arrange a guide and accommodation. Visitors must first sign in and pay their entrance fee at the **Maya Centre Women's Craft Shop**, the first building on the right at the side of the road (a ticket will be issued) before proceeding to the visitor centre, where they must show their ticket, and re-register.

you'll hear their foghorn-like howls reverberating across the forest), red-eye tree frogs, as seen on many a Central American postcard, as well as pacas, coatis and kinkajous. Over 290 species of **birds** have been recorded here, among them the brightly coloured scarlet macaw.

Cockscomb offers around 12 miles of **trails** varying in length and difficulty, all of which leave from the visitor centre, where you can pick up a map (US$2.50) and hire binoculars (US$2.50). Next door is a small exhibition detailing the sanctuary's work and displaying finds from the area – including a pickled fer-de-lance, the region's most venomous snake. Just outside you can see some of the (rather harsh-looking) cages in which the doctor used to trap jaguars for studying and tagging, and a former logger's pick-up truck, which now sits with a tree growing rather pointedly from its cab.

The easiest route is along a self-guided trail which takes you past a series of numbered stopping points – next to medicinal plants, trees favoured by howler monkeys, jaguar scratching posts, etc. The Tiger Fern Trail offers a more challenging hike into the nearby hills. But if you really want to test yourself, then the 4–5-day hike to Victoria Peak is the one for you. Victoria Peak is, according to some, the highest point in Belize, although others claim it to be Doyle's

Where to Stay at Cockscomb Basin

The **Belize Audubon Society** (t 223 5004, base@btl.net, www.belize audubon.org) offers basic self-catering accommodation within the sanctuary – there's a communal kitchen. The closest food shops are in the Maya Centre, although there isn't exactly a great deal of choice, so you might be better off stocking up in Dangriga/ Placencia. If you ask around, you may be able to get meals prepared in the village and delivered to you. The standard of lodging ranges from very basic dorms (US$8) with pit latrines and dorms with composting toilets

(US$18) to larger cabins (S$53.50) for groups and families. There are no hot-water showers. Camping is allowed, but permission must be granted and a small fee paid (US$2.50). Call or email ahead.

Low-cost accommodation is also available in the Maya Centre at **Tutzil Nah Cottages** (t 520 3044, tutzilnah@ btl.net, www.mayacenter.com), which has screened rooms with shared bathrooms. **Nu'uk Che'il** (t 520 3033) and **Menjentzil's Lodge** (t 520 3032, isaqui@btl.net) also both offer bunk-houses and private rooms. Camping is available at all three, as are meals, tours and kayak rentals.

Delight in the Chiquibul National Park. Either way, it's a long walk to the top of the 3,675ft (1,120 m) mountain. A tour guide and a permit are obligatory.

Placencia

The Placencia peninsula has over the past decade become a sort of tourism hothouse, with development taking place at a feverish pace, and set to accelerate in the near future. The first thing you'll notice as you make your way down the thin 16-mile (26km) strip of land jutting out from the Belizean mainland will no doubt be all the construction sites, dozens and dozens of them marking the position of future resorts, holiday homes, hotels and condominiums. Nobody in the building industry is out of work here. Whether all this building is being done in as environmentally and ecologically sound a way as government regulations prescribe, so as to preserve the integrity of the barrier reef (just 20 miles offshore) and the peninsula's stretches of mangroves (home to a mass of wildlife), is a moot point. It certainly doesn't look as if anyone has much trouble getting planning permission around here. And where there have been obvious examples of environmental laws being flouted, these have rarely led to prosecutions. But then, that's hardly surprising, considering that all this expansion is happening with the full support of the government, who welcome the investment and job opportunities it brings to the area. Some people have even claimed that the greater environmental good might actually be served by the ecological sacrifice of the peninsula, with the profits derived from its touristification used to protect other areas from future development. The fear, of course, is that as tourism continues to boom on the peninsula, so the economic pressure to spread development to other areas will become overwhelming.

Orientation

There is just one sandy road running the entire length of the narrow peninsula. This takes you through **Maya Beach**, a small community of mainly American ex-pats with a few resorts and a couple of bars; **Seine Bight**, 3m further south, a Garifuna village with a population of around 800, and the airport, before finally hitting **Placencia village**. The road continues south through the village to the end of the peninsula, eventually petering out next to the tourist information centre. Note that the road skirts the airstrip's eastern end – look out for planes landing/taking off.

In town the village's other main artery is a narrow concrete path running north–south, which was laid out when the village was constructed to aid the transport of building materials over the sand. Today, according to the Guinness Book of Records, it's the 'narrowest main street in the world' – quite some claim for something that is essentially a reinforced wheelbarrow track. Alongside, you'll see a number of signposts pointing out the direction of the town's various hotels, restaurants and tour operators, which are very handy, as the lack of official streets can sometimes make it feel as if you are simply walking through someone's sandy backyard.

Getting to and around Placencia

By Air

Maya Island Air (t 522 2659, *www.mayaislandair.com*) and **Tropic Air** (t 422 3435, *www.tropicair.com*) both operate several daily flights to/from Belize City (US$81 from Goldson International, US$68.50 from Belize Municipal). They take 45 mins (stopping en route in Dangriga) and touch down at the airstrip 1½m (3km) north of the village, from where you can get a taxi into town (US$5 per carload).

By Bus

National Transport Buses run from Dangriga to Placencia at 12noon and 5pm; **James Buses** make the same journey at 10.30am, 11.30am and 5.15pm. Returning National Transport Buses are at 6am and 1pm; returning James Buses at 5.30am, 11.15am and 2pm. Schedules often change, so it may be worthwhile checking the notice board at the tourist information centre for an up-to-date timetable. Buses drop off/pick up passengers from the main bus stop on the seafront, opposite the tourist office and Shell garage.

By Car

Look for the signposted turning off the Southern Highway around 10 miles (16km) south of the Cockscomb Basin Wildlife Sanctuary/Maya Centre. Follow the road for around 8m (13km) until you reach the village of Riversdale, which marks the start of the peninsula road. The peninsula road is very sandy and dusty, apart from a few paved sections running through the towns (where you'll need to keep a close lookout for unmarked speed humps). If you get stuck behind a truck churning up dust, you probably won't be able to see anything at all. Turn your lights on and drive slowly. Be prepared to pull over for a while to let things clear if visibility gets too bad. The authorities have promised to pave the road ready for the end of 2006, although they've made similar promises before. Still, the sheer amount of development going on at present, and the number of influential parties with a vested interest in the improvement of the road infrastructure, may serve to force their hand slightly.

Barefoot Auto Rentals in the village (t 607 5125 or 610 3214, f 631 7225, *www.barefootautorentals.net*) can arrange to have a car meet you at the airstrip.

Golf carts can also be hired, for getting around, from many of the area's hotels.

By Boat

The **Hokie Pokie Water Taxi** (t 523 2376) departs from Independence/Mango Creek (the village on the other side of the lagoon) for Placencia at 6.30am, 7.30am, 8am, 2.30pm and 4.30pm. Return trips run at 6.45am, 10am, 4pm and 5pm. The journey takes about 20 mins and costs US$5 per person.

The **Gulf Cruza** (t 202 4506/523 4045) runs from Placencia to Puerto Cortés in Honduras, on Fridays. It departs from Placencia village at 9.30am, makes a 10am stop at Big Creek for an hour, before heading off again, arriving in Honduras at 2pm. Tickets are available from the Placencia tourist office (US$50). The return trip leaves Puerto Cortés at 10am on Mon.

One thing, however, is sure. In five years time, Placencia will look completely different from how it does now. For this reason, you should treat the following guide as a moment captured in time, and not as a definitive reference. Expect everything to have grown by about 5–10 per cent by the time you get here.

The region's main attraction for both tourists and developers alike is its **beaches**, generally regarded as among the best in the entire country. The peninsula is home to a number of small communities, including Seine Bight and Maya Beach, the principal one being Placencia village itself, right on the southern tip. Though considerably bulked out in recent years, with new condo developments crowding down from the north, Placencia is still a pretty small-scale, budget-orientated affair of weathered clapboard houses resting on stilts in the sand, with little hand-painted signs pointing you in the direction of the nearest inn or eatery. It exudes a distinctly Caribbean charm and tranquillity.

Though primarily a beach destination, with the emphasis on kicking your shoes off and taking things slowly (the tourist slogan for Placencia is 'Barefoot Perfect'), the village also has a number of **tour operators** offering trips inland to national parks and Mayan sites (the Monkey River Tour is particularly popular, *see* p.196) and out to sea to visit the cayes, dive the reef (around 45 minutes away by boat) and, in season, swim and snorkel with migrating whale sharks (the world's largest fish, but perfectly harmless) out at **Gladden Spit**.

🌟 Gladden Spit

If you're trying to stick to a budget and would rather forego the expense of trips, or are just trying to keep things local and low-key, you'll find that most of the village hotels rent out snorkelling gear (flippers US$2.50, and snorkels and masks US$2.50; these can also be rented from Ocean Motion, *see* 'Tour Companies') and offer free use of their kayaks, which you can use to explore both the sea and the lagoon on the peninsula's western side where manatees, dolphins, Morelet's crocodiles and jabiru storks have all been spotted.

Tourist Information in Placencia

ⓘ Placencia >
t 523 4045,
www.placencia.com;
open 9–5

The **Belize Tourism Board**'s Placencia office is located on the southern sea front, near the bus stop.

There's a full notice board and you can pick up lots of leaflets, as well as a copy of the free local monthly newspaper *Placencia Breeze* (*www. placenciabreeze.com*), which has lots of listings and an up-to-date events guide.

Services in Placencia

Banks: Atlantic Bank, Main Rd, t 523 3431. Its ATM accepts foreign cards.

Internet: De Tatch Café, Seaspray Hotel (access for around US$5 an hour). The Purple Space Monkey can also offer a very slow, temperamental (but, crucially, free) service.

Pharmacies: The Placencia Pharmacy, t 523 3346. Next to Wallen's Market.

Post office: At the south end of the sidewalk in the same building as the Fisherman's Co-op.

Supermarkets: EveryDay Supermarket, Main Rd.

Tour Operators in Placencia

Aahsum Adventures, t 523 3159, *bens adventures2@yahoo.com, www.aahsum belize.com*. Offers a wide range of sightseeing tours, including: Cockscomb Basin Wildlife Sanctuary, with cave-tubing and swimming (US$60); Maya Village of Red Bank to see the scarlet macaws (US$60, late Dec– March only); Mayflower Bocawina National Park (US$60); Actun Tunichil Muknal Cave (US$160); Nim Li Punit & Blue Creek Cave (US$85); Lubaantun, plus swimming in the Rio Blanco River (US$80); Caracol, plus swimming in the falls of the Mountain Pine Ridge Reserve (US$220); Xunantunich with visit to St Hermans Cave (US$110) or Cahal Pech (US$105).

Belize Sailing Charters, t 523 3138, f 523 3251, *sailingbelize@yahoo.com, www. belize-sailing-charters.com*. If you fancy spending a few nights at sea, this hires out fully crewed charter boats from US$500 a night, and catamarans from US$2,600 for a week. Daily sailing rates from US$50–135. Honeymoon charters and live-aboard scuba trips also available.

Joy Tours, t 523 3325, *www.belizewith joy.com*. Tours include: snorkelling on the reef (US$60) and snorkelling with whale sharks at Gladden Spit (US$75). Private diving tours start at US$85 for two dives, or US$195 for whale shark diving at Gladden Spit. Also offers kayaking and camping packages (8 nights for US$1,473) and fishing packages (US$1,848 for 4 nights or US$2,920 for 7 nights).

Ocean Motion, t 523 3363, *www.ocean motionplacencia.com*. Tours include: half-day snorkelling (US$30); full-day snorkelling at Laughing Bird Caye and Silk Caye (US$60); sports fishing (US$325 per day); manatee-watching (US$25); Cockscomb Basin Wildlife Sanctuary and cave-tubing (US$65); Monkey River Tour and manatee-watching (US$55); Nim Li Punit and Blue Creek Cave (US$85); Nim Li Punit and Lubaantun (US$85); Lubaantun and Rio Blanco Waterfalls (US$85); Xunantunich and Cahal Pech (US$125); Xunantunich and St Herman's Cave (US$125); Cahal Pech and Blue Hole National Park (US$125); Belize Zoo and Blue Hole National Park (US$120).

SeaHorse Dive Shop, t 523 3166, *seahorse@btl.net, www.belizescuba. com*. Offers: snorkelling trips (from US$40); two-tank wall or night diving trips (from US$85); two-tank diving trips to Shark Hole, Gladden Spit to see the whale sharks, Glover's Reef atoll (US$150). Fishing trips (including boat, guide and lunch US$300–350) and dive courses also available.

Toadal Adventure, t 523 3207, *www. toadaladventure.com*. Tours include: 5-night sea kayaking and snorkelling trip, camping on the cayes (US$1,125); 3-night river kayaking trip (US$800). Day extensions to these packages are available to include a trip to Cockscomb Basin Wildlife Sanctuary and/or Monkey River.

Where to Stay in Placencia

In Placencia, as is customary in most of Belize's major tourist centres, there is a strict demarcation between budget accommodation, which is mostly found in town, and the more expensive places, which are located out of town, further north up the peninsula. Some of the area's top-end choices are very fancy indeed, offering well-maintained (if not entirely private) stretches of beach, lots of tour options, swimming pools, spas and sparkling facilities (but then, many are only a few years old). Village accommodation is less lavishly equipped, but often has more character. Several of the hotels are long-established family-run places. You may miss out on a bit of pampering, but staying in the village puts you within easy reach of the town's shops, restaurants and nightlife. The downside, of course, is that it can get a bit crowded in high season – you'll often find yourself sharing your stretch of beach with a fair few other people; hotel balconies and patios are often overlooked and it can be a little noisy/lively and fun (depending on your point of view) at night.

Placencia Village

Ranguana Lodge, t 523 3112, *www. ranguanabelize.com* ($$$; US$74/79 fan/a/c). Five simple but comfortable beach cabanas (three units have a/c) with private bathrooms, hot water, fans, refrigerators, coffee makers and sea-facing verandas. It's not a bad option if you want to be in the thick of it, but the cabanas are placed quite close together.

Coconut Cottage, t 523 3234, *kw placencia@yahoo.com, www.coconut cottage.net* ($$$; US$55). A good self-catering option, the Coconut Cottage consists of just one large hardwood cabin situated on the beach with a full kitchen (including all utensils), fans and veranda. The cottage sleeps three.

Pickled Parrot Cabanas, t 604 0278, *www.pickledparrotbelize.com* ($$$; US$50). This popular restaurant between the main road and sidewalk also has two pleasant hardwood cabanas with fridges, fans and balconies.

Westwind Hotel, t 523 3255, *www.west windhotel.com* ($$$; US$50). The Westwind's rooms come with fridges, a/c, private bathrooms and a choice of balcony or terrace. Freshly brewed coffee is served every morning and there's a large *palapa* on the beach for shady hammock naps for when the caffeine kick begins to subside.

Manatee Inn, t 523 4083, **f** 607 0202, *www.manateeinn.com* ($$$; US$45). The Manatee is a professionally run, attractive wooden two-storey inn. Its spotlessly clean rooms have hardwood interiors, private bathrooms and lovely views of the sea.

The Yellow House, t 523 3481, **f** 523 4028, *yellowhouse@gmail.com* ($$; US$35). Bright and cheery rooms, some with fridges and microwaves, all with private bathrooms in a two-storey yellow building with veranda. Located between the main road and the sidewalk.

Seaspray Hotel, t 523 3148, **f** 523 3364, *www.seasprayhotel.com* ($; US$25). The brightly painted seafront rooms of the Seaspray range in size and price (US$25–60), but all come with private bathrooms and fans, and some have fridges, coffee makers and balconies. It's very popular. Prior booking advised.

Lydia's Guesthouse, t 523 3117, **f** 523 3354, *lydias@btl.net* ($; US$23). Lydia's is a budget-orientated two-storey guesthouse whose eight rooms have fridges, fans and shared bathrooms. There are also a couple of slightly fancier two-bedroomed cabanas for rent, which come with kitchenettes.

North of Village (near the airstrip)

⭐ Turtle Inn >

Turtle Inn, t US 1-800 746 3745, **t** 523 3244, *www.turtleinn.com* ($$$$$; US$315). One of the area's most lavish choices, the beach-front Turtle Inn is owned by the Hollywood director Francis Ford Coppola (who also owns the equally fancy Blancaneaux Lodge in the Pine Ridge Mountain Resort, *see* p.169). All the cottages and suites are beautifully decorated in a Balinese style, with hand-carved doors and art, and feature a small private garden area with outdoor showers and private screened porches (they also feature genuinely Balinese-size doors – watch your head). There are also a couple of supremely luxurious two-bedroom suites with kitchenettes, as well as an Italian-inspired restaurant/bar (under a giant thatched roof), a pool, a beach bar, a spa, a dive shop and children's area with an ice-cream counter. Guests have complimentary use of the hotel's pedal boats, kayaks and bikes. As well

equipped as the resort is, it's set to expand in the next few years so as to compete with all the new developments taking place in the area, and so will soon have several new cottages, a second swimming pool, a garden grill and (the most intriguing addition) a Creole restaurant.

Chabil Mar Villas, t 523 3606, **f** 523 3611, *www.chabilmarvillas.com* ($$$$$; US$260/350 1/2 bedrooms). Opened in December 2005, the blue-roofed Chabil Mar is a high-spec condo complex of 22 privately owned apartments, of which 19 are let out to vacationers. The villas range in price and size – from one bedroom one bathroom (US$260) to two bedrooms two bathrooms (US$350–550) – and there is also a lavish honeymoon suite (US$550). All have private balconies, cable TV, a/c, fully equipped kitchens and expensive fittings, but are rather kitschily decorated in a sort of random ethnic style. There are also two swimming pools, a golf-car rental service, but no restaurant. Instead guests order their meals from a kitchen, which are then delivered to their room (although the quality of the cuisine is, for the price, rather poor – better to eat out).

The Inn at Robert's Grove, t US 1-800 565 9757, **t** 523 3565, *www.roberts grove.com* ($$$$$; US$189). With prices that start at $189 for a standard room, rising to US$460 for a suite, this would, were it located anywhere else in Belize, be considered rather expensive. Here, it's just another resort, albeit one of the best equipped, and one that owns two small offshore islands, to which it offers tours (*see* p.194). All rooms are spacious and nicely decorated with rich textiles and tiled floors. Rates include use of the hot tubs, three swimming pools, tennis courts, gym, kayaks and windsurfing boards. The resort also has a dive shop offering a range of tours out to the reef, a spa and two restaurants (Habanero, *see* 'Eating Out', and the Seaside Restaurant).

Rum Point Inn, t 523 3239, **f** 523 3240, *rupel@direcway.com, www.rumpoint. com* ($$$$$; US$179). Today it's just another resort among many, but back in the early 70s Rum Point was a true pioneer when it became the first resort to open in Placencia. It may now be outshone by many of its more modern competitors, but still offers a reasonable level of comfort with 10 concrete dome-shaped beach cabanas, all with ceiling fans, fridges and coffee maker; and 12 more luxurious (and more private) garden suites (US$209), which come with a/c, separate seating areas, and large bathrooms. The main building has a library, a bar, a gift shop, a restaurant, a pool and a dive shop (a range of tours is offered). Guests have free use of the resort's bikes, snorkelling gear, kayaks and dinghies.

Miller's Landing Resort, t 523 3010, f 523 3011, *www.millerslanding.net* ($$$$; US$85). Miller's Landing's cabanas occupy three-storey beachfront 'triplex' buildings, set amid pleasant gardens. All come with wooden floors, queen beds and ceiling fans, while those on the upper level have futons and verandas (US$135, plus US$20 per additional person). Meal packages (including breakfast, lunch and a 5-course dinner) are available for US$40 a day. There's also a swimming pool, and fishing and diving tours on offer.

Seine Bight Village

Nautical Inn, t US 1-800 688 0377, t 523 3595, f 523 3594, *www.nauticalinn belize.com* ($$$$$; US$146). One of the area's more low-key resorts, the Nautical Inn is nonetheless very well equipped, with a number of comfortable two-storey beach-front cabanas. The standard rooms are on the ground floor and come with a/c, TVs, telephones, coffee makers and private bathrooms, while the second floor de luxe versions come with all of the above, but are larger and have king-sized beds (US$156). Family rooms are available as are meal plans, and there's a tackle shop, a dive shop and a reasonably priced restaurant.

Blue Crab Resort, t 523 3544, f 523 3543, *www.bluecrabbeach.com* ($$$$; US$90/100 fan/a/c). The small family-run Blue Crab has two thatched cabanas, both with hardwood floors, fans, private bathrooms and private porches, as well as four slightly larger better-equipped rooms (a/c) set slightly further back from the beach. The restaurant serves a hybrid Asian/Belizean/American menu.

Maya Beach

Barnacle Bill's Beach Bungalows, t 523 8010, *taylors@btl.net* or *barnaclebills@hotmail.com* ($$$$; US$105). Bill's two stilt-set bungalows sleep up to three people (on a queen bed and a sofa bed) and are a decent self-catering option with fully equipped kitchens (complete with utensils), private bathrooms, porches with hammocks and screened windows.

Maya Breeze Inn, t US 1-888 458 8581, t 523 8012, *www.mayabreezeinn.com* ($$$$; US$85/95 room/cabin). The Maya Breeze comprises a main building with four spacious, nicely decorated rooms, all with private bathrooms, a/c, fans, fridges, TVs and balconies, and a further three self-catering cabins on the beach, which come equipped with kitchenettes, and are furnished with Guatemalan arts and crafts.

Singing Sands Inn, t 523 8017, *www.singingsands.com* ($$$; US$75). Occupying a lush tropical garden just back from the beach, the Singing Sands Inn offers six rather attractive cabanas (a mixture of sea and garden views), with hardwood interiors and ceiling fans.

Ranguana Caye and Robert's Caye

The Inn at Robert's Grove in Placencia (*see* p.193) owns these two islands. Contact them (t 523 3565, *www.robertsgrove.com*) for more details. Each island can be rented for US$2,776 per night, if you want it all to yourself.

Ranguana Caye, a 1hr boat ride from Placencia ($$$$$; prices start at US$379 per person per night or US$1,343 for seven nights). Three rustic private cabanas on this 2-acre caye 18 miles from Placencia.

Robert's Caye, a ½hr boat ride from Placencia ($$$$$; prices start at US$402 pp per night or US$1,509 for seven nights). Set in one acre of grounds, with four thatched cabanas built partially over the ocean. 10 miles from Placencia.

Eating Out in Placencia

The advice for eating out is pretty much the same as for accommodation – for budget places stick to Placencia village, for something more fancy head to the restaurants of the neighbouring resorts.

De' Tatch Seafood Beach Grill & Bar, at Seaspray Hotel. Reasonable beach-front *palapa* restaurant. The menu is aimed primarily at passing tourists and, as such, is none too adventurous. But they do serve large portions and offer daily specials. They also do a pretty mean coconut shrimp curry.

Garden Brew Coffee House, t 523 3617. Serves a range of speciality coffees and teas, along with a fine selection of sticky treats, soups and sandwiches. For something a little more filling they also offer a dinner menu featuring some impressive and authentic-tasting Thai dishes (as well as burgers for the less adventurous).

Habenero Mexican Café & Bar, Robert's Grove Marina, **t** 523 3565. A rather good Mexican hotel-restaurant overlooking the lagoon. The menu includes all the expected staples – enchiladas, chimichangas, tacos, fajitas – as well as a pretty decent *ceviche* (cold fish and seafood 'cooked' in lime juice).

John The Baker Man, off the main road. John has long been famed for his fresh breads and delicious cinnamon buns (get there early).

Mare Restaurant, Turtle Inn, **t** 523 3244. As you'd expect of one of the area's most celebrated resorts, the Mare is one of Placencia's very best restaurants (albeit also one of its most expensive), serving a range of authentic Italian dishes – pastas, thin-crust pizzas, calzones – as well as a decent array of steak and seafood choices. There's also a very good bar.

Pickled Parrot Bar & Grill. Hugely popular bar that offers a 'Happy Hour' from 5–6pm daily (when tropical rum punch is just US$1) and a basic menu of pizzas, burgers, fajitas and seafood.

Purple Space Monkey Restaurant and Bar, Main Rd, opposite the football field, **t** 523 4094. A popular local hang-out, the Purple Space Monkey offers a range of services in addition to its decent café (which is open for breakfast and lunch only, when it serves a standard burger/burrito style menu), including a full bar (very popular at night), a book exchange and free (but very slow) Internet access.

The Shack. Catering for Placencia's health-conscious backpacking fraternity, this tiny little place offers fruit smoothies, juices, big seafood salads, and vegetarian lunches, plus a range of other healthy snacks.

Trattoria Placencia, t 623 3394. On the beach front, this is one of the village's fancier, more culinary choices, dishing up a range of good handmade pastas, as well as a decent selection of wines. Open for dinner only.

Wendy's Creole Restaurant and Bar. Good local favourite serving a wide range of Creole dishes. Air-conditioned.

Entertainment and Nightlife in Placencia

Be sure to check the listings in the *Placencia Breeze* for scheduled events such as live music, demonstrations of Garifuna drumming and dancing. The resorts to the north of the village often hold weekend events in their bars and restaurants. On Saturdays, **Robert's Grove**'s pool-side bar has an evening BBQ with live music. In Placencia village itself the hot spots are the **Tipsy Tuna Sports Bar** (this is the place to go if there's a major televised sporting event you want to catch), which has pool tables and footballs and stages karaoke evenings on Saturdays, **J-Byrds** which attracts a nice mix of locals and tourists and often puts on live bands on weekends (both are open till 2am) and the more tourist-orientated **Pickled Parrot Bar**, where patrons come for the happy hour (5–6pm Fri) and stay to sample the wide range of potent cocktails (including the delightfully named 'Parrot's Piss').

Nearby Attractions

There are over 70 small, sandy, palm-dotted islands off the coast of Placencia. Some can be visited on snorkelling and diving trips, but many are privately owned and inaccessible to the general public.

Laughing Bird Caye National Park

Laughing Bird Caye

A popular day-trip destination for tourists and locals alike is the picturesque Laughing Bird Caye (*www.laughingbird.org*), located 13 miles off the coast of Placencia. Co-managed by the Friends of Nature Belize (*www.friendsofnaturebelize.org*) and the Forestry Department, this became a national park in 1991 and in 1996 was declared a World Heritage Site by UNESCO. The name 'Laughing Bird' is a reference to the laughing gulls that used to nest on the island. Though these birds now breed elsewhere, away from prying eyes, they can still often be seen on the island along with brown pelicans and frigate birds. Since 1996 there has been a ban on fishing and camping on the island but it's still open to day visitors wanting to use it as a base for snorkelling and diving, or as a picnic spot. The island rests on the eastern edge of a type of reef known as a faro, a steep shelf of reef surrounding a central lagoon (like an atoll) that provides a home to many different types of coral and sponges, as well as turtles, trumpet fish, eagle rays and queen angelfish.

Monkey River Town

Monkey River Town

'Town' is a bit of an exaggeration. With a population of just 200, this barely qualifies as a village, comprising a few clapboard houses, a couple of basic stores, and a handful of places to sleep and eat. But then, what brings travellers to the area is not so much the town, as the river on which it sits, and in particular the abundant local wildlife. Popular 'Monkey River trips' can be undertaken either from Placencia (14 miles away) or from Monkey River Town itself, and consist of a guided cruise past the river's mangrove banks on the look out for turtles, iguanas, crocodiles, howler monkeys, birds and more, hiking some jungle trails, a spot of swimming and lunch back in the village. If you wish to hang around for a few days, the **Sunset Inn** (t 709 2028, *www.monkeyriverbelize.com*) has eight private rooms with fans and shared balcony, for US$30 per night.

Punta Gorda

Punta Gorda (or 'PG' as it's more commonly referred to) is the capital of the country's most southerly district, Toledo, and marks the end of the Southern Highway. A small port and fishing village, PG was founded in 1832 by a group of Honduran Garifuna. Today, Garifuna still make up the majority of the town's 5,000-strong population, although they've since been joined by Creoles, Maya and Indians. Punta Gorda's remote location, lack of beaches (despite being on the seafront) and often overwhelming humid climate – as evidenced by the lush local vegetation – means that it has traditionally been ignored by tourists. In recent years, however, interest in the

Getting to PG

By air: **Maya Island Air** (t 722 2856, *www.mayaislandair.com*) and **Tropic Air** (t 226 2012, *www.tropicair.com*) both fly into the PG airstrip from Belize International (US$103), Belize Municipal (US$88), Dangriga (US$44) and Placencia (US$40) daily. Flights from Belize City take 55 mins. PG's airstrip lies a few blocks inland, a 5min walk from the centre of town.

By bus: **James Bus** (t 722 2625) operates daily services between Belize City and Punta Gorda at 5.30am, 10am and 2.45pm, stopping at Belmopan, Dangriga and Mango Creek en route and taking 6½hrs. They also operate a direct express service twice a day Mon–Sat at 3.30pm and 5.30pm which takes just 5hrs. Tickets cost US$12. The James Bus terminal is located by the police station. Return buses depart at 6am and 8am with an express service at 3pm on Fri and Sat only.

By car: The journey by car from Belize City takes roughly 6hrs along the paved and relatively well-maintained Southern Highway.

Getting away from PG

By boat: Daily boats leave the main pier in Punta Gorda bound for Puerto Barrios in Guatemala. The journey takes around an hour. The service departs PG at 9am, returning at 2pm, and is provided by **Requena Watertaxis** (t 722 2070, *watertaxi@btl.net*). Tickets (US$17.50) can be bought either from Requena's office at 12 Front St or at the pier. Boats also go from here to Livingston in Guatemala on Tues and Fri at around 10am (US$17.50, 1hr).

Punta Gorda

town and its surrounding area (which is home to numerous Maya villages) has begun to grow steadily, with a few more up-market hotels opening. For now, however, it's still a place largely visited by (and catering for) independent travellers and backpackers, who use it as a low-cost base from which to explore the region's Mayan sites and take advantage of the easy access to neighbouring Guatemala. Those travellers that do venture here will find a pretty relaxed place, where people are left to wander and explore as they like, free from hassle. Just be sure to bring an umbrella with you, as this is the country's wettest region and heavy bursts of rainfall are guaranteed pretty much year-round.

The Town

Punta Gorda is laid out according to a rough grid pattern. The centre of town is marked by the small triangular **Central Park** in which stands a **clock tower**. **Front Street**, which runs along the shoreline, is the main artery where you'll find the bus stop, customs and immigration, post office, police station and tourist information office. The town's **market** is also held here from 6am four days a week – Mon, Wed, Fri and Sat. Saturday is the busiest day when people flock here from surrounding villages and across from Guatemala to sell their crafts and food. The town is small and easy to navigate on foot but taxis are available. Trips within PG should cost around US$3.

Tourist Information and Services in PG

The **Tourist Information Office**, which shares its premises with the Toledo Ecotourism Association Office, is on Front St. Do also check out the town's official website, *www.puntagorda belize.com*.

Banks: Belize Bank, Main St, t 722 2324.

Hospital: Main St, t 722 2026.

Internet: V-Comp Technologies, t 722 0093, 29 Main St; Earth Runnings, Middle St.

Pharmacies: Front Street Pharmacy, Front St.

Police: Front St, t 722 2022.

Post office: Front St, t 722 2087.

Tour Companies in PG

TIDE Tours, corner of Prince and Main St, t 722 2129, *www.tidetours.org*. TIDE Tours is a subsidiary of the Toledo Institute for Development and Environment (*www.tidebelize.org*) and was formed to promote ecotourism in the Toledo district and generate funds for the TIDE conservation group. It offers a range of day tours including: historical bike tour of Punta Gorda (US$19); kayak and bird-watching along the Joe Taylor Creek, located in the northern part of PG (US$26.50); kayaking on the Moho River (US$60 for 7–8hrs); cycling tour to Boom Creek (US$26.50); Cerro Hill Garifuna Heritage Tour (US$28); Lubaantun tour, followed by lunch with Mayan family and swimming (US$41.50); wildlife river trip (US$43.50), jungle and cave exploration (US$50.50); fishing and snorkelling at Snake Caye (US$71). It also offers 4- and 7-day adventure and cultural packages.

Where to Stay in PG

Coral House Inn, 151 Main St, t 722 2878, *www.coralhouseinn.com* ($$$$$;

US$150). Set in a pleasant garden, this renovated 1930s home has four rather grand air-conditioned rooms with private bathrooms, wireless Internet access and TVs. Guests get free continental breakfast and complimentary use of the hotel's bikes. There's also a small swimming pool.

El Pescador >

El Pescador, t US 800 742 2017, t 722 0050, *www.elpescadorpg.com* ($$$$$; US$150, fishing packages start from US$1,445 for 2 per boat per room for 3 nights and 2 days fishing). This fancy jungle lodge is actually located around 6 miles north of Punta Gorda off the Southern Highway, but is well worth seeking out, particularly if you're a fishing fan (although this is by no means obligatory in order to enjoy the lodge's facilities). Perched on a hill overlooking nearly 500 acres of private jungle, the lodge offers great panoramic views out over the canopy. Its 12 cabanas come with two queen-sized beds, sitting areas, private bathrooms and private verandas. There's a fly and tackle shop on site, and an open-air tram to transport guests down the hill to the Rio Grande below. Additional facilities include nature trails, canoes, a billiard table and a swimming pool.

Hickatee Cottages, Ex-Servicemen Rd, t 662 4475, *www.hickatee.com* ($$$; US$60). Located just over a mile out of town, these three beautiful family-run cottages have hardwood furniture and floors, and verandas with garden views. There's good home-cooked food on offer along with tours, free bikes and nature trails around the grounds.

St Charles Inn, 23 King St, t 722 2149, *stcharlespg@btl.net* ($; US$25). The St Charles offers simple, well-equipped rooms with private bathrooms, fans and TVs. There is a shared veranda with hammocks and chairs where you can relax and chat to other travellers.

Charlton's Inn, 9 Main St, t 722 2197, *wagnerDM@btl.net* ($; US$20). Superior budget choice with clean, cosy, homely rooms, all with a/c, cable TV and private bathrooms. The communal areas include a nice courtyard and a sea-facing veranda.

Pallavi's Hotel, 21 Main St, t 702 2414, *gracemcp@hotmail.com* ($; US$20). Owned by the same people as Grace's restaurant next door, the Pallavi is a two-storey motel-style building. Its rooms are small and plain, but come with private bathrooms, fans and cable TV.

Eating Out in PG

Earth Runnings, 11 Middle St. A tasty range of healthy (hummus, pasta, salads) and not so healthy (burgers) meals as well as all the usual Belizean favourites. Indoor and outdoor eating areas. Internet access available.

Emery's Restaurant, North St. Decent local restaurant offering staples such as fried chicken, rice and beans and plenty of fresh seafood. Outdoor seating available.

Gomier's, Vernon St. This vegetarian restaurant serves tofu, grains, soy ice cream plus plenty of other veggie and organic treats.

Grace's Restaurant, 21 Main St. Grace offers hearty breakfasts and good-value Belizean fare, such as seafood, rice and beans and soups.

Marenco's Ice Cream Parlour, Main St. In PG's ultra-sultry, humid climes, this understandably does a lot of business, and you'll probably find it something of a godsend during your stay here. It also serves snacks and a few basic rice and bean dishes.

Entertainment and Nightlife in PG

The two major hot spots in town are the **PG Sports Bar**, on the corner of Prince St and Main St, and **Waluco's Beach Bar** on Front St. The former shows televised sports events and has a DJ on Fri and Sat, and also hosts occasional live bands and karaoke. Waluco's is located a mile from the centre of town and is a popular spot during the day with sunbathers and swimmers (it has a pier) as well as a happening night-time venue. Check out the Sun afternoon barbecue. The restaurants and bars of Punta Gorda often put on live performances of **Garifuna drummers** or local **Punta Rock bands**, which are worth keeping an eye out for.

Around Punta Gorda: The Toledo District

The Cayes

Just to the north of Punta Gorda is the **Port Honduras Marine Reserve** (PHMR), a great 500-square-mile (1,295-sq-km) swathe of aquatic territory incorporating a large section of the barrier reef and over 100 cayes, which was only declared a protected area in 2000. Co-managed by the Fisheries Department and TIDE (the Toledo Institute for Development and Environment), the reserve is home to a great deal of wildlife, some of it expected – Morelet's crocodiles, manatees, sharks, rays, etc. – some of it rather less so. The **Snake Cayes**, for instance, a group of four islands, are so named because they support a population of boa constrictors. The West Snake Caye is the most visited of these islands, popular for its wide white coral beaches and pleasant snorkelling. The cayes take about 45 minutes to reach from Punta Gorda by boat. To the southeast of the PHMR, around 40 miles (64km) from Punta Gorda, is the **Sapodilla Caye Marine Reserve**, the highlight of which is Hunting Caye, with its beautiful pristine coral beaches and clear waters offering great swimming and snorkelling. Tours to here can be arranged in Punta Gorda.

Mayan Sites

Lubaantun

Lubaantun
open 8–5; adm US$5

Lubaantun, which means 'place of the fallen stones' (the name was coined in 1924 by the explorer Thomas Gann), was a middle-ranking Mayan administrative centre occupied during the latter part of the Classic Period, until approximately AD 900. At its peak it probably supported around 20,000 people. Lubaantun differs from many other Mayan sites of the period, in that it lacks any stelae (inscribed tablets) and its pyramids were built without using mortar. Instead each limestone block was carved to fit exactly to the next. Unfortunately, the site is now rather overgrown and many of its major buildings have partially collapsed, making it difficult to appreciate the craftsmanship that must have gone into creating the centre. Still, the site's setting, amid lush jungle, is extremely beautiful, and it's worth visiting for that reason alone.

In all, five main plazas with 11 major structures and three ball courts have been found (if not fully excavated) as well as an array of smaller artefacts including pottery fragments, obsidian blades and ceramic figurine whistles (a selection of which can be seen in the visitor centre). The site's most famous artefact, however, has long since been dismissed as a hoax. In 1926 the 17-year-old daughter of the American explorer Frederick Mitchell-Hedges claimed to have found a full-size, 11lb (5kg) Maya carving of a human-sized skull

Getting to Lubaantun

The site lies around 1½ miles (2.4km) from the village of San Pedro Columbia. From Punta Gorda, head north up the Southern Highway for around 15 miles (24km), and then follow the signs down a dirt track towards San Antonio. Follow this road for 2 miles (3.2km), and then take a right to San Pedro Columbia (another 2½ miles away). Drive through the village, over the river until you reach a sign for the site.

Getting to Nim Li Punit

The site is around half a mile (0.8km) from the Southern Highway. Take any bus going along the Highway and ask to be dropped at the turn-off.

made from a single piece of quartz crystal, the like of which had never been seen before. Today, however, most experts believe the carving was of a much more recent vintage, planted at the site to gain the explorer publicity (which it did).

Nim Li Punit

Nim Li Punit
open 9–5; adm US$5

This hill-top ceremonial centre was only discovered in the 1970s and is believed to have been inhabited during the Late Classic Period. Although a fairly small site, excavations have revealed three royal tombs and no less than 26 stelae (great stone slabs commemorating important Mayan events, such as battles), the largest of which measures an impressive 30 feet (9m), and depicts a Mayan ruler wearing a large headdress. It is from this stele that the site gets its name, 'Nim Li Punit' meaning 'Big Hat' in Kekchi Maya. Several of these stelae can be seen in the visitor centre.

The Toledo Villages

The Toledo district around Punta Gorda supports a number of small 'ethnic' villages where populations of Maya and Garifuna still live traditional agrarian lifestyles far removed from mainstream Belizean society. These villages – which include the settlements of San Antonio (the largest and most developed of the region's Mayan villages, 19 miles (30km) northwest of Punta Gorda), San José (which still lacks electricity), Blue Creek (which has a population of just 300) and the coastal Garifuna town of Barranco – lie within range of a number of interesting archaeological and natural attractions, including the 6,000-acre Aguacaliente Wildlfe Sanctuary, the Lubaantun Mayan ruins (*see* p.200), the 500-acre Rio Blanco Waterfall Park and the Temash/Sarstoon National Park.

If you are interested in spending some time in one of the villages and visiting some of the nearby sites in the company of a knowledgeable local guide, then an interesting and inexpensive way to do it is though the **Toledo Ecotourism Association's** (**t** 722 2096, **f** 722 2199, *ttea@btl.net*, *www.ecoclub.com/Toledo*) award-winning ecotourism guesthouse programme. The TEA is owned and managed by a group of Mopan, Kekchi and Garifuna villages (eight Maya, one

Garifuna) and was founded in 1990 to allow the villagers to control and profit from tourism in their district. Within each village is a rustic but clean guesthouse for visitors to stay, constructed by the villagers from hardwood and thatch in the manner and style of their own homes, with bunk beds and basic bathroom facilities. The families within the villages then take it in turns to provide meals, entertainment (usually demonstrations of drumming or dance) and to act as guides for the visitors, thus ensuring that the income derived is spread fairly throughout the village. To arrange a stay in one of these guesthouses, contact the TEA either in person at their office in Punta Gorda (see p.198), by telephone or via their website. Lodging costs US$9.25 per person per night. Tours around the nearby attractions and activities (such as storytelling, cooking and language lessons) are priced at US$3.50 per person per hour. Traditional meals, usually including freshly made tortillas, rice and beans and a meat dish, cost US$3.25 for breakfast or dinner and US$4 for lunch (traditionally the largest meal of the day).

The North

Primarily agricultural with a small resident population, northern Belize tends to be somewhat neglected by tourists, most taking only a brief trip to the Mayan site of Lamanai (one of the country's most spectacular) before heading straight back south, or over to the cayes.
This is a pity, for while the north can't boast the same number of attractions (or the same level of tourist infrastructure) as some of the country's more developed areas, there's still much here for visitors to enjoy, even if they do have to spend rather longer searching it out.

12

Don't miss

❶ Dramatic Mayan ruins
Lamanai **p.210**

❷ Exploring botanical trails
Shipstern Nature Reserve **p.218**

❸ Relaxing by the bay
Consejo **p.218**

❹ Searching for big cats
Rio Bravo Conservation and Management Area **p.212**

See map overleaf

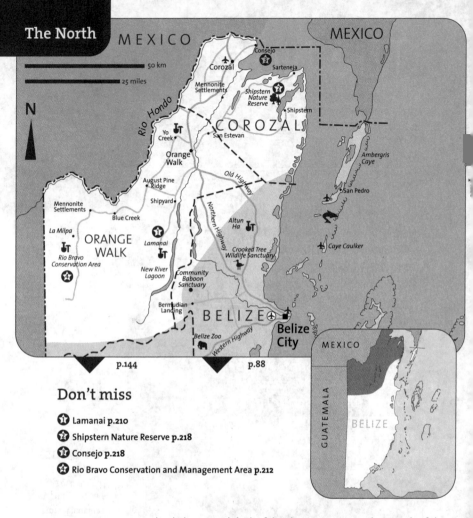

MEXICO

MEXICO

50 km

25 miles

N

Rio Hondo

Consejo

Corozal

Sarteneja

Mennonite
Settlements

Shipstern
Nature
Reserve

Shipstern

COROZAL

Yo
Creek

San Estevan

Orange
Walk

Old Highway

Ambergris
Caye

August Pine
Ridge

San Pedro

Mennonite
Settlements

Shipyard

Caye Caulker

La Milpa

Blue Creek

ORANGE
WALK

Lamanai

Altun
Ha

Rio Bravo
Conservation Area

New River
Lagoon

Crooked Tree
Wildlife Sanctuary

Community
Baboon
Sanctuary

Northern Highway

Bermudian
Landing

BELIZE

Belize Zoo

Western Highway

Belize
City

MEXICO

p.144

p.88

GUATEMALA

BELIZE

Don't miss

1 Lamanai **p.210**

2 Shipstern Nature Reserve **p.218**

3 Consejo **p.218**

4 Rio Bravo Conservation and Management Area **p.212**

Indeed, the region's lack of development means that much of the area (that has escaped being turned into farmland) remains essentially wild, providing great nature-watching opportunities. The coastal plains, lagoons and wetlands are bursting with birdlife (not to mention manatees, crocodiles and turtles), while the thick jungle of the Rio Bravo Conservation Area, in the west, hides the highest concentration of wild cats in the country. The region is also littered with dozens of Mayan sites, including Cerros, near Corozal town, and Nohmul (and the aforementioned Lamanai) near Orange Walk.

The area is made up of two districts: the 1,790-sq-mile (4,636-sq-km) Orange Walk, which borders Belize District to the west and north, and which has a population of just under 40,000; and the rather smaller district of Corozal to the north, whose population numbers less than 20,000, most of whom reside in or around the district's eponymous seaside town.

You may require a phrase book for a visit to these parts, as Spanish is the dominant language, mestizos (many of whom are the descendants of refugees from the Yucatán Caste Wars of the late 19th century) making up a large percentage of the population. The region is also home to the country's largest number of German-speaking Mennonites, who reside in the communities of Blue Creek, Little Belize, Progresso and Shipyard.

Orange Walk District

Orange Walk Town

Located on the Northern Highway, 57 miles (91km) north of Belize City, Orange Walk is the largest and most populated town in northern Belize. It's still a pretty small place, however, made up of a rather unkempt-looking, ragtag collection of streets, with few facilities for visitors. But then the primary business here is agriculture, not tourism. Lying at the heart of a vast sugar-growing region (which has led to it being given the slightly grandiose nickname, 'Sugar City'), Orange Walk is the main market town and source of services for a network of surrounding farms and plantations, as well as local communities of Mennonites, who can often be spotted on the streets in their traditional uniform of dungarees and straw hats. The town's lack of visitor appeal is perhaps best summed up by the fact that its most famous landmark is its sugar refinery, which can be spotted belching out sickly-sweet smoke just north of the town's tollbooth.

Though there's little to see in the town itself, aside from one small museum, Orange Walk does have some reasonable accommodation and eating options – although you should note that those at the budget end of the spectrum are primarily aimed at the truck drivers who haul the great loads of sugar cane up and down the highway – and it can serve as a handy gateway to nearby Mayan sites (particularly Lamanai) and the Rio Bravo Conservation Area. There are a couple of operators in town offering tours.

History

This area had long been settled by Icaiche Maya when British Baymen arrived in the 18th century to begin logging the region's mahogany. It's been suggested that Orange Walk may have derived its name from the orange trees that lined the banks of the New River, along which the trees were floated down to the coast. The settlement remained little more than a basic logging camp until the mid-19th century when mestizo refugees fleeing the Yucatán Caste Wars (1847–1901) began to arrive en masse, seeking the protection of

Getting to and away from Orange Walk

Orange Walk is a pretty straightforward place to get to. By **car**, simply follow the Northern Highway north from Belize City (or south from Corozal). A toll of US$0.35 must be paid a couple of miles south of the town.

Novelo's (t 302 2858) operates hourly **buses** (between 6am and 6pm) running to and from Belize City and Corozal (but *see* p.66). The journey from Belize City takes around 2hrs and should cost around US$4–6. It should cost under US$5 to get from Corozal (a 1hr journey). You'll be dropped in the town centre on Queen Victoria Avenue (the stretch of the Northern Highway running through the centre of Orange Walk). Buses to nearby villages usually leave from outside the fire station on Queen Victoria Avenue.

the British. The local Maya, who had come to an uneasy accommodation with the British presence, considered this a migration too far. Believing his people's territory to be under threat the Mayan chief, Marcus Canul, led an attack on Orange Walk on 1 September 1872 with the intention of driving the mestizos and their British protectors out. In the event, British troops won the day, defeating the Mayan army and killing their leader. However, fearing that the Mayans might regroup and launch another attack, the British constructed two forts in Orange Walk: Fort Mundy (named after one of the Lieutenant-Governors of the time, Major Robert Mundy) looking over the river at the north end of town where Independence Plaza now sits; and Fort Cairns (named after one of the other Lieutenant-Governors of the time, William Wellington Cairns) in the centre of town (it's now marked by Fort Cairns Market Plaza), the

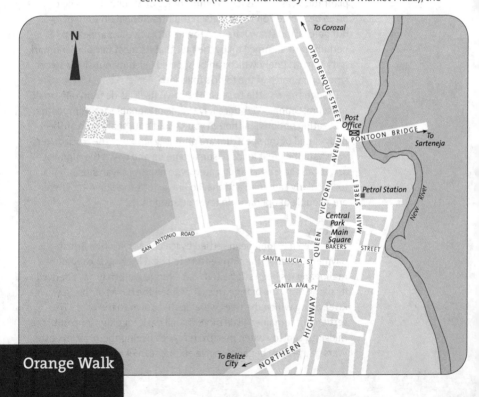

Orange Walk

ruins of which can still be seen. These were eventually to prove redundant, however, the Mayans never again having the numbers (or the will) to launch a further offensive. In the years following, the town, bolstered by the large influx of refugees, developed into a major centre of sugar production, something it continues to be today. The only blip in its history came in the late 20th century when a fall in international sugar prices led to many local farmers switching to the production of marijuana, for which there was a more readily available market at the time. For a while Belize become one of the America's major drug exporters. A clampdown by the authorities, however (under pressure from the US government who provided spotter planes for the purpose of identifying illicit farms), largely eradicated the practice, although it does still take place on a small scale in some of the region's remoter areas.

The Town

Laid out just east of the New River, Orange Walk is a reasonably compact and easy-to-navigate place. Most of its hotels and restaurants are located on one of two main roads – Queen Victoria Avenue, the name given to the stretch of the Northern Highway running through town (which is also rather confusingly referred to by locals as the Belize–Corozal road), and the parallel Main Street. Around this nexus is spread a higgledy-piggledy assortment of minor roads. The official centre of the town is the town hall ('Palacio Municipal'), which adjoins a formal plaza around halfway up Queen Victoria Avenue.

Banquitas House of Culture
t 322 017; open Tues–Fri 10–6, Sat 8–1

The town's only formal tourist attraction is the recently opened (2002) **Banquitas House of Culture**, one of only three such houses of culture in the country, on the corner of Main and Bautista's Streets, which contains a small museum on the history and industry of the Orange Walk area. It also puts on temporary displays by local artists, and has a small restaurant and a pleasant landscaped riverside garden.

Tourist Information and Services in Orange Walk

There is no tourist information office, but your hotel should be able to provide some information on the area.
Banks: Belize Bank, 34 Main/Park St, **t** 322 2019; Scotiabank, corner of Park and Main St, **t** 322 2194. Both have ATMs.
Hospital: Orange Walk Hospital, Northern Highway, **t** 322 2073.
Internet: Cyber Walk NetCafé, 115 Otro Benque Rd, **t** 322 3024; Orange Walk Information & Technology Centre,

Town Hall, Queen Victoria Ave (opposite Central Park).
Library: The Sandy Hunter Library, Hospital Crescent, **t** 322 2345.
Pharmacy: Fuente, 14 Main St, **t** 322 3651.
Post office: Sub-Treasury Building, corner of Main St and Hospital Crescent, **t** 322 2196.
Supermarkets: M & A Supermarket, 30 Cinderella St, **t** 322 2809; The People's Store, 51 Main St, **t** 322 2003.
Tour companies: **Jungle River Tours**, 20 Lovers Lane, **t** 302 2293. Offer river trips to Lamanai.

Where to Stay in Orange Walk

Inexpensive ($$)–Budget ($)
Akihito Hotel, 22 Queen Victoria Ave, t 302 0185, *www.akihitobelize.com*. Offers a variety of budget options, from the very basic (bunk beds in dormitories for US$7.50) through the moderately basic (doubles with shared bathrooms for US$22.50) to the reasonably comfortable (doubles with private bathrooms for US$30). Additional services include high-speed Internet access, cable TV, laundry service and a Jacuzzi.

D*Victoria Hotel, 40 Queen Victoria Ave, t 322 2518, f 322 2847, *www. dvictoria.com* (US$37.50). One of the town's best-known hotels, the D*Victoria Hotel's 31 rooms are pleasantly furnished and come with private bathrooms, cable TV and a/c. There's also a decent restaurant and a swimming pool. Note, a popular disco is held here on Fri and Sat nights, when you might want to request a quieter room (unless, of course, you're planning on bopping the night away with everyone else). Camping is also permitted on site.

Hotel de la Fuente, 14 Main St, t 322 2090, f 322 3651, *www.hoteldelafuente. com* (US$25/30 fan/a/c). The Hotel de la Fuente has nine light, airy and fairly well-equipped rooms – the de luxe ones (US$40) come decked out with sofas, fridges, toasters and coffee makers (complimentary coffee is supplied), while the junior suites (US$70) have full kitchens. Check-in is at the adjacent pharmacy, which is run by the same management.

Mi Amore Hotel, 19 Queen Victoria Ave, t 322 2031, f 322 3462, *miamore@btl.net* (US$30). As with the D*Victoria, the Mi Amore holds a popular weekend disco. This is a reasonable main-road choice: the rooms are clean, comfortable and spacious and have private bathrooms.

St Christopher's Hotel, 10 Main St, t 322 2420, f 322 1064, *rowbze@btl.net*, *www. stchristophershotelbze.com* (US$30). Located at the north end of town, by the New River, this hotel's leafy garden by the water's edge is a lovely spot to wind down after a hard day spent trekking around Maya sites. All rooms have tiled floors, cable TV and private bathrooms. Some have river views.

Eating Out in Orange Walk

If you're on a budget, you can pick up a range of cheap eats – including tacos and tamales – from the vendors in Central Park. The food court on the market square next to the town hall also offers a large range of cheap local dishes and you can pick up a decent selection of vegetables here if you're self-catering. The town also has several (largely similar) Chinese restaurants.

The Diner, 37 Clark St (behind the hospital), t 322 2137. A little out of the way (it's around a 20min walk from town), but nonetheless well worth a visit, this extremely popular thatched-roof restaurant serves up a more adventurous menu than most of its in-town competitors, featuring a number of international dishes (including lobster thermidor). It makes a welcome change from the otherwise ubiquitous Chinese/Belizean cuisine.

Juanita's, 8 Santa Ana St, t 322 2677. Serving up typical Belizean and Mexican dishes, Juanita's has long been a favourite with locals who stop off for fry-jacks and breakfast burritos in the morning, cow-foot soup at lunch, and rice and beans in the evening. It's cheap, cheerful and clean.

New China Restaurant, Queen Victoria Ave, t 322 2650. One of the best of the town's glut of Chinese restaurants. There are no great surprises on the menu here, but the food is tasty, reasonably priced and there are plenty of vegetarian dishes available.

Nightlife in Orange Walk

It's not exactly party central, but there are a few choices if you want to make a night of it. Both the **Mi Amore Hotel** and **D*Victoria Hotel** have decent bars and hold popular discos on weekends. The **Acuario Bar**, 33 San Francisco St (t 322 2542), is another local favourite, regularly hosting live bands and DJs (it's open from 11pm).

Around Orange Walk – Mayan Sites

Cuello and Nohmul

The closest Mayan site to Orange Walk town is unfortunately also the least interesting. Located just 2½ miles (4km) west of town, and named after the family who own the land on which the ruins (and the adjacent rum distillery) sit, **Cuello** (pronounced *kway-yo*) was occupied from around 1000 BC. Although the site has yielded some intriguing discoveries over the years, including human remains and pieces of carved jade, suggesting that it was involved in long-distance trade and acted as some sort of ceremonial centre (albeit, because of its size, necessarily a minor one), most of these have been shipped off to museums.

Today, the site comprises little more than a few mounds and a small pyramid. Entry to the site is free, though prior permission must be sought from the landowners to look around. Visitors should check in at the gate on arrival. There's no public transport to the site. A taxi from Orange Walk town will cost around US$10 round trip (for more information, contact Cuello Brothers Distillery, San Antonio Road, Yo Creek Road, **t** 322 2141).

Of more interest to the casual visitor is **Nohmul**, a large Mayan site around 10 miles (16km) north of Orange Walk town near the village of San Jose. Nohmul means 'Great Mound' in Maya, and the raised site certainly dominates the surrounding acres of sugar-cane plantations, although the 'great' seems a bit of an exaggeration. The central temple may be the tallest structure in the whole of Orange Walk District, but it's still only 25 feet (8m) above ground level. Still, the views from the top are very impressive.

The settlement, which covers an area of 12 square miles (19 sq km), enjoyed two main periods of occupation: from around 350 BC–AD 200, and then again in the Late Classic period, from around AD 600–900. Indeed, evidence suggests that the site may have been at its most populous in the 10th century, a time when most lowland Maya communities had begun to collapse, something which has led scholars to suggest that the site may have been taken over at this time by Yucatec Maya from the north. The site consists of two ceremonial groups of plazas (numbering ten in total) connected by a raised causeway (known as a *sacbe*).

To get to Nohmul by car, take the Northern Highway north from Orange Walk town till you reach San José. Turn left at the far end of the village by the sign for Nohmul. Keep right until you arrive at the sight. Buses heading north to Corozal will stop in San José (you can ask to be dropped by the turning), from where you'll have to walk the final mile to the site.

① Lamanai
*open Mon–Fri 8–5, Sat
and Sun 8–4; adm US$5*

Lamanai

The Lamanai ruins are generally regarded as the most spectacular of all the Mayan sites in Belize, and one of the country's 'must-see' attractions. The settlement enjoys an isolated location, in the midst of the jungle on the New River Lagoon, something that no doubt largely contributed towards its remarkable longevity. Lamanai was the longest continuously occupied site in the Maya lowlands, still inhabited at the time of the Spanish arrival in the 16th century, hundreds of years after most of the region's other settlements had been abandoned. As a result the settlement's name is (almost uniquely for the region) the original Mayan one. It means, according to translations made by those original Spanish invaders, 'submerged crocodile', although doubts have been expressed recently as to the accuracy of this translation (the slightly less poetic 'drowned insect' has been put forward as an alternative). Still, the sheer number of representations of crocodiles found at the site, in carvings, pottery and inscriptions, suggest that, whatever the site's true name, the creature certainly featured prominently in local mythology.

Occupation of the 950-acre site is thought to have begun around 1500 BC, although most of the structures visible today were constructed several hundred years later. It was both an important trade hub – various items that originated in other early Mayan, Olmec and Aztec cities have been found here – and a major ceremonial centre. At its peak, it may have supported up to 35,000 people. Its population was still relatively healthy when the Spanish appeared on the scene, although it wouldn't remain so for long. Spanish attempts to convert the Maya to Christianity, which saw the Europeans build two churches at the settlement, were met at first with disinterest and later with outright hostility. In 1640, the Maya launched a rebellion, burning the churches down. The settlement was abandoned shortly afterwards. Over the succeeding centuries, the great city was gradually swallowed back up by the jungle, the only subsequent man-made structure being a British-built sugar mill erected (and hastily abandoned) in the late 19th century. It now stands wrapped in tree roots.

Incredibly, around 95 per cent of Lamanai's structures have not yet been excavated (principally due to a lack of funding) and remain covered in foliage. It's been estimated that there may be as many as 700 temples here. Still, the 5 per cent of the site that can be seen is pretty impressive, and the jungle setting provides both a romantic backdrop and plenty of wildlife-spotting opportunities – toucans, vultures and howler monkeys are all regularly spotted in the fringing trees (as are crocodiles in the adjacent lagoon).

Getting to Lamanai

Although Lamanai is accessible by car (via the villages of Yo Creek, August Pine Ridge and San Felipe), the most scenic and enjoyable route to the site is via a **boat trip** from Orange Walk town along the New River, spotting wildlife (crocodiles, monkeys, toucans) as you go. Several companies now offer tours out of Orange Walk and Ambergris Caye for around US$40 per person, including lunch and guided tours of the river and ruins. The journey takes around 1hr 45mins. There is no bus service.

The Site

Lamanai's docking area (*see* 'Getting to Lamanai', above), entrance and museum (which houses a collection of pottery and other finds from the area) lie at the site's eastern end, by the lagoon. West of here stands the site's most striking structure, the 105ft- (33m-)tall **High Temple** (or N10-43 to give it its correct, if slightly less catchy, label). First erected around 100 BC, it underwent, as was common with most Mayan pyramids, several subsequent modifications and expansions, the last of which probably took place around AD 600. By the time the Maya had finished with it, it was absolutely huge, the largest Pre-Classic building yet found in the Maya lowlands. The views from the top are astounding, reaching across the river and tree tops and stretching all the way to Guatemala.

Northeast of the High Temple is the **Mask Temple** (N9-56), another large (albeit not quite as large) pyramid, built around 200 BC, in which was found a giant, 13ft- (4m-)high carved mask of a face sporting a crocodile headdress (hence the name), while to the south is the city's **ball court**, the large centre marker of which (when compared with other ball courts) was found to be covering a mysterious chamber containing liquid mercury and several pieces of jade.

Further south is a stela (tablet) believed to show a representation of Lord Smoking Shell, who ruled the area in the 7th century, as well the **Jaguar Temple** (N10-9), so named because of a jaguar mask found here.

The remains of the Spanish churches and the British sugar mill are located ½ mile south of here.

Where to Stay at Lamanai

(★) Lamanai Outpost Lodge >

Lamanai Outpost Lodge, t 223 3578, f 220 9061, www.lamanai.com ($$$$$; US$120). If you want to see a bit more of the region's wildlife after a day at the ruins, then this up-market lodge is the place to go. Set on the banks of the New River Lagoon, the lodge's rustic, thatched cabanas have verandas overlooking the surrounding jungle. There is a whole host of nature-themed activities on offer, including bat walks, birding expeditions, night tours and trips out onto the lagoon. The highly recommended open-air dining room also has panoramic views of the grounds. All-inclusive packages (including meals, two activities and transfers from Belize City international airport) are available.

Getting to Rio Bravo

Driving to Rio Bravo takes a rather bumpy 3hrs from Orange Walk, so make sure you have a full tank and get the complete directions from the PFB (*see* below) when you notify them of your interest in visiting. The PFB can also organize a **pick-up** from Orange Walk if you don't have your own transport.

Rio Bravo Conservation and Management Area (RBCMA)

⚙ RBCMA
t 207 5616, f 207 5635,
pfbel@btl.net,
www.pfbelize.org;
adm $20 (includes
guided tour)

Owned and managed by the Programme for Belize (PFB), a non-profit conservation organization, this is the largest private reserve in the country, encompassing approximately 260,000 acres of northwest Orange Walk District. It's a hugely varied area made up of a diverse selection of habitats – broadleaf forest, rainforest, savannah, marshland, lagoons – and is dotted with numerous Mayan sites (many of which remain unexcavated and unexplored). The array of flora and fauna found here is pretty staggering: 390 species of bird, 200 species of tree and 70 mammals. This last group includes monkeys, coatimundis and all of Belize's cat species. In fact, Rio Bravo has the largest population of jaguars in the whole of Central America, which means your chances of seeing one in the wild are better here than almost anywhere else on earth (that still means basically no chance, but it's nice to know that the odds have moved marginally in your favour).

As successful as the reserve has proved, its creation was not without a struggle. Amazingly, this area actually stood on the brink of environmental destruction in the 1980s, earmarked as the site of a new power station (to be fuelled by the wood of the surrounding forests) and a Coca Cola fruit farm. However, sustained protests by a group of concerned environmentalists – who would go on to form the nucleus of the Programme for Belize – got the government to change its plans. Today, the park's two field stations, La Milpa and Hill Bank, conduct a good deal of important scientific research into conservation techniques and sustainable forestry. Because this is

Where to Stay at Rio Bravo

★ Chan Chich
Lodge ›

Chan Chich Lodge, t/f 223 4419, *www.chanchich.com* ($$$$$; US$250). Fringed by jungle and occupying the central plaza of the Chan Chich (meaning 'Little Bird') Maya site, this lodge enjoys a spectacular setting, which the thatched-roof accommodation does its best to live up to. The standard cabanas come with two queen-sized beds, while the spacious de luxe

(US$280) have king-sized beds and walk-in wardrobes. All cabanas have wraparound verandas complete with hammocks for observing the local wildlife. There's also a Jacuzzi and over nine miles of trails within the grounds (guides and maps can be supplied). Horse-riding and canoeing are also offered. The easiest (not to say the most expensive) way to get here is by a 30min charter flight to the nearby Gallon Jug airstrip, which can be arranged when booking.

Mennonites

Mennonites, members of a German-speaking religious sect, are a common sight throughout the country. You'll spot them in many Belizean towns, dressed in their obligatory uniform of dungarees and straw hats, perhaps trotting a horse and buggy along the street or selling furniture at the side of the road. If their dress seems strangely archaic, that's because it is. And it's deliberately kept that way. Indeed, as exemplars of the notion of 'sticking to your beliefs', the Mennonites have few rivals. They've managed to uphold a rigid system of beliefs and follow a pretty strict way of life (not to mention code of dress) for centuries, often in the face of outright hostility from the surrounding community.

Ironically, the sect was founded during a period of great social flux, in mid-16th-century Europe, at the height of the Reformation, a time when rigidly held dogmas and belief systems were being regularly questioned and transformed. Into this Protestant maelstrom stepped a Dutch Anabaptist priest, Menno Simons, who sought to challenge the prevailing orthodoxies of the day. His solution was to create a new dogma and orthodoxy, which his eponymous followers have been adhering to rigidly ever since.

From the outset, the Mennonites were nothing if not contrary. Though their creed is notionally harmless (a commitment to pacifism forms the very core of their ideals), many Mennonite tenets seem almost wilfully designed to invoke the hostility of the state – refusing to pay taxes, refusing to recognize official institutions, refusing to send their children to school and refusing to undertake military service. As a consequence, Mennonites have often tested the patience of their fellow communities to breaking point, and have been obliged to move on several times during their history. After their foundation, their search for a tolerant homeland took them, in succession, to Switzerland, Prussia and Russia. Initially, Russia seemed pretty welcoming. Its government was even willing to exempt the Mennonites from joining its armed forces. However, in the late 19th century, with Europe's great nations growing increasingly belligerent and the storm clouds of war brewing, Russia decided it was time for all hands to come to the military pump. They revoked the exemption, obliging the Mennonites to make their most jarring transition yet, as they travelled from the Old World to the New, pitching up in Canada. Their thick German accents, however, didn't go down well with the locals after the First World War, forcing them to move again, this time south to Mexico. But, once more, after a few decades of relative peace and anonymity, their lifestyle began to be questioned by the authorities. And so, in 1958, they arrived in Belize. To begin with things didn't look too promising here either, with the British government and the local Caribbean population regarding the strangely dressed, German-speaking, aloof arrivals with a good deal of suspicion. However, the British were canny enough to realize that, even if they weren't going to get any military participation or much in the way of community service out of the Mennonites, they could still be of benefit to the country. The Mennonites were given access to land on which they were encouraged to utilize their centuries-worth of finely honed farming techniques (techniques by now perfected in locales around the world). The result was the creation of a number of hugely successful industries – dairy farming, furniture-making and house-building. The Mennonites have also been responsible for much of the country's road-building programme. Despite never fully participating in Belize's culture, the sect has over the past 40 years or so played an important role in the development of the country, helping to maintain its infrastructure and contributing significantly to the economy (even if their famous cheese is some of the worse you've ever tasted in your life).

Though all Mennonites still adhere to a lifestyle notably different from the rest of mainstream Belizean society, these days some are stricter in their beliefs than others. Indeed, there is growing tension between two main groups (as much as you can get tension between groups of devout pacifists): traditionalists, who believe in admitting to as little change as possible – refusing to use electricity or motorized vehicles or dress in anything other than their strict traditional uniforms (some refuse to speak anything other than German); and modernizers, who have made greater efforts to adapt to (and benefit from) the modern world – driving trucks, using power tools and keeping fridges and telephones in their homes.

The north is home to four of the six main Mennonite communities in Belize: Shipyard and Little Belize (both of which are traditional); and Blue Creek and Progresso (both of which are more modern). The other two are Barton Creek and Spanish Lookout in Cayo. Remember, if visiting, that these are living communities, not tourist attractions. The Mennonites have spent a good portion of their history scrupulously avoiding interacting with the wider community. Though they may be used to the attention of tourists, that doesn't mean they like it. So, be respectful, and don't take photographs without permission.

primarily an area set aside for conservation and research, rather than a tourist attraction (it's funded largely by commercial donations), all that potential visitors need to do is contact the Programme for Belize to inform them of their plans before arriving. Access to the reserve is via the La Milpa station, from where trails lead into the surrounding jungle. Your entry fee includes the price of a guided tour. It's also possible to stay at La Milpa, provided that space isn't taken up by visiting students (always a possibility). The accommodation isn't cheap – dormitory bunks from US$100 per day, private rooms US$115 – but it is very ecofriendly, and the price includes three meals a day and guided tours around the site, as well as access to the research library and lectures.

Just 3 miles (5km) from the station lies **La Milpa** itself, the third largest Mayan site in Belize (behind Caracol and Lamanai), which is currently being excavated by archaeologists from Boston University and the University of Texas. The site dates back to around 400 BC (Late Pre-Classic) and comprises 11 plazas and over 50 structures. You're welcome to explore, although you may find some of the areas closed off while the excavation work continues.

Corozal District

Corozal Town

Overlooking a pretty bay, Corozal is an easy-going, unassuming seaside town with a safe, laid-back vibe. Just 9 miles (14km) from the Mexican border, it's largely Spanish-speaking, and indeed its culture and layout are more Mexican than Caribbean- (or British-) influenced. Despite being the capital of the district, there isn't a great deal for tourists to do here, beside stroll the seafront, although the town does provide a pleasant-enough base from which to explore nearby attractions, which include a couple of Mayan sites and the Shipstern Nature Reserve. With many of the town's visitors simply passing through the town en route to Mexico, Corozal can at times have something of a border town feel to it. Long-stay visitors tend to head to the surrounding area, particularly the pretty nearby village of Consejo, which has enjoyed something of a property boom in recent years fuelled by the arrival of a large influx of US ex-pats.

The town was founded in 1849 by refugees fleeing the Yucatán Caste Wars, who built a small fortified settlement (the remains of pillboxes from this time can still be seen around the post office opposite the plaza), on the site of an abandoned waterfront Mayan city, Chetumal. Those parts of the Mayan settlement that escaped being built over can be visited just north of town at Santa Rita. The word 'Corozal' refers to a type of palm regarded by the Maya as a

Getting to Corozal

By air: Both **Maya Island Air** (**t** 422 2333 in Corozal, **t** 226 2435 in San Pedro, *www.mayaislandair.com*) and **Tropic Air** (**t** 226 2012, *www.tropicair.com*) operate flights to/from Corozal and San Pedro on Ambergris Caye (US$40.50 one way). To get here from Belize City, you'll have to fly to San Pedro first.

By boat: Thunderbolt (**t** 226 2904, *thunderbolttravels@yahoo.com*) run a daily San Pedro–Corozal service at 3pm, and a Corozal–San Pedro service at 7am, costing US$40 one way, US$70 roundtrip. Services arrive and depart from Corozal's main pier.

By bus: **Novelo's** (**t** 422 2132) run an hourly service from Belize City to Chetumal in Mexico, stopping en route in Corozal (but *see* p.66). Passengers are set down at the bus station, two blocks west of Central Park/Plaza.

symbol of fertility, a fitting name for a town that would go on to become a major regional centre of agriculture, specifically sugar production, which still forms the bedrock of the local economy.

On 27 September 1955, Hurricane Janet hit Corozal, obliterating most of its rickety, stilt-set wooden houses. In the years that followed, the whole town was completely redesigned and rebuilt according to a Mexican template. As a consequence Corozal is now laid out according to an easy-to-follow grid system of inter-connecting avenues and streets. The centre of the town is the Mexican-style plaza 'Central Park', with its central fountain and clock tower (not to mention street vendors selling taco and hot dogs) at 1st Street South and 1st Street North (and 4th and 5th Avenue), adjacent to which are the main post office and town hall. Most of the town's restaurants and hotels are located on 5th, 4th or 1st Avenue, the last of which runs along the seafront and is dotted with a number of nice ornamental parks, picnic areas and swimming spots.

12   The North | Corozal Town

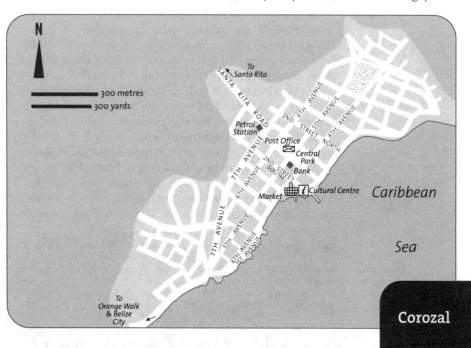

Cultural Centre
t 422 3176; open 8–5,
adm US$1.50

The town's main attraction is the yellow-roofed **Cultural Centre**. Built in 1886 and formerly used as a market, it now houses a collection of Mayan artefacts, including a traditional thatched hut and cooking utensils, along with displays of historical photos, bottles and sugar-industry relics. The building is also home to the town's **tourist information** office.

Also worth checking out in town is the huge, vivid mural painted by artist Manuel Villamor Reyes, depicting the history of Belize, which spans an entire wall in the **Town Hall**. This can be viewed close up during normal business hours or through the window of the door when the town hall is closed.

Santa Rita

Just a mile northwest of the centre of town is this partially excavated site that once formed part of the ancient city of Chetumal (or Chactemal), on which Corozal town was built. Founded in around 2000 BC and still occupied some three and a half millennia later when the Spanish arrived, the site enjoyed a strategically important location, set at the hub of a network of trade routes, from which it transported honey, cacao and vanilla around the region via two nearby rivers. Unfortunately there isn't much to see here now other than a single, partly restored temple. To get to the site, head north past the bus station up the Santa Rita Road and go left towards the hospital. The temple is opposite the Coca Cola factory.

Cerros (Cerro Maya)

Cerros
open 8–5

Looking from Corozal town out across Corozal Bay, you should just about be able to make out a small mound poking above the trees. This is the Mayan site of Cerros (the name derives from the Spanish *cerro*, which means 'hill'). During the Late Pre-Classic period (around 350 BC–AD 250), this was an important coastal trade centre controlling routes through the New River and Río Hondo, and was the site of several grand building projects. The Maya constructed a huge canal system around the site to accommodate their large canoes and developed special raised fields to supply their agricultural needs. Several temples can be seen here, the largest of which is around 70ft (21m) high. It's a fairly stiff climb, although the views out across the bay are worth it. The simplest (and quickest) way to get to the site is by boat (either hire your own or take a tour from town), although you can also get there by car in the dry season.

Services in Corozal

① Corozal
Tourist Information
Cultural Centre >
off 1st Ave, t 422 3176

Banks: Atlantic Bank, corner of 3rd Ave and 3rd St North, t 422 3473; Belize Bank, 5th Ave and 1st St South, t 422 2087; Scotiabank 4th Ave, t 422 2046).

You can also exchange money at M&D Casa de Cambio, at 36 5th Ave, t 422 2175.
Books: Charlotte's Book Exchange, 78 5th Ave, t 422 0135.

Hospital: On the Santa Rita Rd, **t** 422 2076.

Internet: Charlotte's Web Cyber Café, 78 5th Ave, **t** 422 0135.

Library: Corozal Library, 1st St South, **t** 422 3751.

Pharmacies: Evergreen Pharmacy, 8 2nd St South/Park St, **t** 422 0362 (*open Mon–Sat 8.30–1 and 3–9, Sun 9–1 and 4–8*).

Post office: 5th Ave (on Fort Barlee site), **t** 422 2462.

Supermarkets: U-Save Supermarket, 4th Ave, 2nd St, **t** 422 3739.

Where to Stay in Corozal

Corozal Bay Inn, Almond Drive, **t** 422 0078, **f** 422 3498, *www.corozalbayinn. com* ($$$$; US$90). If you just can't be without a swimming pool while on holiday then this small resort-style accommodation is your only choice in Corozal town. It also has its sandy beach (albeit a man-made one that is separated from the sea by a sea wall), complete with palm trees and hammocks for true Caribbean-esque lounging. All 10 beach cabanas come with two double beds, coffee makers, fridges, cable TV, wireless Internet access and private bathrooms.

Tony's Inn & Beach Resort, South End, **t** US 1-800 447 2931, **t** 422 2055/422 3555, **f** 422 2829, *www.tonysinn.com* ($$$$; US$80). Tony's consists of 24 rooms (with TV, a/c and private bathrooms) spread over a two-storey hacienda-style building within pleasant, leafy, landscaped grounds. There is an artificial sandy beach and a pretty good (and very popular) palapa restaurant/bar, the 'Y* Not Grill & Bar'.

★ The Copa Banana >

The Copa Banana, 409 Bay Shore Drive, **t** 422 0284, **f** 422 2710, *www. copabanana.bz* ($$$; US$55). Extremely popular, good value, and (inevitably) yellow, the Copa Banana comprises two adjoining guesthouses offering a total of five suites, all of which have TVs, a/c, fans, queen-sized beds (apart from one with twin beds), private bathrooms, and are individually decorated in homely styles. The rooms are self-contained, but each guesthouse has its own communal veranda and living room as well as a fully equipped kitchen where guests can prepare their meals. Free bicycles, and complimentary coffee, tea and juice in the mornings also offered.

Hok'ol K'in Guest House, 89 4th Ave, **t** 422 3329, **f** 422 3569, *www.corozal.net* ($$$; US$50/57 fan/a/c). Ten lovely guest rooms with views of the bay. The family room is particularly good value sleeping up to six people (US$70 for full occupancy), and there's a decent restaurant selling 'American-style' cuisine, as well as a new Internet café with wireless access.

Las Palmas Hotel, 123 5th Ave, **t** 422 0196/602 5186, *www.laspalmashotel belize.com* ($$$; US$40). Previously 'Nestor's Hotel', the newly renovated Las Palmas is a good choice for groups, offering a 'Backpacker's Special' for US$60, based on four people sharing a room. The rooms are clean with private bathroom, TVs, a/c and fridges, albeit rather simply decorated.

Hotel Maya, South End, **t** 422 2082, **f** 422 2827, *www.hotelmaya.net* ($$; US$30). Twenty clean and basic rooms are available in this friendly budget hotel, all with private bathrooms, TVs and fans. Tours can be arranged and cheap (and tasty) meals ordered in the veranda restaurant.

Eating Out and Nightlife in Corozal

The public market and street vendors in Central Park are good for picking up cheap eats, or you could grab a few snacks from one of the grocery stores and have a picnic on the seafront if you want a table with a bay view.

Nightlife is pretty low-key with what action there is revolving around the hotel bars. **Tony's Inn** and the neighbouring **Corozal Bay** are two of the most popular.

Al's Café, 5th Ave, **t** 422 3654. Popular breakfast-time haunt for the area's ex-pats, who stop by for a quick (and cheap) fry-jack or breakfast burrito on the way to the beach.

Cactus Plaza, 6 6th St South, **t** 442 0394. Fill up on cheap (US$2–3), fresh Mexican staples, such as tostadas and tacos, at this popular restaurant/bar.

Le Café Kela >

Le Café Kela, 37 1st Ave, **t** 422 2833. By far the best restaurant in Corozal, this little *palapa*-cum-bistro-style eatery may seem an unlikely portal into fine French cuisine, but the crêpes here are genuinely fantastic. They also do a good selection of grilled fish, pasta and pizzas. The prices are reasonable (mains US$4–10) although you may have to book ahead (it's very popular).

Marcello's Pizza, 25 4th Ave at 3rd St, **t** 422 0157. Reasonable pizzas for around US$6 for those days when only a pie can satisfy.

Patty's Bistro, 13 4th Ave, **t** 402 0174. A range of Belizean favourites, such as cow-foot soup (US$4), stewed pinto beans with meat (US$3.75) and coconut curry with shrimp (US$6) served up alongside a few international selections, including cheeseburgers and T-bone steaks. Eat in or take away.

Around Corozal

Consejo

⑬ Consejo

Around 8 miles (13km) north of Corozal is the small fishing village of Consejo and the adjoining retirement development of Consejo Shores. As with Ambergris Caye just out to sea, this area has attracted a large influx of US ex-pats in recent years come to buy (or build) their own place in the tropical sun. The area certainly ticks all the right property-development boxes – sandy beaches, swaying palms, turquoise waters, a low crime rate and plenty of available land. For those who aren't planning to buy, it's a pleasant spot to hang out on the way to Mexico but be warned, a few hours here may have you considering putting a foot on the Belizean property ladder (you'll certainly see enough adverts).

Sarteneja

East of Corozal, across the bay, is the Sarteneja peninsula, at the northern tip of which lies the picturesque fishing village of Sarteneja. The name is Mayan for 'water between rocks', and refers to a large stone well in the centre of the village. As was the case with several of the region's towns, Sarteneja was founded in the 19th century by refugees from the Yucatán Caste Wars and is built over a former Mayan site. Although rather off the beaten track, the town does have a couple of decent hotels and restaurants and lies just a few miles from the entrance to the Shipstern Nature Reserve.

Shipstern Nature Reserve

 ㉔ Shipstern Nature Reserve
3 miles (5km) from Sarteneja, **t** *423 2247; open 8–5; adm US$5 (includes guided tour)*

Home to every species of Belizean mammal, including jaguars, peccaries and manatees, not to mention 250 species of bird, 60 species of reptiles and 200 butterfly species, the 22,000-acre Shipstern Nature Reserve represents one of your best chances of seeing some of the country's famed wildlife (which, unfortunately, also includes a multitude of bugs, so be sure to bring suitable supplies of repellent). The reserve, which is co-managed by the Belize Audubon Society and the Swiss International Conservation

Getting to Sarteneja

The Corozal–San Pedro Thunderbolt **boat** will stop at Sarteneja if requested (*see* p.215). Otherwise, if **driving**, head south to Orange Walk and then take the road east out of town up to San Estevan, from where you can follow a bumpy unpaved road to Sarteneja. Daily **bus** services operate to the town from Belize City, Orange Walk and Corozal, passing by the entrance to the reserve.

Foundation, encompasses a wide variety of different habits, including mangroves, savannah, forests and lagoons. Visits are by guided tour only (included in the entrance fee), which last 45 minutes and take you along the Chiclero Botanical Trail, where you can find out about the medicinal uses of various trees and plants, and on a visit to the reserve's butterfly farm.

If you want to explore further after this, you'll have to pay your guide a further US$2.50 an hour. Full-day tours with boat trips, and night tours, are also available.

Basic dormitory accommodation is provided at the visitor centre for US$10 per person, which includes use of the kitchen facilities. Tents can be pitched for US$10.

Chetumal, Mexico

Day trips to Chetumal in Mexico can be easily arranged from Corozal. It's a well-worn path regularly taken by many Belizeans and ex-pats en route to the town's American-style **mall** (complete with American fast-food restaurants). The easiest way to get there is by bus from Corozal's bus station, which takes around 45 minutes, or you can take a taxi the 8 miles (13km) to the border town of Santa Elena (around US$14) and cross on foot. There will be plenty of buses and taxis waiting on the other side in Subteniente López ready to ferry you the final 7 miles (11km) to Chetumal.

At the **border**, tourists are required to present their passport for stamping and pay an exit tax of US$28. There is a tourist office on the Belizean side of the border if you require assistance.

Where to Stay around Corozal

Consejo

CasaBlanca by the Sea, t 423 1018, f 423 1003, *www.casablancabelize.com* ($$$; US$75). The CasaBlanca has well-groomed grounds, a good seafood restaurant and comfortable rooms with queen-sized beds, a/c and views of the Bay.

The Smuggler's Den, t 614 8156, *http://smugglersdenbelize.tripod.com* ($$/$$$; US$30/50). The Smuggler's Den offers a choice of three types of beach-front accommodation: the basic 'Casa Leo' bungalows (US$30), which come with private bathrooms and fans; the standard bungalows (US$50) which also have TVs and kitchenettes; and the family-sized and very fancy 'Casa Kyle' (US$100), which have all of the above, plus living rooms and DVD players. In addition, there's a good restaurant, a volleyball court, and bikes and canoes for rent.

Sarteneja

Krisami's Bayview Lodge, Front St (west end), t 423 2283, *www.krisamis. com* ($$$; US$60). It's a bit motel-like, but this lodge, run by the friendly Verde family, has spacious rooms with twin beds, tiled floors and a/c plus complimentary coffee. Transfers to Shipstern Nature Reserve, as well as a variety of other tours, can be arranged. Meals by request only.

Fernando's Seaside Guesthouse, Front St, t 423 2085, *sartenejabelize@hotmail. com, www.cybercayecaulker.com/ sarteneja.html* ($$; US$30). Four large, good-value rooms with twin double beds, fans and tiled bathrooms. An extra US$10 will get you an even bigger one with a high thatched roof.

Last Resort, Main Rd, Copper Bank, t 606 1585 ($$; US$30). Remote and rustic with 10 thatched-roof cabanas, a library and a restaurant serving a good range of Belizean and international dishes. Bikes can be hired, as can canoes for exploring the adjacent lagoon. Camping is also allowed in the grounds.

Language

Although **English** is the official language of Belize, taught in all the country's schools, many Belizeans also speak one (or, in some cases, more than one) of the country's various other tongues. In fact, despite English's official status, the majority of Belizeans do not speak it as a first language, but as a second. Following the large influx of immigrants from neighbouring Central American countries in the past 20 years, **Spanish** is now the most widely spoken tongue, although its use is mainly concentrated in villages in the north near the Mexican border, and in the west near Guatemala. Even in those central eastern areas where English is still dominant, including Belmopan, Belize City and the cayes, the locals tend to converse, not in formal English, but in creole (or *kriol*), an amalgamation of the African languages spoken by slaves brought to Belize from the 17th to the early 19th century, and the English spoken by British loggers (and slave owners). Belize creole is unique to the country, although it does share some similarities with other English-based creole languages, including Jamaican creole. While many words will be familiar to English speakers everywhere, the grammar and strong Caribbean lilt with which the words are pronounced can make it pretty difficult to understand. For more information on Belize creole, log on to the official website of the **National Kriol Council of Belize** (*www.kriol. org.bz*). which aims to promote Belize's creole culture and language.

The Garinuga (or Garifuna) communities of Dangriga, Hopkins and Punta Gorda in southern Belize speak their own language, known as **Garifuna**, an Arawak language that originated on the island of St Vincent from where the Garifuna people hail. It's spoken not just in Belize, but in Garifuna communities throughout the region, including in Honduras and Guatemala. An unusual aspect of the Garifuna language is that the version spoken by males is slightly different from that spoken by females (*see* p.175 for more information on Garifuna/Garinuga).

Belize's communities of Mennonites also have their own language, in this instance a form of Low German known as **Plautdietsch**, but it's almost as common to hear them chattering in creole (*see* p.213 for more information on Mennonites).

Finally, there are the Mayan languages, of which three are spoken in Belize: **Kekchi** (or Q'eqchi'), the use of which is restricted mainly to southern Belize; **Mopan**, which is also spoken in southern regions as well as the western Cayo district; and **Yucatan** (or Yucatec) **Mayan**, which is spoken in the west and in some northern villages.

Some Creole Phrases

Belize creole is written phonetically so English speakers should have little difficulty with pronunciation.

I like Belize *Mee laik Bileez*

What is your name? *Weh yu nayhn?*

Good morning *Gud maanin*

How are you? (informal hello) *Weh di go aan?*

Further Reading

Beletsky, Les, *Belize and Northern Guatemala: Ecotraveller's Wildlife Guide* (Academic Press, 1999). A handy field guide for identifying habitats and wildlife (including marine life) as well as information on conservation and ecotourism.

Conroy, Richard Timothy, *Our Man in Belize: A Memoir* (Thomas Dunne Books, 1997). Anecdotal memoirs of a US Foreign Service Officer posted to British Honduras in 1959.

Edgell, Zee, *Beka Lamb* (Heinemann, 1982). A Belizean author's fictional account of a young girl's life in Belize during the 1950s. Also by the same author, *The Festival San Joaquin* (Heinemann, 1997) and *In Times Like These* (Heinemann, 1991).

King, Emory, *Driver's Guide to Beautiful Belize* (Tropical Books, 2000). A detailed guide to exploring the country by car. Emory King has also written several other books detailing the history and culture of the country and life there as a US ex-pat. Details can be found on King's website, *www.emoryking.com*.

Jones, H. Lee, *Birds of Belize* (University of Texas Press, 2004). An exhaustive and very useful guide to the 500-plus species of bird that make Belize their home.

Portis, Charles, *The Dog of the South*, (Bloomsbury, 2005, originally published in 1979). A novel following one man's road trip from Arkansas, USA, to Belize City.

Rabinowitz, Alan, *Jaguar: One Man's Battle to Establish the World's First Jaguar Reserve* (Island Press, 2000). An interesting account of Rabinowitz's two-year stay in the Cockscomb Basin studying jaguars, integrating with the Mayan community and helping to found the Cockscomb Reserve.

Stray, P.J., *Danger on Lighthouse Reef* (Silver Burdett Press, 1997). A children's mystery from the Passport Mystery Series set in Lighthouse Reef.

Sutherland, Anne, *The Making of Belize: Globalization in the Margins* (Greenwood Press, 1998). A look at how globalization has affected Belize.

Thomson, P. A. B., *Belize: A Concise History* (MacMillan Caribbean, 2005). An in-depth delve into Belize's colourful history.

Wright, Donald, *Time Among the Maya: Travels in Belize, Guatemala and Mexico* (Grove Press, 2000, originally published in 1989). An informative, accessible overview of the history, culture and architecture of the Maya people.

Ellis, Zoila, *On Lizards, Heroes and Passion* (Cubola, 1997). Seven short Belizean-set stories. Also by the same author: *Mmmm...a Taste of Belizean Cooking* (Cubola 2003), a collection of recipes from restaurant chefs across the country. Both titles are only published within Belize.

Useful Websites

General

www.belize.gov.bz official website of the government of Belize

www.belizenet.com website of Belize by Naturalight, a destination guide to the regions of Belize, with links to related sights

www.belizeforum.com website of the Belize Forums, which has an active message board for locals and tourists

www.belize2nite.com event listings for the whole of Belize with an emphasis on nightlife

www.toucantrail.com website of the budget-orientated Belize Toucan Trail, which provides tourist information on Belize, plus listings for US$60 a night or less lodgings

www.travelbelize.org official site of the Belize Tourism Board

www.embassyofbelize.org official site of the Embassy of Belize, which provides information on retiring to Belize

www.scubadivingbelize.com information on diving, providing photos, maps and tips

News and Media Sites

www.Amandala.com.bz website of the *Amandala*, Belize's biggest selling newspaper

www.belizemagazine.com Internet magazine with interviews, articles on culture, sights, food and drink, etc.

www.belizetimes.bz the somewhat selective website of the *Belize Times*, which carries some of the articles from the weekly newspaper

www.7newsbelize.com website of the Channel 7 Daily News, providing daily transcripts of the Belizean news channel

www.channel5belize.com website of the Belizean news channel, it provides transcripts of news reports from across the entire country

Index

Main page references are in **bold**. Page references to maps are in *italics*.

Authors' Acknowledgements

Many, many thanks to everyone in Belize who took the time to talk to us and help us on our voyage of discovery around the country, particularly Mike, Norma and Karina in Belize City, Jeff and Vivian on Ambergris Caye, Michael in Cayo, Peter in Dangriga and Diane way down south, as well as everyone at Cadogan.

First edition published 2006

Cadogan Guides
2nd Floor, 233 High Holborn,
London, WC1V 7DN
info@cadoganguides.co.uk
www.cadoganguides.com

The Globe Pequot Press
246 Goose Lane, PO Box 480, Guilford,
Connecticut 06437–0480

Copyright © Joseph Fullman and
  Nicola Mainwright 2006

Cover design by Sarah Rianhard-Gardner
Book design by Andrew Barker
Cover photographs: © Mark Lewis/Alamy; index
  stock/Alamy
Introduction photographs: © Susannah Sayler
Maps © Cadogan Guides 2006,
  drawn by Map Creation Ltd

Art Director: Sarah Rianhard-Gardner
Managing Editors: Natalie Pomier and
  Antonia Cunningham
Editor: Dominique Shead
Assistant Editor: Nicola Jessop
Proofreading: Elspeth Anderson
Indexing: Isobel McLean

Printed in Italy by Legoprint
A catalogue record for this book is available
  from the British Library
ISBN-10: 1-86011-341-9
ISBN-13: 978-1-86011-341-3

The author and publishers have made every effort to ensure the accuracy of the information in this book at the time of going to press. However, they cannot accept any responsibility for any loss, injury or inconvenience resulting from the use of information contained in this guide.

Please help us to keep this guide up to date. We have done our best to ensure that the information in this guide is correct at the time of going to press. But places and facilities are constantly changing, and standards and prices in hotels and restaurants fluctuate. We would be delighted to receive any comments concerning existing entries or omissions. Authors of the best letters will receive a copy of the Cadogan Guide of their choice.